REGICIDE
The Official Assassination
of John F. Kennedy

Regicide

The Official Assassination

of John F. Kennedy

by

Gregory Douglas

Monte Sano Media
Huntsville, AL, 2002

Gregory Douglas:
Regicide. The Official Assassination of John F. Kennedy.
Dust Cover: Michael Martin
Huntsville (Alabama): Monte Sano Media, April 2002
ISBN 1-59148-297-6

Set in Century Schoolbook 9 pt.

In this work, quotations are surrounded by quotation marks, except where
entire chapters consist of quotations (WCR quotes).

Let us sit upon the ground

and tell sad stories

about the death of Kings.

William Shakespeare, *King Lear*

Treason doth never prosper,

what's the reason?

For if it prosper,

none dare call it treason.

John Harrington

Table of Contents

Foreword

The assassination of President John Fitzgerald Kennedy in Dallas, Texas, on November 22, 1963, continues to generate an enormous amount of popular controversy, more so than any other historical happening in recorded memory. The killing took place in a major American city in full view of hundreds of people and in broad daylight, yet years after the event, a dispassionate overview of the incident is impossible to achieve. The act and its consequences are as cluttered as the dense Indian jungle that so thoroughly hides the gaudy tiger from the sight of its prey.

The initial stunned confusion in Dallas has continued, with much official connivance, into succeeding decades, with an immense proliferation of books, magazine articles, motion picture productions, and television dramas, which are equally divided between assaults on previous productions and the presentation of even more confusion, theory, and supposition.

One camp consists entirely of what can best be termed the "official version" and in the other camp are the "revisionist versions." There is only one of the former and a multitude of the others.

There is no question in the minds of anyone that John F. Kennedy was shot dead in Dallas, Texas, in November of 1963. The real issue is who shot him and why.

Is the report of the official Warren Commission correct?[1] Was the President killed by a disaffected man who acted entirely alone? Was his subsequent murder perpetrated by another disaffected man who also acted entirely alone?

Are the legions of revisionists correct? Was the Kennedy assassination the result of a plot? And if there was a plot, who were the plotters and what were their motives?

---

[1] The Warren Commission Report, pb. edition, New York: St. Martin's Press [no year, ISBN 0-312-08257-6]; hereinafter WCR.

The overwhelming majority of the public, who are the final arbiters of whatever may pass for historical truth, has, in the intervening years, come to believe less in the determined certainty of officialdom and more in the questions raised by those who cannot accept official dictums.

In a very strong sense, the Kennedy assassination marked an important watershed in the relationship between the American public and its elected and appointed officials. Before that event, what the government said was almost universally accepted as the truth. There was unquestioning and simplistic belief, and more, there was trust in the pronouncements from the Beltway and its numerous and often very slavish servants in academia and the American media. It is true, people would say, because it is printed in my newspaper and supported by important and knowledgeable savants.

That the media and academia might be influenced by, if not actually commanded by, the government rarely occurred to anyone outside of a small handful of chronic malcontents.

The questions that were raised by the Warren Commission's lengthy and thoroughly disorganized report were certainly in many cases very important. That there were many errors in this hasty attempt to allay national anxieties is clearly evident, but in retrospect, and in view of recently disclosed evidence, these are more errors of commission than omission.

The Warren Report was prepared and released to the public not to encourage questioning but to silence it as quickly as possible. There are many cogent reasons for this desire for silence and acceptance, not the least of which was the urgent desire for self-preservation and the maintenance of the integrity of the governmental system.

In actuality, the American currency is not backed by gold or silver holdings but by the blind faith of the public. If the concept of unquestioning belief in governmental currency stability is questioned, economic chaos can be the result, and this applies equally to government probity.

To quote from the title of the first and very important revisionist work on the Kennedy assassination, there was a great "rush to judgment" and a frantic desire on the part of the official establishment to completely bury not only the murdered President but also any questions his killing might have engendered with him.

Was the primary reason for this desire for closure merely a desire to placate public opinion or were there other, and far more sinister, reasons for this rush to judgment?

Those who question the official chronicle have been severely hampered by the fact that all the records, documents, interviews, and other evidentiary material are securely under governmental custody and control. It is beyond the belief of any reasonable person to think that an official agency would release to the public any material that would bring the official judgment into question. This is not only institutional maintenance but also, all things in evidence now considered, a frantic effort at self-preservation.

Not all documents, however, lie under government control, and there exist reports that do not only question the Warren Report's findings but are also of such a nature as to both thoroughly discredit it and, in the final analysis, bring it to ruin.

Such a historical land mine lay for years in the personal files of Robert Trumbull Crowley, once Deputy Director for Operations for the Central Intelligence Agency. Crowley, who had authored books on Soviet intelligence, died in October of 2000 after a long illness.

When Crowley retired from the CIA in the 1980s, he took a significant quantity of important historical documents with him and, prior to his death, gave a number of these to various historians with whom he occasionally cooperated.

Among these documents was a lengthy paper prepared by the Defense Intelligence Agency (DIA) in 1978 as a commentary on Soviet intelligence evaluations of the Kennedy assassination.

The Defense Intelligence Agency, a branch of the Department of Defense, specializes in the analysis of foreign military technical intelligence.

This document was considered highly sensitive, for reasons that shall shortly become very evident, and its distribution was limited to a handful of copies with severely restricted circulation.

Crowley had a copy of this explosive document because he had personal knowledge of the factors and personalities behind the assassination and had, in fact, prior professional knowledge of the information contained in the DIA secret paper.

The second and certainly even more important document is a 98 pages long paper entitled "OPERATION ZIPPER Conference Record." This document is a long list of decisions and activities of various U.S. authorities in a project with the code name "Operation ZIPPER." The distribution of this document was restricted to five persons, one of them being R. T. Crowley, in whose papers a copy of it was found.

This book uses the official DIA Report and the "Operation ZIPPER" document as its framework. In addition to that, the author uses the notes he made during endless hours of conversation he had with R. T. Crowley in the years between 1993 and 1996, and has dug deeply into the great body of literature on the assassination of J. F. Kennedy to flesh out what has proven to be a very ugly skeleton. In sum, it puts sinews and flesh on the bones of a monster.

The loss of faith is a terrible matter, and one can say after reading these papers and with bitter truth: "Who then will guard the guardians?"

Gregory Douglas

Acknowledgments

It is generally the custom for beginning writers to thank anyone and everyone even remotely connected with his book. Book
editors, typists, library personnel, former teachers, family members, and pets are all given their five seconds of fame (or far less
depending upon the sales of the book).

However, that having been said, the author would like to offer
the most sincere and grateful, albeit posthumous, thanks to the
late Colonel Robert T. Crowley of Washington, D.C., and his co-
worker, Colonel William Corson, USMC (United States Marine
Corps), of Potomac, Maryland, for all of the very important advice
and assistance they have rendered to the grateful author. Also
their friend and co-worker, Joe Trento of Front Royal, Virginia, for
his valuable commentary and excellent advice, especially concerning the activities of James Jesus Angleton.

As opposed to acknowledging others who aided in the actual
preparation of this study, recognition ought to be given on the author's part for research into American intelligence matters.

David Lifton's work, *Best Evidence*,[2] is a brilliant analysis of
the Kennedy autopsy; Thomas C. Reeves, *A Question of Character*[3]
is one of the best revisionist views of the life and political career of
John F. Kennedy; Thomas Dale Scott's work, *Deep Politics and the
Death of JFK*[4] is a sensible and studied work on the backgrounds
of Kennedy adversaries; and Seymour Hersh's work *The Dark Side
of Camelot*[5] gives a far more detailed revisionist look into JFK and

[2] David S. Lifton, *Best Evidence: Disguise and Deception in the Assassination of
     John F. Kennedy*, New York: Carroll & Graf, 1980.
[3] Thomas C. Reeves, *A Question of Character: A Life of John F. Kennedy*, New York:
     Macmillan, 1991.
[4] Peter Dale Scott, *Deep Politics and the Death of JFK*, Berkeley: University of Cali-
     fornia Press, 1993.
[5] Seymour Hersh, *The Dark Side of Camelot*, New York: Brown, 1998 (pb. edition).

provides considerable background on his Soviet connection. Almost
every book on the subject, regardless of how bizarre it might appear to the average reader, contains small nuggets of value to be
mined by the thorough researcher.

Former CBS news director and documentary producer, Los An-
geles-based Ted Landreth has done prodigies investigating certain
highly sensitive CIA operations inside the United States.

Also, an important work is Gerald Posner's *Case Closed*.[6] This
work is an excellent overview and defense of the *official* establishment point of view. That the American media lavishly praised
it when it appeared in 1993 is a commentary on the objectivity of
the media.

---

[6]   Gerald Posner, *Case Closed*, New York: Doubleday, 1993.

Obituary

Tuesday, October 10, 2000: Page B06, *Washington Post*:
"Robert Trumbull Crowley
Senior CIA Officer
Robert Trumbull Crowley, 76, a senior CIA officer whose career spanned from the agency's inception in 1947 until his retirement in the mid-1980s, died Oct. 8 at Sibley Memorial Hospital. He had congestive heart failure and dementia.

Mr. Crowley became assistant deputy director for operations, the second in command in the clandestine directorate of operations. After retiring, he co-wrote a book with former CIA intelligence officer and Marine Corps officer William R. Corson, "The New KGB: Engine of Soviet Power," published by William Morrow in 1985.

Mr. Crowley, a Washington resident, was a Chicago native and attended the U.S. Military Academy at West Point, N.Y. He served in the Army in the Pacific during World War II and retired from the Army Reserve in 1986 as a lieutenant colonel.

Survivors include his wife since 1948, Emily Upton Crowley of Washington; a son, Greg Upton Crowley of Washington; and two granddaughters."[7]

In 1996, Robert Crowley entered a Washington hospital for major surgery. It was believed that he might have cancer of the lungs. The operation was successful, but Crowley, who had been suffering from short-term memory problems, slipped into a state of chronic dementia from which he never recovered.

---

[7] *Washington Post*, October 10, 2000, p. B6; see the WP online archive at www.washingtonpost.com; doc-ref: http://nl11.newsbank.com/nl-search/we/Archives?p_action=doc&p_docid=0EB2C4671708A4E7&p_docnum=1.

Before entering the hospital, Crowley, known in the CIA as the "Crow," sent off two packets of documents from his extensive files to the author of this book with instructions to return the papers if he survived the operation. After the operation, it was evident to Crowley's family that he would do no more writing, and I was told to keep the papers and not to return them.

As one of the most powerful men in the Central Intelligence Agency and one of the least known outside of the Agency, Crowley was involved in most of the important CIA operations during his tenure. His personal files are of great value to researchers and cover both foreign and domestic intelligence operations.

Among these papers was the above mentioned DIA Report, a 1978 in-depth analysis of a Soviet intelligence report on the assassination of President John Kennedy. At one time, the Russians were held suspect in this act, and in the intervening years, their intelligence organs had been compiling data in refutation of this thesis. It should be noted that Lee Oswald, the purported assassin, had defected to the Soviet Union and, while resident in that country, married the niece of an MVD[8] intelligence officer.

Although the DIA Report makes it very clear that Oswald was a source for the Office of Naval Intelligence and that his defection was spurious, his openly avowed Marxism, public support of the Communist government of Cuban dictator Fidel Castro, and his repeated pro-Communist utterances made him a very handy weapon with which to attack the Russians.

The DIA Report, signed by Army Colonel Vedder B. Driscoll, chief of the Soviet Intelligence division of the DIA, appears to be the first official analysis of the Kennedy assassination that does not follow the official line, and which survived the post-assassination shredding frenzy that seized the American intelligence community.[9]

Theories, opinions, and arguments abound concerning the Kennedy assassination, and while many authors will applaud Dris-

---

[8] Soviet Secret Police under the State Security Committee, successor to the NKVD and predecessor to the KGB; Otto Heilbrunn, *The Soviet Secret Services*, New York: Praeger, 1956, pp. 127, 134.

[9] See Appendix.

coll's DIA Report, others will reject it. Rejection or acceptance depends entirely on what an author may have previously published on the subject.

The other surviving official paper, the already mentioned "Operation ZIPPER" document, will most likely cause an even more heated controversy, since it does not have a cover document and consists merely of a brief listing of persons and agencies involved, decisions made, and events that took place during and after the preparation of Kennedy's assassination.

Over 2,500 works on the assassination have appeared in print to date, but nothing approaches what can best be termed the "Driscoll Report" and the "ZIPPER Document" for brevity and accuracy. The reader is given a unique view of the events in Dallas and Washington post-November 22, 1963.

The facts behind the Kennedy assassination are found in the Driscoll Report and the ZIPPER Document. For the first time, the actual motives of those who organized and instigated the act are clearly and decisively exposed, as are the techniques of the actual shooting, the nature of the weapons used, and the means by which the shooters escaped.

These documents do not challenge the famous Warren Report that has been ridiculed by many and supported by few; they merely supersede it.

The ZIPPER Document reveals, most importantly, the names and official positions of those who directed the killers. For example, the man who instigated the attack was one of the highest level American intelligence officials, and the man to whom he entrusted the supervision of the assassins was someone who had been involved in one of the most important American intelligence-gathering actions against the Soviet Union, an operation that the Driscoll Report now reveals had been known to the Soviets even before it was launched! The fate of the shooters is also revealed; only one of them lived more than a month after Kennedy died.

In this work, rather than present the endlessly chewed arguments of others to dazzle or bore the reader, the Driscoll Report and the ZIPPER Document are presented in full with appropriate commentary.

This study is organized into a number of chapters. The assassination itself is covered by a translation of the Soviet intelligence report, followed by pertinent and parallel excerpts from the official Warren Commission Report and the Defense Intelligence Agency analysis. The observations of the author conclude each section.

The next chapters will cover the more important players. Again, first a Soviet report, followed by the pertinent sections of the Warren Report, the DIA analysis, and concluding with the author's comments. The Warren Commission Report basically covered the actual assassination and the subsequent murder of the alleged assassin, Lee Harvey Oswald. Both the Soviet and Driscoll Reports contain additional material not covered in the Warren Commission Report.

Subsequent chapters addressing the real history of the Kennedy assassination are based mainly on the ZIPPER Document, with some use of the Driscoll Report, and are backed by information the author received during his many conversations with R. T. Crowley.

Long years of suspicion, investigation, and revisionist commentary have ended with the discovery and publication of the Driscoll Report and the ZIPPER Document from the papers of top CIA official, Robert Crowley.

The deadly international plots, assassinations of unpopular foreign politicians, active involvement in the world-wide drug market, ruthless manipulation of the United States government to include the office of the President, counterfeitings, the fomenting of revolts and bloody uprisings in nations friendly to the United States, the infiltration and control of the American and foreign print and film media, and the general belief that their opinions should dictate America's domestic and foreign policy have led directly to such anti-American incidents as the murder of American citizens and such explosive outrages as the recent attack on the World Trade Center.

The Central Intelligence Agency, which likes to picture itself as the protective shield of the American people, has proven itself to be consistently wrong in its analysis of almost every problem presented to it and has alienated by its actions a good part of the world which at one time had been neutral in its opinion of America if not sympathetic. It is beyond belief that a complicated, yearlong international plot against America, which culminated in the WTC attack and which involved hundreds of people, could not have been observed by the CIA. This is either an example of gross incompetence at best or connivance at worst.

The Crowley Papers give all of us a true understanding of the meaning of Lord Acton's dictum, "Power corrupts and absolute power corrupts absolutely."

The Assassination

DEFENSE INTELLIGENCE AGENCY
WASHINGTON, D. C. 20301

20 APRIL 1978

SUBJECT: Soviet Intelligence Report on Assassination of President KENNEDY

TO: Director

The following report has been prepared at your request in response to a Soviet report on the assassination of President John F. KENNEDY on 22 NOV 1963. The Soviet document (see Enclosure a) has been obtained from a fully reliable source and duly authenticated.

This report is an analysis of the Soviet document and is done on a paragraph-by-paragraph basis.

Material in this analysis has been taken from a number of sources indicated in the Appendix and is to be considered classified at the highest level. Nothing contained in this report may be disseminated to any individual or agency without prior written permission of the Director or his appointed deputy.

This agency does not assume, and cannot verify, the correctness of the material contained herein, although every reasonable effort has been made to do so. Any use of information contained in this report must be paraphrased and sources, either individual or agency, must not be credited.

VEDDER B. DRISCOLL
Colonel, USA
Chief, Soviet/Warsaw Pact
Division
Directorate for Intelligence
Research

1 Enclosure
Appendix

NOTE: The Russian language file is not attached to this report and exists in official translation only.

The following chapters will consist of facsimile reproductions of the DIA's translation of the Soviet intelligence study, of its own analysis, and of quoted excerpts of the official Warren Commission Report, followed by commentary.

The Facts of the Assassination

The Soviet Intelligence Study (translation)

ENCLOSURE A

THE SOVIET INTELLIGENCE STUDY (translation)

1. On 22 November, 1963, American President John Kennedy was shot and killed during a political motor trip through the Texas city of Dallas. The President was riding at the head of the procession in his official state car, seated in the right rear with his wife on his left side. Seated in front of him was the Governor of Texas and his wife, also on his left side. The vehicle was an open car without side or top protection of any kind. There was a pilot car in front, about 30 meters, and the President's car was flanked by motorcycle outriders located two to a side roughly parallel with the rear wheels of the State car.

2. The President and his party were driving at a speed of about 20 kilometers per hour through the built-up area of Dallas and greeted the many people lining the streets along his route. Security was supplied by the Secret Service supplemented by local police. There were two Secret Service agents in the front of the car. One was driving the car. Other agents were in cars following the Presidential vehicle and Dallas police on motorbikes were on both sides of the Presidential car but at the rear of it. There was a pilot car in front of the President's car but it was some distance away.

3. The course of the journey was almost past all the occupied area. The cars then turned sharply to the right and then again to the left to go to the motorway leading to a meeting hall where the President was to speak at a dinner. It is considered very bad security for such an official drive to decrease its speed or to make unnecessary turnings or stops. (Historical note: It was just this problem that led directly to positioning the Austrian Heir in front of wating assassins at Sarajevo in 1914) The route was set by agents of the Secret Service and published in the Dallas newspapers before the arrival of the President and his party.

4. After the last turning to the left, the cars passed a tall building on the right side of the street that was used as a warehouse for the storage of school books. This building was six stories tall and had a number of workers assigned to it. There were no official security people in this building, either on the roof or at the windows. Also, there were no security agents along the roadway on either side. All security agents were riding either in the Presidential car (two in the front) and in the following vehicles.

5. As the President's state car passed this building, some shots were heard. The exact source and number of these shots was never entirely determined. Some observers thought that the shots came from above and behind while many more observers in the area stated that the shots came from the front and to the right of the car. There was a small area with a decorative building and some trees and bushes there and many saw unidentified people in this area. Many people standing in front of this area to watch the cars stated that shots came from behind them.

-1-

6. When the first shots were fired, the President was seen to lean forward and clutch at his throat with both hands. Immediately when this happened, the Secret Service driver of the President's state car slowed down the vehicle until it was almost stopped. This was a direct breach of their training which stated that in such events where firing occurred, the driver of the President's car would immediately drive away as quickly as possible.

7. At the same time as the first shot, there was a second one, this one from above and behind. This bullet struck the Governor, sitting in front of the President and slightly to his right, in the right upper shoulder. The bullet went downwards into the chest cavity, breaking ribs, struck his wrist and lodged in his left upper thigh. There were then two shots fired at the President's car. The first shot initiated the action and this one appears to have hit the President in the throat. If so, it must have been fired from in front of the car, not behind it.

8. Right at this moment, there was one other shot. The shell, obviously struck the President on the upper rear of the right side of his head, throwing him back and to the left. Also, at this time, blood, pieces of skull and brains could be seen flying to the left where the motorbike police guard was struck with this material on his right side and on the right side of his motorbike.

9. Immediately after this final shot, the driver then began to increase his speed and the cars all went at increasing speed down under the tunnel.

10. The fatally injured President and the seriously injured Governor were very quickly taken to a nearby hospital for treatment. The President was declared as dead and his body was removed, by force, to an aircraft and flown to Washington. The badly wounded Governor was treated at the hospital for his wounds and survived.

11. Within moments of the shots fired at the President, a Dallas motorcycle police officer ran into the book building and up to the second floor in the company of the manager of the establishment. Here, the policeman encountered a man later positively identified as one Lee Harvey Oswald, an employee of the book storage company. Oswald was drinking a Coca-Cola and appeared to be entirely calm and collected. (Later it was said that he had rushed down four flights of steps past other employees in a few moments after allegedly shooting the President. It is noted from the records that none of the other employees on the staircase ever saw Oswald passing them.) The elevator which moved freight and personnel between the floors was halted at the sixth floor and turned off so that it could not be recalled to persons below wishing to use it.

The Warren Commission Report

At 11:40 a.m., CST, on Friday, November 22, 1963, President John F. Kennedy, Mrs. Kennedy, and their party arrived at Love Field, Dallas, Tex. Behind them was the first day of a Texas trip planned 5 months before by the President, Vice President Lyndon B. Johnson, and John B. Connally, Jr., Governor of Texas. After leaving the White House on Thursday morning, the President had flown initially to San Antonio where Vice President Lyndon B. Johnson joined the party and the President dedicated new research facilities at the U.S. Air Force School of Aerospace Medicine. Following a testimonial dinner in Houston for U.S. Representative Albert Thomas, the President flew to Fort Worth where he spent the night and spoke at a large breakfast gathering on Friday.

Planned for later that day were a motorcade through downtown Dallas, a luncheon speech at the Trade Mart, and a flight to Austin where the President would attend a reception and speak at a Democratic fundraising dinner. From Austin he would proceed to the Texas ranch of the Vice President. [WCR, pp. 1-2.]

The Secret Service was told on November 8 that 45 minutes had been allotted to a motorcade procession from Love Field to the site of a luncheon planned by Dallas business and civic leaders in honor of the President. After considering the facilities and security problems of the several buildings, the Trade Mart was chosen as the luncheon site. Given this selection, and in accordance with the customary practice of affording the greatest number of people an opportunity to see the President, the motorcade route selected was a natural one. The route was approved by the local host committee and White House representatives on November 18 and publicized in the local papers starting on November 19. This advance publicity made it clear that the motorcade would leave Main Street and pass the intersection of Elm and Houston Streets as it proceeded to the Trade Mart by way of the Stemmons Freeway.

By midmorning of November 22, clearing skies in Dallas dispelled the threat of rain and the President greeted the crowds from his open limousine without the "bubbletop," which was at that time a plastic shield furnishing protection only against inclement weather. To the left of the President in the rear seat was Mrs. Kennedy. In the jump seats were Governor Connally, who was in front of the President, and Mrs. Connally at the Governor's left. Agent William R. Greer of the Secret Service was driving, and Agent Roy H. Kellerman was sitting to his right. [WCR, p. 2]

At the extreme west end of Main Street, the motorcade turned right on Houston Street and proceeded north for one block in order to make a left turn on Elm Street, the most direct and convenient approach to the Stemmons Freeway and the Trade Mart. As the President's car approached the intersection of Houston and Elm Streets, there loomed directly ahead on the intersection's northwest corner a seven story, orange brick warehouse and office building, the Texas School Book Depository. [WCR, p. 2]

The President's car which had been going north made a sharp turn toward the southwest onto Elm Street. At a speed of about 11 miles per hour, it started down the gradual descent towards a railroad overpass under which the motorcade would proceed before reaching the Stemmons Freeway. The front of the Texas School Book Depository was now on the President's right, and he waved to the crowd assembled there as he passed the building. Dealey Plaza—an open, landscaped area marking the western end of downtown Dallas—stretched out to the President's left. A Secret Service agent riding in the motorcade radioed the Trade Mart that the President would arrive in 5 minutes.

Seconds later shots resounded in rapid succession. The President's hands moved to his neck. He appeared to stiffen momentarily and lurch slightly forward in his seat. A bullet had entered the base of the back of his neck slightly to the right of the spine. It traveled downward and exited from the front of the neck, causing a nick in the left lower portion of the knot in the President's necktie. Governor Connally had been facing towards the crowd on the right. He started to turn toward the left and suddenly felt a blow on his back. The Governor had been hit by a bullet which entered at the extreme right side of his back at a point below his right armpit. The bullet traveled through his chest in a downward and forward direction, exited below his right nipple, passed through his right wrist, which had been in his lap, and then caused a wound to his left thigh. The force of the bullet's impact appeared to spin the Governor to his right, and Mrs. Connally pulled him down into her lap. Another bullet then struck President Kennedy in the rear portion of his head, causing a massive and fatal wound. The President fell to the left into Mrs. Kennedy's lap. [WCR, p. 3]

The first person to see Oswald after the assassination was Patrolman M. L. Baker of the Dallas Police Department. Baker was riding a two-wheeled motorcycle behind the last press car of the motorcade.

Baker testified that he entered the lobby (of the Texas Book Depository) and "spoke out and asked where the stairs or elevator was*** and this man, Mr. Truly, spoke up and says, it seems to me like he says 'I am a building manager. Follow me, officer, and I will show you.'"

Meanwhile, Truly had run up several steps towards the third floor. Missing Baker, he came back to find the officer in the doorway to the lunchroom "facing Lee Harvey Oswald." Baker turned to Truly and said, "Do you know this man, does he work here?" Truly replied, "Yes." Baker stated later that the man did not seem to be out of breath; he seemed calm. [WCR, p. 152]

That Oswald descended by stairway from the sixth floor to the second-floor lunchroom is consistent with the movements of the two elevators, which would have provided the other possible means of descent. When Truly, accompanied by Baker, ran to the rear of the first floor, he was certain that both elevators, which occupy the same shaft, were on the fifth floor. In the few seconds which elapsed while Baker and Truly ran from the first to the second floor, neither of these slow elevators could have descended from the fifth to the second floor. Furthermore, no elevator was at the second floor when they arrived there. [WCR, p. 153]

The DIA Analysis

18. The Dallas trip had been in train since late July of 1963. Texas was considered to be a key state in the upcoming 1964 Presidential elections. It was the disqualification of over 100,000 Texas votes, in conjunction with the known fraudulent voting in Chicago in 1960 that gave President Kennedy and his associates a slim margin of victory.

The actual route of Kennedy's drive through downtown Dallas was made known to the local press on Tuesday, November 19. The sharp right turn from Main St. onto Houston and then the equally sharp left turn onto Elm was the only way to get to the on ramp to the Stemmons Freeway. A traffic divider on Main St precluded the motorcade from taking the direct route, from Main St. across Houston and thence right to the Stemmons Freeway exit.

20. Just after the President's car passed the Texas Book Depository, a number of shots were fired. There were a total of three shots fired at the President. The first shot came from the right front, hitting him in the neck. This projectile did not exit the body. The immediate reaction by the President was to clutch at his neck and say, "I have been hit!" He was unable to move himself into any kind of a defensive posture because he was wearing a restrictive body brace.

21. The second shot came from above and behind the Presidential car, the bullet striking Texas Governor Connally in the upper right shoulder, passing through his chest and exiting sharply downwards into his left thigh.

-12-

22. The third, and fatal, shot was also fired at the President from the right front and from a position slightly above the car. This bullet, which was fired from a .223 weapon, struck the President above the right ear, passed through the right rear quadrant of his head and exited towards the left. Pieces of the President's skull and a large quantity of brain matter was blasted out and to the left of the car. Much of this matter struck a Dallas police motorcycle outrider positioned to the left rear of the Presidential car.

23. Photographic evidence indicates that the driver, SA Greer, slowed down the vehicle when shots were heard, in direct contravention of standing Secret Service regulations.

24. Reports that the initial hit on the President came from above and behind are false and misleading. Given the position of the vehicle at the time of impact and the altitude of the alleged shooter, a bullet striking the back of the President's neck would have exited sharply downward as did the projectile fired at Governor Connally purportedly from the same shooter located in the same area of the sixth floor of the Texas Book Depository.

25. The projectile that killed the President was filled with mercury. When such a projectile enters a body, the sudden decrease in velocity causes the mercury to literally explode the shell. This type of projectile is designed to practically guarantee the death of the target and is a method in extensive use by European assassination teams.

26. The disappearance of Kennedy's brain and related post mortem material from the U.S. National Archives was motivated by an official desire not to permit further testing which would certainly show the presence of mercury in the brain matter.

27. Official statements that the fatal shot was fired from above and behind are totally incorrect and intended to mislead. Such a shot would have blasted the brain and blood matter forward and not to the left rear. Also, photographic evidence indicates that after the fatal shot, the President was hurled to his left, against his wife who was seated to his immediate left.

28. The so-called "magic bullet" theory, i.e., a relatively pristine, fired Western Cartridge 6.5 Mannlicher-Carcano projectile produced in evidence, is obviously an official attempt to justify its own thesis. This theory, that a projectile from above and behind struck the President in the upper back, swung up, exited his throat, gained altitude and then angled downwards through the body of Governor Connally, striking bone and passing through muscle mass and emerging in almost undamaged condition is a complete impossibility. The bullet in question was obtained by firing the alleged assassination weapon into a container of water.

29. Three other such projectiles were recovered in similar undamaged condition. One of these was produced for official inspection and was claimed to have been found on Governor Connally's stretcher at Parkland Hospital. As a goodly portion of the projectile was still in the Governor's body, this piece of purported evidence should be considered as nothing more than an official "plant."

-13-

Author's Comments

Almost all of the revisionist works on the Kennedy assassination deal with forensics. The main and only purpose for the existence of the Warren Commission was to firmly establish that a lone individual who had no accomplices had shot President Kennedy. Any evidence in existence at the time the commission sat that furthered this thesis was used; any evidence that would refute their thesis was ignored.

Oswald, the lone individual with no accomplices, had to have shot the President and Governor Connally with a surplus Italian Army 6.5-mm Mannlicher-Carcano rifle equipped with a cheap telescopic sight. He had to have fired from the sixth floor of a building, down at a moving target and have fired three shots in a five-second period of time. The Carcano was a very clumsy bolt-action rifle. The turned-down bolt handle was difficult to manipulate, and the field of vision of the scope was so small as to virtually render it useless against a moving target.[10]

Tests by numerous firearms experts were never able to duplicate either the rate of fire or the alleged accuracy of the weapon purported to have been the sniper's only weapon.[11] While the muzzle velocity of the 6.5-mm round tip bullet was very low, nevertheless, if it hit a human being within a reasonable distance, it could inflict a fatal shot.

The "magic bullet" thesis is a piece of impossible nonsense that nevertheless was eagerly accepted and promulgated by the Warren Commission and, decades after the event, is still shrilly supported by those members of the media who have a vested interest in doing so. The nearly pristine bullet conveniently planted on a stretcher at Parkland Hospital could never have hit or passed into anything other than a container of water.

---

[10] Terry Gander and Peter Chamberlain, *Weapons of the Third Reich*, Doubleday: New York, 1979.

[11] Robert J. Groden and Harrison E. Livingstone, *High Treason,* New York: Conservatory Press, 1989, p. 58. Carl Oglesby, *Who Killed JFK?* Berkeley: Odonian Press, 1992, pp. 26f.

Lee Harvey Oswald

The Soviet Intelligence Study (translation)

18. During the course of the interrogations, Oswald was repeatedly led up and down very crowded corridors of the police headquarters with no thought of security. This is an obvious breach of elementary security that was noted at the time by reporters. It now appears that Oswald's killer was seen and photographed in the crowds in the building.

19. The American Marine defector, Lee Harvey Oswald, entered the Soviet Union in October of 1959. Initially, Oswald, who indicated he wanted to "defect" and reside in the Soviet Union, was the object of some suspicion by Soviet intelligence authorities. He was at first denied entrance, attempted a "suicide" attempt and only when he was more extensively interrogated by competent agents was it discovered that he was in possession of material that potentially had a great intelligence value.

20. Oswald, who as a U.S. Marine, was stationed at the Atsugi air field in Japan, had been connected with the Central Intelligence Agency's U2 intelligence-gathering aircraft program and was in possession of tecnhical manuals and papers concerning these aircraft and their use in overflights of the Soviet Union.

21. The subject proved to be most cooperative and a technical analysis of his documentation indicated that he was certainly being truthful with Soviet authorities. In addition to the manuals, Oswald was able to supply Soviet authorities with a wealth of material, much of which was unknown and relatively current. As a direct result of analysis of the Oswald material, it became possible to intercept and shoot down a U2 aircraft flown by CIA employee Gary Powers.

22. On the basis of the quality of this material, Oswald was granted asylum in the Soviet Union and permitted to settle in Minsk under the supervision of the Ministry of the Interior. This was partially to reward him for his cooperation and also to remove him from the possible influence of American authorities at the Embassy in Moscow.

23. Oswald worked in a radio factory, was given a subsidized apartment in Minsk and kept under constant surveillance. He was very pro-Russian, learned

to speak and read the language, albeit not with native fluency, and behaved himself well in his new surroundings.

24. Although Oswald was a known homosexual, he nevertheless expressed an interest in women as well and his several casual romantic affairs with both men and women were duly noted.

25. Oswald became involved with Marina Nikolaevna Prusakova, the niece of a Minsk-based intelligence official. He wished to marry this woman who was attractive but cold and ambitious. She wished to leave the Soviet Union and emigrate to the United States for purely economic reasons. Since his marrying a Soviet citizen under his circumstances was often most difficult, Oswald began to speak more and more confidentially with his intelligence contacts in Minsk. He finally revealed that he was an agent for the United States Office of Naval Intelligence and had been recruited by them to act as a conduit between their office and Soviet intelligence.

26. The official material on the CIA operations was entirely authentic and had been supplied to Oswald by his controllers in the ONI. It was apparent, and Oswald repeatedly stated, that the CIA was completely unaware of the removal of sensitive documents from their offices. This removal, Oswald stated, was effected by the ONI personnel stationed at Atsugi air field. Oswald was unaware of the reasons for this operation but had been repeatedly assured that the mission was considered of great national importance and that if he proved to be successful, he would be afforded additional and profitable future employment. It appears that Oswald was considered to be a one-time operative and was expendable. His purpose was to establish a reputation as a pro-Russian individual who would then "defect" to the Soviet Union and pass over the U2 material. He did not seem to realize at the time he "defected" that once he had been permitted to live in the Soviet Union on an official governmental subsidy, returning to America would be very difficult, if not impossible.

27. Now, with his romantic, and very impractical, attachment to Prusakova, he was being pressured by her to marry and then take her with him back to the United States. Oswald was informed that this was not a possible option for him. He became very emotional and difficult to deal with but finally made the suggestion that if he were allowed to marry and return to the United States, he would agree to work in reality for the Soviet Union.

28. After referring this matter to higher authority, it was decided to accede to Oswald's requests, especially since he was of no further use to Soviet intelligence and might well be of some service while resident in America.

29. Marriage was permitted and his return was expedited both by the Soviet authorities and the Americans who were informed, via a letter from Oswald, that he was in possession of intelligence material of value to them. This valuable information was duly given to him, a reversal to be noted on his original mission!

30. Oswald was given prepared information of such a nature as to impress American intelligence and permitted to contact intelligence officials in the American Embassy in Moscow. He was then permitted by the Americans to return to the United States with his new wife.

31. In America, Oswald no longer worked with the ONI because he was not able to further assist them. Besides, he was viewed as dangerous because he had knowledge of the ONI theft and use of CIA documents.

32. While in America, Oswald then worked as a paid informant for the Federal Bureau of Investigation who had contacted him when he returned and requested his assistance with domestic surveillance against pro-Soviet groups. He was assigned, in New Orleans, the task of infiltrating the anti-Castro groups which were nominally under the control of the CIA.

33. It is noted that there exists a very strong rivalry between the FBI and the CIA. The former is nominally in charge of domestic counterintelligence and the latter in charge of foreign intelligence. They have been fighting for power ever since the CIA was first formed in 1947. Oswald has stated that the FBI was aware of this ONI-sponsored defection with stolen CIA U2 documents but this is not a proven matter.

34. Later, Oswald was transferred to Dallas, Texas, by the FBI and he then secured a position in a firm which dealt in very secret photographic matters. Here, he was able to supply both the FBI and Soviet intelligence with identical data.

35. FBI reports, kept secret, show clearly that Oswald was paid by the FBI as an informant.

36. In New Orleans, a center of Cuban insurgent activity, Oswald was in direct contact with FBI officials and worked for a Guy Bannister, former FBI agent. Oswald infiltrated the ranks of Cuban insurgents and reported his findings to the FBI.

44. Oswald was a part of the FBI surveillance of the Cuban insurgents in the New Orleans area.

45. Oswald made a number of public appearances passing out pro-Castro leaflets in order to ingratiate himself with the insurgents.

46. At the FBI request, a local television station filmed Oswald passing out these leaflets and had this film shown on local stations in order to enhance Oswald's image. When his mission was finished, Oswald was then sent to Dallas to observe and penetrate the Russian colony there.

Russian Intelligence Study, *Driscoll Report*, p. 3-5, 6

The Warren Commission Report[12]

Lee Harvey Oswald was openly committed to Marxist ideology; he defected to the Soviet Union in 1959, and resided there until June of 1962, eventually returning to the United States with a Russian wife. [WCR, p. 254]

According to Oswald's diary he attempted suicide when he learned his application for citizenship had been denied. [WCR, p. 260]

While in Atsugi, Japan, Oswald studied the Russian language, perhaps with some help from an officer in his unit who was interested in Russian and used to "talk about it" with Oswald occasionally. [WCR, p. 257]

He may have begun to study the Russian language when he was stationed in Japan, which was intermittently from August 1957 to November 1958. [WCR, p. 256]

According to Oswald's "Historic Diary" and the documents furnished to the Commission by the Soviet Government, Oswald was not told that he had been accepted as a resident of the Soviet Union until about January 4, 1960. Although November 13 and 16 Oswald informed Aline Mosby and Priscilla Johnson that he had been granted permission to remain in the country indefinitely, the diary indicates that at that time he had been told only that he could remain "until some solution is found with what to do with me." [WCR, p. 265]

Once he was accepted as a resident alien in the Soviet Union, Oswald was given considerable benefits which ordinary Soviet citizens in his position in society did not have. The "Historic Diary" recites that after Oswald was informed that he could remain in the Soviet Union and he was being sent to Minsk he was given 5,000 rubles by the "Red Cross***" for expenses." He used 2,200 rubles to pay his hotel bill and another 150 rubles for a train ticket. [WCR, p. 269]

---

[12] The excerpts from the Warren Commission Report are designed to reflect the paragraphs in the Soviet Intelligence Study, hence are out of sequence on a number of occasions, but not out of context.

[...] about 6 weeks after his arrival he did receive an apartment, very pleasant by Soviet standards, for which he was required to pay only 60 rubles ($6.00) a month. Oswald considered the apartment "almost rent free." Oswald was given a job in the "Byelorussian Radio and Television Factory," where his pay on a per piece basis ranged from 700 to 900 rubles ($70-$90) a month. [WCR, p. 269]

The Commission has also assumed that it is customary for Soviet intelligence agencies to keep defectors under surveillance during their residence in the Soviet Union, through periodic interviews of neighbors and associates of the defector. Oswald once mentioned that the Soviet police questioned his neighbors occasionally.

Moreover, it is from Oswald's personal writings alone that the Commission has learned that he received supplementary funds from the Soviet "Red Cross." In the notes he made during the return trip to the United States Oswald recognized that the "Red Cross" subsidy had nothing to do with the well-known International Red Cross. He frankly stated that the money had come from the "MVD." [WCR, p. 272]

Marina Oswald said that by the time she met him in March 1961 he spoke the language well enough so that at first she thought he was from one of the Baltic areas of her country, because of his accent. She stated that his only defects were that his grammar was sometimes incorrect and that his writing was never good. [WCR, p. 257]

Oswald's marriage to Marina Prusakova on April 30, 1961, is itself a fact meriting consideration. A foreigner living in Russia cannot marry without the permission of the Soviet Government. [WCR, p. 274]

When Oswald arrived at the Embassy in Moscow, he met Richard E. Snyder, the same person with whom he had dealt in October of 1959. Primarily on the basis of Oswald's interview with Snyder on Monday, July 10, 1961, the American Embassy concluded that Oswald had not expatriated himself. On the basis of this tentative decision, Oswald was given back his American passport, which he had surrendered in 1959. The document was due to

expire in September 1961, however, and Oswald was informed
that its renewal would depend upon the ultimate decision by the
Department of State on his expatriation. On July 11, Marina
Oswald was interviewed at the Embassy and the steps necessary
for her to obtain an American visa were begun. In May 1962, after
15 months of dealing with the Embassy, Oswald's passport was
ultimately renewed and permission for his wife to enter the United
States was granted. [WCR, p. 277]

The Director of the FBI J. Edgar Hoover, Assistant to the Director Alan H. Belmont, FBI agents John W. Fain and John L.
Quigley, who interviewed Oswald, and FBI Agent James P. Hosty,
Jr., who was in charge of his case at the time of the assassination,
have testified before the Commission. All declared, in substance,
that Oswald was not an informant or agent of the FBI, that he did
not act in any other capacity for the FBI, and that no attempt was
made to recruit him in any capacity. [WCR, p. 327]

On October 4. 1963, Oswald applied for a position with the
Padgett Printing Corp., which was located at 1313 Industrial
Boulevard, several blocks from President Kennedy's parade route.
Oswald favorably impressed the plant superintendent who
checked his prior job references, one of which was Jaggars-Chiles-
Stovall, the firm where Oswald had done photography work from
October 1962 to April 1963. [WCR, p. 246]

The DIA Analysis

30. Soviet commentary on Oswald is basically verified from both KGB
and CIA sources. Oswald, however, was not being run by the ONI but instead
by the CIA. Their personnel files indicate that Oswald was initially recruited
by ONI for possible penetration of the very pervasive Japanese Communist
intelligence organization. Atsugi base was a very important target for these
spies.

31. Because of a shift in their policy , the CIA found it expedient to
exploit their U2 surveillance of the Soviet Union as a political rather than
intelligence operation.

32. The Eisenhower administration's interest in the possibility of achieving
a rapproachment with the Soviet Government created a situation that might have
proven disasterous to the CIAs continued functions.

33. Internal CIA documents show very clearly that as their very existence was dependent on a continuation of the Cold War, any diminution of East-West hostility could easily lead to their down sizing and, more important, to their loss of influence over the office of the President and also of U.S. foreign policy.

34. It was proposed, according to top level CIA reports, to somehow use their U2 flights to create an increase in tension that could lead to a frustration of any detente that might result from a lessening of international tensions.

35. It was initially thought that certain compromising documents could be prepared, sent to the CIA base at Atsugi, Japan, and then somehow leaked to the aggressive Japanese Communists. However, it was subsequently decided that there was a strong possibility that the documents might not be forwarded to Soviet Russia and kept in Japan for use in the anti-west/anti-war domestic campaigns.

36. CIA personnel stationed at Atsugi conceived a plan to arrange for select documents to be given directly to the Soviets via an American defector. It was at this point that Oswald's name was brought up by an ONI man. A CIA evaluation of Oswald convinced them that he would be the perfect defector. Psychological profiles of Oswald convinced them that he was clever, pro-Marxist, a person of low self-esteem as manifested in his chronic anti-social attitudes coupled with homosexual behavior.

37. As Oswald had developed a strong friendship with his ONI control, it was decided to allow him to think that he was working for the U.S. Navy rather than the CIA.

38. Oswald was told that he was performing a "special, vitally important" mission for the ONI and would be given a very good paying official position when he "successfully returned" from the Soviet Union. CIA and ONI reports indicate that he was never expected to return to the U.S. after he had fulfilled his function of passing the desired documents to the Soviet intelligence community.

39. The subsequent interception and shooting down by the Soviets of a U2 piloted by CIA agent Gary Powers using the leaked CIA material was sufficient to wreck the projected Eisenhower/Khruschev meeting and harden the Soviet leader's attitude towards the West.

-14-

40. It should be noted that the Powers U2 was equipped with a delayed action self-destruct device, designed to be activated by the pilot upon bailing out. This device was intended to destroy any classified surveillance material on the aircraft. In the Powers aircraft, the device was later disclosed to have been altered to explode the moment the pilot activated it. This would have resulted in the destruction of both the pilot and his aircraft.

41. After his return to the United States, Oswald was a marked man. He was a potential danger to the CIA, whose unredacted personnel reports indicate that Oswald was considered to be unstable, hostile, intelligent and very frustrated. He was, in short, a loose cannon.

42. While resident in Dallas, Oswald became acquainted with a George S. De Mohrenschildt, <u>a CIA operative.</u> De Mohrenschildt, a Balt, had family connections both in Poland and Russia, had worked for the German Ausland Abwehr and later the SD during the Second World War. He "befriended" Oswald and eventually an intimate physical relationship developed between the two men. This infuriated Marina Oswald and their already strained relationship grew even worse. She had come to America expecting great financial rewards and instead found poverty, two children and a sexually cold husband.

43. It was De Mohrenschildt's responsibility to watch Oswald, to establish a strong inter-personal relationship with him and to learn what information, if any, Oswald might possess that could damage the CIA if it became known.

44. The CIAs subsequent use of Oswald as a pawn in the assassination was a direct result of this concern.

Author's comments

On November 25, 1963, three days after Kennedy's assassination, U.S. Deputy Attorney General Nicholas Katzenbach, later a high Department of State official under Lyndon Johnson, wrote the following memorandum to Bill Moyers, aide to President Lyndon Johnson:

"It is important that all of the facts surrounding President Kennedy's assassination be made public in a way which will satisfy people in the United States and abroad that all the facts have been told and that a statement to this effect be made now.

1. The public must be satisfied that Oswald was the assassin; that he did not have confederates who are still at large; and that the evidence was such that he would have been convicted at trial.

2. Speculation about Oswald's motivation ought to be cut off, and we should have some basis for rebutting thought that this was a Communist conspiracy or (as the Iron Curtain press is saying) a right-wing conspiracy to blame it on the communists. Unfortunately the facts on Oswald seem too pat—too obvious (Marxist, Cuba, Russian

wife, etc.). The Dallas police have put out statements on the Communist conspiracy theory, and it was they who were in charge when he was shot and thus silenced.

3. The matter has been handled thus far with neither dignity nor conviction. Facts have been mixed with rumor and speculation. We can scarcely let the world see us totally in the image of the Dallas police when our President is murdered.

I think this objective may be satisfied by making public as soon as possible a complete and thorough FBI report on Oswald and the assassination. This may run into the difficulty of pointing to inconsistencies between this report and statements by Dallas police officials. But the reputation of the Bureau is such that it may do the whole job."[13]

On November 29, FBI Director Hoover wrote an in-house memo (see Appendix) that, in part, stated:

"I told him [President Johnson] I thought it would be very bad to have a rash of investigations. He then indicated the only way to stop it is to appoint a high-level committee to evaluate my report and tell the House and Senate not to go ahead with the investigation. I stated that would be a three-ring circus."[14]

And, in fact, the reputation of the Bureau was such that the whole job was well and truly accomplished. The FBI was in sole charge of assembling evidence for the Warren Commission, and almost simultaneously with the Katzenbach letter, Director Hoover had been committing himself on paper to express his firm determination that Oswald, and Oswald alone, was responsible for the assassination.

This determination was reflected in a flood of teletypes from FBI headquarters to the agency offices in Dallas, New Orleans, Miami, and Chicago. Regardless of what information was uncovered by local agents, all of it had to be given to the local agent-in-

---

[13] *House Select Committee on Assassinations*, HSCA 567, vol. 3, Washington, D.C.: U.S. Government Printing Office, 1976.

[14] Memo of J. Edgar Hoover to Staff, 29 November 1963, Crowley Papers. See Appendix.

charge who then forwarded it to Washington. There, the numerous reports on Oswald's activities and personal connections, along with reports on the Chicago mob, the CIA activities in Louisiana and Florida, and the late President and his activities and personal connections, were skillfully tailored to present a seamless series of reports, interviews, photographic and other forensic evidence for presentation to the waiting commission.

Any witness statements that contradicted the official version of events were excluded from this presentation, as were photographs that might have contradicted the lone-assassin theory.

The Soviet intelligence report mentions the discovery of Oswald in the second floor employee's lounge by a Dallas police officer immediately after the shooting. It is commented by them, and reflected in the official report, that Oswald appeared to be very calm and certainly not out of breath as he would have been from running down four flights of steps only moments before. Further, other employees of the Texas Book Depository who had been using the stairs had not seen Oswald rush down past them. He could not have used the building's elevators to go from his work area on the sixth floor to the lunchroom, because persons unknown stopped one on the sixth floor and the other was on another floor. There were no elevators stopped on the second floor near the employee lunchroom.

The forensics have been equally confusing. Dallas Deputy Sheriff Seymour Weitzman was one of three deputy sheriffs who discovered a rifle on the sixth floor of the Book Depository. Weitzman was a firearms expert and owned two gun shops. Initially, he positively identified the rifle as a German Mauser, 7.65-millimeter weapon. This is the so-called Argentine Mauser, which was manufactured by the Germans for the Argentine army. Unlike later models of the Mauser, it has a straight bolt handle, and the top of the receiver is plainly marked with the coat of arms of Argentina. The Argentine Mauser, a very well built and easy to use weapon, had been offered as military surplus to the buying public for some years previously and was easily available to collectors, gun shops, and hunters.

The physical differences between the 7.65-mm Argentine Mauser surplus rifle and the 6.5-mm Italian Mannlicher-Carcano surplus rifle are very evident, and no-one with the professional background of Deputy Weitzman could possibly mistake one for the other.

In his book *Case Closed,* New York author and avid Warren Commission supporter Gerald Posner states:

> "Seymour Weitzman and Luke Mooney, two Dallas policemen [sic], thought at first glance that the rifle was a 7.65 [mm] bolt action Mauser. Although the officers quickly admitted their mistake, that initial misidentification led to speculation that a different gun was found on the sixth floor and that Oswald's Carcano was later swapped for the murder weapon. <u>There are considerable similarities between a bolt-action Mauser and a Carcano. Firearms experts say they are easy to confuse without a proper exam.</u>" [Emphasis added][15]

Aside from his slavish adherence to the conclusions of the Warren Commission Report, Posner has obviously no knowledge of firearms whatsoever. The immediate visual differences between the two weapons are very clear and obvious. The Carcano has a distinctive box magazine protruding in front of the trigger guard, and the Mauser has none. The Mauser has a straight bolt handle, and the Carcano has a turned-down bolt handle.[16]

Weitzman was a gun dealer, and both surplus weapons were very common in the trade at the time of the assassination. The supporting comments by Posner attributed to government experts are obviously self-serving, like the majority of such statements found in the Warren Commission Report, and have absolutely no probative value whatsoever.

After the Mauser was turned in to local authorities, it suddenly was transformed into a Carcano rifle, one that allegedly had been purchased by Oswald using an alias. The Mauser vanished from

---

[15] G. Posner, *op. cit.* (note 6), p. 270n.
[16] See footnote 10.

the sight of living men, but the Carcano was presented to the world as the murder weapon.

The so-called "magic bullet" was certainly fired from the suspected Carcano, but by whom and when is certainly not known at this remove. Because of the pristine condition of the bullet, it is clearly evident that it had never, under any remote circumstances, been fired into or passed through a human body.

In his November 29, 1963 report, FBI Director Hoover said:

> "I said no, that three shots were fired at the President and we have them. I stated that our ballistic experts were able to prove the shots were fired by this gun; that the President was hit by the first and third bullets and the second hit the Governor; that there were three shots; that one complete bullet rolled out of the President's head; that it tore a large part of the President's off; that in trying to massage his heart on the way into the hospital they loosened the bullet which fell on the stretcher and we have that."[17]

When he was arrested, Oswald proclaimed to the media that he was a patsy and had nothing to do with the killing of John F. Kennedy. Katzenbach's dictum that the evidence had to be such as to secure a conviction was certainly quickly and officially implemented.

Since Oswald was very shortly and most conveniently dead, all manner of innuendo, deliberate error, and patently manufactured evidence was put together into a pastiche that never needed to be examined and cross-examined in a court of law. Oswald had been tried and found publicly guilty *in absentia*, and in the event that there existed other, even more provable suspects, they were entirely safe in the knowledge that they had escaped whatever manipulated creativity had passed for the process of justice and were certainly well protected.

The few works that support the findings of the Warren Commission contain a number of errors, which strongly indicate that their authors have done little research and have no genuine un-

---

[17] Hoover letter, *op. cit.* (note 14), p. 3.

derstanding of their subjects. As a case in point, referring once again to the Posner book, this author shows an appalling lack of knowledge of the Soviet intelligence structure in the 1950s and 1960s.

Posner comments on a statement allegedly made by a *faux* Soviet defector that the uncle of Marina Oswald was "MVD. It's like being a local policeman, nothing more. He was completely unimportant."[18] At another point, Posner shows a picture of Oswald and his wife's relatives with the comment that Colonel Ilya Vasillyevich Prusakova, her uncle, was mistakenly believed to have been a KGB officer when he was "actually the equivalent of a local U.S. policeman."[19]

Posner is referring here to the false Soviet defector Nosenko who was sent by the Soviet government to the United States immediately after the assassination to allay American fears that the Soviets had been involved with the Kennedy assassination via Oswald. He very obviously had no knowledge of the intelligence agencies he purported to have served. The MVD was, at that time, the name of the Soviet secret police controlled by the State Security Committee. It was later renamed into KGB.[20] A serving colonel in the Minsk office of the MVD was most certainly not the "equivalent of a local U.S. policeman."

The Warren Report and its supporters have attached a considerable amount of importance to the comments and very supportive testimony of Oswald's Russian wife, Marina. On this subject, Hoover wrote in his November 29 memo:

> "I advised the President that his wife had been very hostile, would not cooperate and speaks only Russian; that yesterday she said, if we could give assurance she would be allowed to remain in the country, she would cooperate; and that I told our agents to give that assurance and sent a Russian-speaking agent to Dallas last night to interview her."[21]

---

[18]   G. Posner, *op. cit.* (note 6), p. 54n.

[19]   *Ibid.*, Plate iii.

[20]   See footnote 8.

[21]   Hoover letter, note (14), p. 4.

Jack Rubenstein ("Ruby")

Soviet Intelligence Study (translation)

47. Two days after the shooting of the American President, the alleged assassin, Oswald was shot to death in the basement of the Dallas Police Department while he was being transferred to another jail. On the day of the assassination, November 22, FBI Chief Hoover notified the authorities in Dallas that Oswald should be given special security.

48. This killing was done in the presence of many armed police officers by a known criminal and associate of the American Mafia named Jack Rubenstein, or "Ruby" as he was also known. "Ruby" had a long past of criminal association with the Mafia in Chicago, Illinois, a major area of gangster control in America. "Ruby" had once worked for the famous Al Capone and then for Sam Giancana. This man was head of the Chicago mob at the time of the assassination.

49. "Ruby" was the owner of a drinking establishment in Dallas that specialized in dancing by naked women and was also a close friend of many police officers in Dallas. "Ruby" had been seen and photographed in the Dallas police department while Oswald was being interrogated. It should be noted here that suspect Oswald was very often taken by Dallas police out into the completely unguarded hallways of the building and in the presence of many persons unknown to the police. This is viewed as either an attempt to have Oswald killed or a very incompetent and stupid breach of basic security.

50. The timing by "Ruby" of his entrance into the guarded basement was far too convenient to be accidental. Also, the method of his shooting of Oswald showed a completely professional approach. "Ruby" stepped out from between two policemen, holding a revolver down along his leg to avoid detection. As he stepped towards the suspect, "Ruby" raised his right hand with the revolver and fired upwards into Oswald's body. The bullet severed major arteries and guaranteed Oswald's death.

51. Although "Ruby" subsequently pretended to be mentally disturbed, his actions showed professional calculation to a degree. This play-acting was continued into his trial and afterwards. "Ruby" was convicted of the murder of

and sentenced to death. H died in prison of cancer in January of 1967 after an appeal from his sentence had been granted by the court judge. Information indicates that he was given a fatal injection.

52. "Ruby's" statements should not be confused with his actions. He was a professional criminal, had excellent connections with the Dallas police, had been involved with activities in Cuba and gun running into that country and some evidence has been produced to show that he and Oswald had knowledge of each other.

53. Like Oswald, "Ruby" too had homosexual activities and one public witness firmly placed Oswald in "Ruby's" club prior to the assassination.

54. In view of later developments and disclosures, the use of a Chicago killer with local Mafia connections to kill Oswald is not surprising. Stories of "Ruby's" eccentricity were highlighted by American authorities to make it appear that he, like suspect Oswald, was an eccentric, single individual who acted out of emotion and not under orders.

55. As in the case of Oswald, there was never a proven motive for "Ruby's" acts. Oswald had no reason whatsoever to shoot the President, had never committed any proven acts of violence. Although he was purported to have shot at a fascist General, it was badly presented and in all probability was a "red herring" to "prove" Oswald's desire to shoot people. "Ruby", a professional criminal with a long record of violence, claimed he shot Oswald to "protect" the President's wife from testifying. This statement appears to be an obvious part of "Ruby's" attempt to defend himself by claiming to be mad.

56. It is obvious that "Ruby" killed Oswald to silence him. Since Oswald was not involved in the killing of the President, continued interrogation of him leading to a court trial would have very strongly exposed the weakness of the American government's attempt to blame him for the crime.

57. Silencing Oswald promptly was a matter of serious importance for the actual killers.

58. That Oswald could not be convicted with the evidence at hand, his removal was vital. He could then be tried and convicted in public without any danger.

The Warren Commission Report

Concerned that there might be an attempt on Oswald's life, FBI Director J. Edgar Hoover sent a message to [Dallas Police] Chief Curry on November 22 through Special Agent Manning C. Clements of the FBI's Dallas office, urging that Oswald be afforded the utmost security. Curry does not recall receiving the message. [WCR, p. 225]

Jack Ruby shot Lee Harvey Oswald at 11:21 a.m., on Sunday, November 24, 1963, shortly after Ruby entered the basement of the Dallas Police Department. Almost immediately, speculation arose that Ruby had acted on behalf of members of a conspiracy who had planned the killing of President Kennedy and wanted to silence Oswald. [WCR, p. 333]

Ruby is known to have made his way, by about 11:30 p.m., to the third floor of the Dallas Police Department where reporters were congregated near the homicide bureau. [WCR, p. 340]

(A photograph of Ruby taken in Dallas Police Headquarters about midnight November 22, 1963 is Commission Exhibit 2424)

Video tapes confirm Ruby's statement that he was present on the third floor when Chief Jesse E. Curry and District Attorney Henry M. Wade announced that Oswald would be shown to the newsmen at a press conference in the basement. [WCR, p. 342]

Sunday morning trip to police department—Leaving his apartment a few minutes before 11 a.m., Ruby went to his automobile taking with him his dachshund, Sheba, and a portable radio. He placed a revolver which he routinely carried in a bank moneybag in the trunk of his car. [WCR, p. 354]

Ruby parked his car in a lot directly across the street from the Western Union office. He apparently placed his keys and billfold in the trunk of the car, then locked the trunk, which contained approximately $1,000 in cash, and placed the trunk key in the glove compartment. He did not lock the car doors. [WCR, p. 357]

Ruby entered the police basement through the auto ramp from Main Street and stood behind the front rank of newsmen and police officers who were crowded together at the base of the ramp awaiting the transfer of Oswald to the county jail. As Oswald emerged from a basement office at approximately 11:21 a.m., Ruby moved quickly forward and, without speaking, fired one fatal shot into Oswald's abdomen before being subdued by a rush of police officers. [WCR, p. 357]

The assembly of more than 70 police officers, some of them armed with tear gas, and the contemplated use of an armored truck, appear to have been designed primarily to repel an attempt of a mob to seize the prisoner. [WCR, p. 227]

If Oswald had been tried for his murders of November 22, the effects of the news policy pursued by the Dallas authorities would have proven harmful both to the prosecution and the defense. The misinformation reported after the shootings might have been used by the defense to cast doubt on the reliability of the State's entire case. [WCR, p. 238]

The DIA Analysis

57. The use of Jack Ruby to kill Oswald has been explained by the official reports as an aberrant act on the part of an emotional man under the influence of drugs. The Warren Commission carefully overlooked Ruby's well-known ties to the Chicago mob as well as his connections with mob elements in Cuba.

58. Ruby's early Chicago connections with the mob are certainly well documented in Chicago police files. This material was not used nor referred to in the Warren Report.

59. Ruby's close connection with many members of the Dallas police infrastructure coupled with a very strong motivation to remove Oswald prior to any appointment of an attorney to represent him or any possible revelations Oswald might make about his possible knowledge of the actual assassins made Ruby an excellent agent of choice. If Oswald had gained the relative security of the County Jail and lawyers had been appointed for him, it would have proven much more difficult to remove him.

60. The Warren Commission was most particularly alarmed by attempts on the part of New York attorney Mark Lane, to present a defense for the dead Oswald before the Commission. Lane was refused this request. A written comment by Chief Justice Earl Warren to CIA Director Allen Dulles was that "people like Lane should never be permitted to air their radical views...at least not before this Commission..."

61. Ruby had been advised by his Chicago mob connections, as well as by others involved in the assassination, that his killing of Oswald would "make him a great hero" in the eyes of the American public and that he "could never be tried or convicted" in any American court of law.

62. Ruby, who had personal identity problems, accepted and strongly embraced this concept and was shocked to find that he was to be tried on a capital charge. Never very stable, Ruby began to disintegrate while in custody and mixed fact with fiction in a way as to convince possible assassins that he was not only incompetent but would not reveal his small knowledge of the motives behind the removal of Oswald.

-16-

63. In the presence of Chief Justice Warren, Ruby strongly intimated that he had additional information to disclose and wanted to go to the safety of Washington but Warren abruptly declared that he was not interested in hearing any part of it.

64. A polygraph given to Ruby concerning his denial of knowing Oswald and only attempting to kill him as a last minute impulse proved to be completely unsatisfactory and could not be used to support the Commission's thesis.

65. During his final illness, while in Parkland Hospital, Ruby was under heavy sedation and kept well supervised to prevent any death bed confessions or inopportune chance remarks to hospital attendants. An unconfirmed report from a usually reliable source states that Ruby was given an injection of air with a syringe which produced an embolism that killed him. The official cause of Ruby's death was a blood clot.

66. It was later alleged that Ruby had metastated cancer of the brain and lungs which somehow had escaped any detection during his incarceration in Dallas. It was further alleged that this terminal cancer situation had existed for over a year without manifesting any serious symptoms to the Dallas medical authorities. This is viewed by non-governmental oncologists as highly unbelievable and it appears that Ruby's fatal blood clot was the result of outside assistance.

Author's comments

Although the American public was badly shaken by the events of November 22, 1963, the killing of Oswald two days later was a matter that brought into serious question the entire developing official explanation of the assassination.

The Katzenbach letter is an excellent indication of which way the official wind was blowing. At the same time, Director Hoover wrote similar letters, one to President Johnson about cutting off debate and clearly defining Oswald as the sole assassin.[22]

Oswald was *not* the sole assassin. In point of fact, Lee Harvey Oswald had nothing whatsoever to do with the assassination of John Kennedy. Oswald was a very convenient scapegoat for the murder and was set up for it by the real killers.

---

[22] Hoover wrote several documents for President Johnson. See especially the Hoover Memorandum, note 14.

The question has been asked that if the FBI had been entrusted with the investigation, would they not have found evidence of a conspiracy, assuming there was one?

The answer would be affirmative. If there had been a conspiracy, the FBI would certainly have discovered it. That having been said, consider several important factors.

Oswald had been employed by a number of official U.S. agencies: the ONI,[23] the CIA, and, finally, the FBI. Given the intense and growing public concern over the stunning act in Dallas, it would have been political suicide for Hoover to acknowledge that an FBI paid informant had killed the President of the United States.

Hoover had found his position very insecure during the Kennedy administration. The President's brother, Robert Kennedy, had been Attorney General and detested Hoover, calling him "an old faggot" and trying to find some way to leverage him out of his office.[24] It was only the fact that Hoover had enormous files on all the important personalities in Washington, including the President and members of his family, that kept him in office. Hoover's files on the President included information on the illegal and socially outrageous activities of John Kennedy and his father Joe.[25]

The apparent ease with which Oswald's killer had been able to penetrate a heavy screen of Dallas police officers was addressed by Hoover in his memo of November 29:

> "The President asked if we have any relationship between the two (Oswald and Rubenstein) as yet. I replied that at the present time we have not; that there was a story that the fellow had been in Rubenstein's nightclub but it has not been confirmed. [... Ruby] knew all of the police officers in the white light district; let them come in and get food and liquor, etc.; and that is how I think he got into po-

---

[23] Office of Naval Intelligence, the Navy's secret service.

[24] The bitter animosity between the Attorney General and the Director of the FBI has been well covered in a number of works. See William Sullivan, *The Bureau: My Thirty Years in Hoover's FBI*, New York: Norton, 1979.

[25] For a study of the criminal activities of Joseph P. Kennedy, as they are mentioned hereafter, see S. Hersh, *op. cit.* (note 5), pp. 44-60.

lice headquarters. I said if they ever made any move, the pictures did not show it even when they saw his approach and he got right up to Oswald and pressed the pistol against Oswald's stomach; that neither officer on either side made any effort to grab Rubenstein—not until after the pistol was fired. I said, secondly, the chief of police admits he moved Oswald in the morning as a convenience and at the request of the motion picture people who wanted daylight."[26]

The truth of the Kennedy assassination is not to be found in the deliberate obfuscations, untruths, and omissions of the Warren Report but in the files of the Director of the FBI and, more especially, in the files of the CIA.

If, as postulated here, Kennedy was not killed by a lone, disgruntled societal misfit, who then did kill him and why?

The answers are to be found in both the Soviet intelligence report and the DIA commentary. Additional answers can be found in current FBI and CIA files, but as these are not available for public viewing, nor are ever likely to be, it is to these other papers that one must look.

Files aside, the most important tool that a historian can use is logic. A very complex series of theories, postulations, and presentations may simply be reduced to a very common denominator. By not multiplying entities beyond necessity, the truth quickly becomes evident to the investigator. Cutting away the concealing jungle growth brings the stalking tiger into full view.

As the Warren Commission Report obviously has nothing to say about any reasonable suspects other than the unfortunate Lee Harvey Oswald and his friends, its comments are not included in the final chapters of the drama.

Persons with an interest in going into government service are encouraged to read the Warren Commission Report to learn how to conceal their mistakes in a matrix of literary and historical nonsense. The Brothers Grimm with their classic fairy tales were

---

[26] Hoover letter, *op. cit.* (note 14), pp. 2f.

doubtlessly the first governmental spin doctors, but then, no-one ever was expected to take *them* seriously.

The Official Cover Up

Soviet Intelligence Study (translation)

62. A very large number of published books about the assassination have appeared since the year 1963. Most of these books are worthless from a historical point of view. They represent the views of obsessed people and twist information to suit the author's beliefs.

63. There are three main ideas written about:
a. The American gangsters killed the President because his brother, the American Attorney General, was persecuting them;
b. Cuban refugees felt that Mr. Kennedy had deserted their cause of ousting Cuban chief of state Castro;
c. Various American power groups such as the capitalist business owners, fascist political groups, racists, internal and external intelligence organizations either singly or in combination are identified.

64. American officials have not only made no effort to silence these writers but in many cases have encouraged them. The government feels, as numerous confidential reports indicate, that the more lunatic books appear, the better. This way, the real truth is so concealed as to be impenetrable.

65. It was initially of great concern to our government that individuals inside the American government were utilizing Oswald's "Communist/Marxist" appearance to suggest that the assassination was of a Soviet origin.

66. In order to neutralize this very dangerous theme, immediately after the assassination, the Soviet Union fully cooperated with American investigating bodies and supplied material to them showing very clearly that Oswald was not carrying out any Soviet design.

67. Also, false defectors were used to convince the Americans that Oswald was considered a lunatic by the Soviet Union, and had not been connected with the Soviet intelligence apparatus in any way. He was, of course, connected but it was imperative to disassociate the Soviet Union with the theory that Oswald, an American intelligence operative, had been in collusion with them concerning the assassination.

68. The false defector, Nosenko, a provable member of Soviet intelligence, was given a scenario that matched so closely the personal attitudes of Mr. Hoover of the FBI that this scenario was then officially supported by Mr. Hoover and his bureau.

69. Angleton of the CIA at once suspected Nosenko's real mission and subjected him to intense interrogation but finally, Nosenko has been accepted as a legitimate defector with valuable information on Oswald.

70. Because of this business, Angleton was forced to resign his post as chief of counter intelligence. This has been considered a most fortunate byproduct of the controversy.

71. The FBI has accepted the legitimacy of Nosenko and his material precisely because it suited them to do so. It was also later the official position of the CIA because the issue dealt specifically with the

-8-

involvement, or non-involvement, between Oswald, a private party, and the organs of Soviet intelligence. Since there was no mention of Oswald's connection with American intelligence, this was of great importance to both agencies.

The DIA Analysis

71. The concerns of Soviet intelligence and governmental agencies about any possible Soviet connection between defector Oswald and themselves is entirely understandable. It was never seriously believed by any competent agency in the United States that the Soviet Union had any part in the assassination of Kennedy.

72. Because of the emotional attitudes in official Washington and indeed, throughout the entire nation immediately following the assassination, there was created a potentially dangerous international situation for the

-17-

Soviets. Oswald was an identified defector with Marxist leanings. He was also believed to be a pro-Castro activist. That both his Marxist attitudes and his sympathies and actions on behalf of the Cuban dictator were enhanced simulations was not known to the Warren Commission at the time of their activities.

73. To bolster their eager efforts to convince the American authorities that their government had nothing to do with the assassination, men like Nosenko were utilized to further support this contention. It is not known whether Nosenko was acting on orders or whether he was permitted access to created documentation and given other deliberate disinformation by the KGB and allowed to defect. A great deal of internal concern was expressed upon Nosenko's purported defection by Soviet officials but this is viewed as merely an attempt, and a successful one, to lend substance to his importance.

74. James Angleton's attitude towards Nosenko is a commentary on the duality of his nature. On the one hand, Angleton was performing as Chief of Counter Intelligence and openly showed his zeal in searching for infiltraters and "moles" inside his agency while on the other hand, Angleton had very specific personal knowledge that the Soviet Union had nothing to do with the Kennedy assassination.

Author's Comments

The death of President Kennedy was, on the surface at least, a straightforward act. He was shot to death while riding in a motorcade. The shooting itself was photographed by a number of bystanders in Dealy Plaza (and subsequently, the FBI seized a number of these pictures and none of them have ever been seen again), and the famous Zapruder motion picture has been viewed by a large number of people.

The murder of Oswald two days later by a petty criminal in a heavily guarded police facility clearly sowed the seeds of the following cloud of controversy and doubt that has surrounded this act.

The hastily cobbled together Warren Report was of such a nature as to raise far more questions than it answered, and the attempts on the part of establishment supporters to validate it merely lend credence to the suspicions of growing legions of doubters.

When the establishment formulates an official version of an important incident, this version is strongly supported by not only the establishment itself, but by the sections of the media and academia that are beholden to them.

Anyone who entertains or, even more importantly, presents for public consumption views that are in opposition to the establishment are either ignored or trivialized. In the case of the growing number of those who have brought the Warren Commission Report into question, the usual dismissive phrase is "conspiracy buff." The implication is that anyone who questions the Warren Report is merely a gadfly amateur, protected under the First Amendment, but, of course, just another eccentric. And, as such, to be ignored.

On the other hand, authors like Gerald Posner who support the Warren Report are given prominent coverage in the establishment papers, and one sees such comments as "Persuasive...brilliantly illuminating...more satisfying than any conspiracy theory." This is credited to a reviewer for the *New York Times*,[27] a newspaper that has always been a powerful supporter of the establishment point of view of the Kennedy assassination.

The official version of this event is always given the most positive adjectives in media comment while anything that would negate the official version is always termed "conspiracy theory" and generally dismissed as being the product of a disordered mind and, certainly, not having been proven.

There have been, of course, no other documents available to the public other than the ones under governmental control, and this absence has powerfully strengthened the establishment position.

Should any documents appear that would seriously question that position, the formula for negation is already well in place. Proof would be demanded, and if it were forthcoming, it would be rejected.

The motives of the supporters of the government's thesis and their methods will be discussed in a separate chapter.

---

[27] G. Posner, *op. cit.* (note 6), dust jacket comments.

The Alternative Theory

There is no question that President John F. Kennedy was murdered in Dallas, Texas on Friday, November 22, 1963.

There *is* a question of whether the official government report is accurate. There is a further question as to whether this report is a deliberate attempt to confuse and hide what might actually have happened.

The key issue is whether Lee Harvey Oswald, acting entirely alone, shot and killed President Kennedy and shot and wounded Texas Governor John Connally from a so-called sniper's nest on the sixth floor of the Texas Book Depository where he was employed.

There is a question of the weapon used. Did Oswald use a surplus Italian army rifle, a 6.5-mm Mannlicher-Carcano, equipped with an American telescopic sight?

If Oswald did not act alone, who may have acted with him?

If Oswald did not act at all, who then shot the President to death and wounded the Governor?

If persons other than Oswald assassinated the President, who were they and, more importantly, why did they act?

If there were other assassins, were they politically motivated?

Were they professionals, merely performing their work for money?

If professionals were hired to kill the President, who hired them and why?

These are all questions that will hopefully be fully addressed in the following pages, but certainty is always illusion, and cases of such complexity are never closed, contrary to the title of Posner's book. And wishing does not make it so, ever.

While there were a significant number of groups and individuals who disliked and even hated John Kennedy, most of them possessed neither the means nor the ability to terminate his presidency.

However, there were a very few who did. Leaving out the chronically displeased and the lunatic fringe and concentrating on those who might have had not only the means but also the ability to assassinate a heavily guarded President, here is the primary question:

Who were these groups?

There was, first and foremost, organized American crime. At the time of the assassination, Robert Kennedy, the President's brother, was conducting a serious campaign against organized crime. He was doing so at the request of his father, multimillionaire and former Ambassador to Great Britain, Joseph P. Kennedy.[28]

The Mafia, most especially the Chicago branch of that confederation, was enraged at these attacks on them. They felt that because the "Ambassador" (as he liked to be called) had openly solicited their active assistance for the candidacy of his son, John, during the presidential campaign of 1960, attacks by the Kennedy administration on them were not in order.

They had agreed with Joseph Kennedy to work in conjunction with the Chicago political machine, under the capable hands of Mayor Richard Daley, to secure blocks of vital votes for John F. Kennedy. In this, they were very successful. In Chicago it is still said that in 1960, people voted early and often. So great was the enthusiasm for a Kennedy victory that even the dead were said to have voted, again, early and often.

The presence of Texas Senator Lyndon Johnson on the ticket as Vice President somehow secured the negation of over 100,000 votes in Texas, and this dubious act, coupled with the successes in Chicago, secured Kennedy's election but by the slimmest of margins.

The *quid pro quo* stated in the beginning, and fully expected to be operable by the Chicago group, was that the ongoing prosecution, and, as they saw it, persecution of Teamsters' Union Presi-

---

[28] S. Hersh, *op. cit.* (note 5), p. 153.

dent James R. Hoffa by the government be halted. Organized crime had been making effective use of the Teamsters' Union's enormous pension fund to build casinos in Las Vegas, and Hoffa was considered to be more than friendly and very useful to their business projects.

By accepting the aid of Chicago mob boss Sam Giancana in the election, it was generally, and not unreasonably, felt by this individual that his terms had been accepted. John Kennedy had been elected with the Chicago mob's vital support, and the actions against Hoffa therefore would cease.[29]

They reckoned, however, without the personality of Joseph Kennedy.

During Prohibition, the elder Kennedy had been deeply involved in the importation and sale of liquor that had been officially banned in the United States. This activity was the real basis for the large Kennedy fortune, and Joe Kennedy had formed a partnership in the Chicago area with gang leader Al Capone during this period.

There was an incident in which Kennedy attempted to cheat Capone over a large shipment of illegally imported liquor, and the enraged Capone threatened to kill the future ambassador. In order to prevent this, Kennedy was forced to bring two suitcases filled with money to Chicago to seek to repair the dangerous breach between himself and the brutally effective Capone:

75. The senior Kennedy, it is known, was heavily involved with rum-running during the Prohibition era and had extensive mob connections. He had closely been associated with Al Capone, mob boss in Chicago, and had a falling out with him over an allegedly hijacked liquor shipment. Capone, Chicago police records indicate, had threatened Kennedy's life over this and Kennedy had to pay off the mob to nullify a murder contract.

Driscoll Report, p. 18

Kennedy had never forgiven Capone for his threats, for the loss of money, and most especially for the humiliations he had suffered by his *mea culpa*.[30]

---

[29] *Ibid.*, pp. 131-154.
[30] See footnote 25.

The "Ambassador" was a man who never forgot and never forgave, and when his son was safely in the White House, he demanded that the new President appoints his younger brother as the Attorney General of the United States. Robert Kennedy had been slated for a less important post in the new administration, but Joe Kennedy demanded it, and when he demanded, he was obeyed.

The children of Joseph Kennedy were completely under the influence and certainly the domination of their ferocious father, and they did as they were told, even if they occupied the Oval Office.[31]

When Bobby Kennedy became Attorney General, he immediately, on his father's instructions, instituted a reign of terror against organized crime in general and specifically the Chicago branch. The targets of this vengeance must have viewed these renewed and greatly intensified attacks on themselves as a gross breach of faith and a betrayal by a long-time business associate.

The Mafia certainly had the means of assassinating someone, although perhaps not the President of the United States, and they certainly had the motivation.

In fact, they did play a significant part in the plot but not as a prime mover, only as a very willing and able subcontractor. Professional crime, then, is one significant player on the board. Well organized, intelligent, and completely ruthless as they may be, this segment of the American business community did not achieve its position in American society because they were stupid. Had they personally attempted to assassinate a sitting President, if caught before or after the act, the reprisals would have been swift and deadly.

However, the mob's connections reached well up into various governmental structures, and if they had an even more powerful patron guiding and ultimately protecting them, the chances of detection and subsequent retribution would be greatly lessened:

---

[31] *Ibid.*, pp. 153f.

> 72. It is known now that the American gangsters had very close relations with the Central Intelligence Agency. This relationship began during the war when the American OSS made connections with the Sicilian members of the American gangs in order to assist them against the fascists. The man who performed this liaison was Angleton, later head of counter intelligence for the CIA. These gangster contacts were later utilized by the CIA for its own ends.

Russian Intelligence Study, *Driscoll Report*, p. 9

> 45. The connections of Angleton, Chief of Counter Intelligence for the CIA with elements of the mob are well known in intelligence circles. Angleton worked closely with the Sicilian and Naples mobs in 1944 onwards as part of his duties for the OSS.
>
> 46. The connections of Robert Crowley another senior CIA official, with elements of the Chicago mob are also well known in intelligence circles.

Driscoll Report, p. 15

The American mob is one of the major pieces on the chessboard but there are others to consider.

The next significant group to consider is the Cuban exiles. In 1959, when Fidel Castro and his revolutionary movement over-threw Cuban dictator Fulgencio Batista, the U.S. backed and thoroughly corrupt Cuban head of state, a massive influx of upper and professional class Cubans fled to the protection of the United States.

Castro soon made his Marxist leanings very clear and by doing this became an immediate player in the ongoing Cold War. While elements of the CIA had actively assisted him in achieving power, others began a campaign against him, using every means to remove him, including plotting his assassination.

Not only did Castro nationalize American business holdings, he also forced out the Mafia owners of Cuba's very lucrative casino industry. Since the CIA had strong and often useful contacts with the Mafia, the anger of the mob because of the dispossession of its assets matched or surpassed that of American business interests and strongly motivated the powerful anti-Castro movement, which was sponsored and maintained by the CIA.[32]

---

[32] S. Hersh, *op. cit.* (note 5), pp. 268-293; Anthony Summers, *Conspiracy*, New York: McGraw-Hill, 1980, pp. 264-272; Peter Grose, *Gentleman Spy: The Life of Allan Dulles*, Amherst: The University of Massachusetts Press, 1994, pp. 493-518.

Paramilitary cadres of Cuban anti-Castro activists were organized, armed, and funded by the CIA, and in April of 1962, these units attacked the island with the intention of initiating a revolt against Castro. The landing was met by Cuban regular military units under Castro's command and was decisively crushed.

Kennedy did not back up the commando units with armed support by U.S. military units, and the fury of the rebel Cubans was intense.

More promises to liberate their country were made by the CIA, and the units were increased in size and armament. It was their continuing commando raids against Cuba that eventually led directly to the Cuban missile crisis of October 1962.[33]

A combination of Kennedy's perceived weakness coupled with the CIA's commando raids convinced Soviet leader Nikita Khrushchev that he could threaten the United States with possible military reprisals while shoring up the Soviet Union's relations with its Western Hemisphere ally.

Kennedy proved to be far stronger than the Soviet leader had bargained for, and the risk of war, which was great, diminished quickly as the result of a significant rapprochement between the two leaders.

As a result of this rapprochement, Kennedy agreed to halt the incursions, and Khrushchev agreed to withdraw Soviet missiles from Cuba.

This demarche infuriated the volatile Cubans who felt they had been betrayed twice by the Kennedy administration in general and specifically by the President himself.[34]

The CIA condoled with the Cuban rebels and, in spite of presidential orders to cease and desist the raids, continued to encourage and support them with unabated zeal.[35]

---

[33] There are many excellent studies of the Cuban Missile Crisis. See especially P. Grose, *op. cit.* (note 32), S. Hersh, *op. cit.* (note 5).

[34] See footnote 33.

[35] R. Groden, H. Livingstone, *op. cit.* (note 11), pp. 248f.; A. Summers, *op. cit.* (note 32), pp. 260f.

Finally, Kennedy ordered the FBI to break up the commando training camps in Florida and Louisiana and seize all their weapons and arrest as many militants as could be found:[36]

---

76. Anti-Castro Cuban militants view Kennedy's abandonment of their cause with great anger and many members of these CIA-trained and led groups made calls for revenge on the President for his abandonment of their cause.

Driscoll Report, p. 18

These FBI raids occurred shortly before the November Dallas visit, and certainly volatile Cuban rage provided another entity that was added to the list of those who not only wanted revenge on Kennedy but also possessed the temperament, the experience, and the motivation to accomplish it.

The third group is one that is only mentioned by most revisionist writers almost in passing, and yet of all of the possible suspects brought before the bar of public and historical inquiry, it had the strongest motive to remove John F. Kennedy as President of the United States.

This group is the Central Intelligence Agency, an entity that had close connections to both organized crime and the militant Cubans. In retrospect, the CIA had the clearest, most logical, and immediate reason for removing John F. Kennedy from the Presidency and the further removal of anyone privy to their instigation and implementation of such an act.

The CIA has, since its inception in 1947, been accused of an unending catalog of instigating rebellions, civil wars, religious upheavals, the planning and execution of assassinations, and numerous other acts of terrorism throughout the world.[37]

It was, after all, the CIA who recruited, trained, and armed Osama bin Laden and his terrorists, a group that then turned on its creator with terrible results.[38]

---

[36] S. Hersh, *op. cit.* (note 5), pp. 381f.

[37] There has been a massive amount of material published on the ruthless activities of the CIA. See the Bibliography for works cited. Specific references may be found in: Victor Marchetti and John Marks, *The CIA and the Cult of Intelligence*, New York: Dell, 1983, John Nutter, *The CIA's Black Ops: Covert Action, Foreign Policy, and Democracy*, Amherst, N.Y.: Prometheus Books, 2000.

[38] Alexander Cockburn, Jeffrey St. Clair, *Whiteout: The CIA, Drugs, and the Press*, London; New York: Verso, 1998, pp. 255-275.

By these actions, which are certainly known to its victims, the CIA has built up a reservoir of suspicion, general animosity, and specific hatred throughout the world, and these perceptions have had serious consequences for the American people. In many of these cases, the sins of the fathers have indeed been visited upon their children.

In order to discomfit and disrupt the Soviet Union when that country occupied Afghanistan, the CIA organized, funded and armed groups of young Muslims to conduct guerrilla warfare in that bleak mountain country.

Russian military units were so badly mauled by the rebels that they eventually withdrew from Afghanistan, leaving the rebels in command of the country. When the Soviets left, so did the CIA. The rebels were left in control of an impoverished country with an obliterated infrastructure and with no support from their erstwhile friends.

A strong sense of betrayal turned into animosity, and then into hatred and ready acceptance of the belief that the United States was an evil entity. From this hardening attitude, it was only a short step to attacking their former allies with the same ruthless zeal they had so effectively practiced against America's previous enemy.

And what are the origins of this official arm of the American people? The Central Intelligence Agency was instituted by the National Security Act in 1947. President Harry S. Truman used the CIA to keep the White House informed of foreign activities that could have an impact on the United States. They were, in fact, a presidential intelligence and information agency and nothing more.[39]

With the expansion of the Cold War, which they helped formulate and encourage, the CIA started on a campaign of empire building that grew to enormous proportions. They convinced the President and key members of his administration as well as the American Congress that the Central Intelligence Agency alone was

---

[39] Though formally created in 1947, the CIA started operating in 1948; see bibliography for references to the early days of the CIA.

able to combat the machinations of the evil Soviet Union, to preserve democracy, and to maintain American economic superiority throughout the world.

Their annual budget grew to astronomical proportions, and none of it was accounted for. Anyone who questioned the actions of the CIA was immediately singled out for attack in the American media as a suspect and unreliable person. Questions by legislators about CIA operations, even very benign operations, were met with a stony refusal of cooperation. The favorite CIA defense was to cite the concept of what they loved to call "National Security" to silence their critics.[40] They were trusted by the White House and, in the minds of many in Washington, became the vital and trusted shield of the United States.

The CIA set American foreign policy to a remarkable degree. They subjected foreign governments and leaders to their brilliant scrutiny, made determinations based on their brilliant scrutiny, and then wrote secret reports concerning these determinations—which then became state policy:

---

73. American foreign policy was, and still is, firmly in the hands of the CIA. It alone makes determinations as to which nation is to be favored and which is to be punished. No nation is permitted to be a neutral; all have to be either in the U.S. camp or are its enemies. Most often, the wishes of American business are paramount in the determination as to which nation will receive U.S. support and which will not only be denied this support but attacked. It is the American CIA and not the Soviet Union, that has divided the world into two warring camps.

Russian Intelligence Study, *Driscoll Report*, p. 9

Like historical events, government bureaucracies are complex, diverse, and beyond simple understanding.

The entity that had the greatest reason to remove John Kennedy from his office was divided and subdivided into many sections and branches, many of which operated as semi-independent entities, answerable in theory to their superiors but in fact to no-one.

In the compartmentalization of an agency with a fanatic fascination with secrecy, the opportunities for indulgence in private actions were immense and, in almost every instance, entirely secure.

---

[40] A. Cockburn, J. St. Clair, *op. cit.* (note 38), pp. 29-62.

The CIA was headed by a Director, and beneath him, during the period in question, was the Deputy Director, the Deputy Director for Community Relations, and beneath them were: the Directorate of Intelligence, the Directorate of Science and Technology, the Directorate of Management and Services, and, finally, the Directorate of Operations, also known as Clandestine Services.[41]

It was in the Directorate of Operations that the initial disaffection with the actions of President Kennedy first surfaced. In light of their wider discoveries of certain of Kennedy's activities, the dissatisfaction had hardened into a resolve to remove him, or, as was said at the time, to "neutralize" him.

The CIA has always found euphemisms for its murderous activities. "Neutralize" is one word, and another euphemism is to "terminate with extreme prejudice" as well as to "close the files" on a successfully terminated "resource" or perhaps what was coming to be viewed as a "rogue" President.[42]

To fully understand the dynamics of the Kennedy assassination, it is necessary to study both the President's actions and the CIA's reactions to them.

A historical incident, for example the sinking of the *RMS Titanic* in 1912, is an excellent example of changing perspectives. There was the immediacy and inaccuracy of the initial newspaper reports. The liner was safe and on its way to Halifax with all saved, the world press reported, when, in reality, the shattered remains of the White Star's luxury liner were actually at the bottom of the Atlantic Ocean.[43]

Initial reports and observations have historical importance by showing often-erroneous primary impressions, but it takes the passage of time, shifting policies, and extensive and objective investigation to show a matter in the round and with far greater accuracy.

---

[41] See Appendix for official organizational chart, taken from V. Marchetti, J. Marks, *op. cit.* (note 37), pp. 60f.

[42] According to personal conversations with R. T. Crowley, these terms were used extensively by members of the CIA.

[43] David G. Brown, *The Last Log of the Titanic*, Camden, Me.: International Marine/McGraw-Hill, 2001, pp. 125-136.

As in so many other cases, it was the personality, actions, and family background of John Kennedy that led to his death.

It has emerged in the decades since his death that Kennedy was a man who enjoyed living on the edge. He acquired his serious flirtations with disaster from his father. The senior Kennedy was a thoroughly ruthless controlling man who let nothing and no-one stand in his way. Pathologically ambitious, Joe Kennedy believed that he should have been destined for political and social greatness, but his treacherous and savage lifestyle effectively blocked his advance in the public arena.[44]

Kennedy thought he could manipulate Franklin Roosevelt, but he was, in turn, used by the President who was far more skilled in Byzantine plottings than the bootlegger and stock market manipulator. Kennedy had been head of the Securities and Exchange Commission and performed outstandingly, but his completely predatory approach to all things he desired was such as to keep Roosevelt from using his genuine talents.[45]

Kennedy essentially purchased the ambassadorship to the Court of St. James in London but, when there, proceeded to perform in a manner that infuriated Roosevelt. Kennedy immediately became involved in stock market manipulations, dealt in foreign holdings, and used his inside connections to add to his already impressive holdings.

Worse, from Roosevelt's point of view, he did everything possible to sabotage the joint program Roosevelt and Churchill were putting forward to involve the United States in Britain's war with Germany.

British intelligence, with a mandate from Prime Minister Winston Churchill, spied on Kennedy, bugging his telephone and intercepting his correspondence, and passed on their findings both to Churchill and Roosevelt. Without realizing it, Kennedy had ef-

---

[44] Michael Beschloss, *Kennedy and Roosevelt*, New York: W. W. Norton, 1980, contains an excellent accounting of the relationship between FDR and his Ambassador to England.

[45] M. Beschloss, *op. cit.* (note 44), pp. 243-254.

fectively destroyed any hope he might have entertained that Roosevelt would support any Kennedy for high political office.[46]

His eldest son, Joe Jr., was killed in the war under circumstances that are still unknown and highly suspect.[47] As Kennedy was planning to put this son forward for the high political offices he himself could never achieve, he then turned his attentions to the next eldest son Jack.

John Fitzgerald Kennedy was not a likely candidate for high political office. He was plagued with ill health, had aspirations to become a professional athlete, and was thoroughly under his father's thumb. He also possessed a good sense of humor, considerable intelligence, youthful good looks, and the ability to make people like him.[48]

Unfortunately for his image, many of the people who liked him were women, and for them, Kennedy had an insatiable appetite. His sexual appetites were of such a voracious nature as to verge on the pathological and posed a terrible public relations threat to the occupant of the White House.[49]

As well as having the potential to destroy his public reputation, his frenzied pursuit of sexual gratification left him and, to a lesser degree, his younger brother Robert in a position to be blackmailed.

If it had not been for the vaulting ambition of his father, it is doubtful if John F. Kennedy would have achieved much more than an elevated position in the business world. Once he became Senator, and then President, his father oversaw his actions to a remarkable degree, and only when the senior Kennedy had a crippling stroke did his son begin to show signs of being his own man.[50]

Beneath his considerable charm, John F. Kennedy was a very ruthless individual who could move with great effect against his

---

[46] *Ibid.*, and also S. Hersh, *op. cit.* (note 5), pp. 62-73.

[47] Gregory Douglas, *Gestapo Chief,* San Jose: Bender, 1995, pp. 64f.; David McCullough, *Truman,* New York: Simon & Schuster, 1992, p. 324.

[48] T. C. Reeves, *op. cit.* (note 3), pp. 414 *et seq.*.; S. Hersh, *op. cit.* (note 5), pp. 29f. *et seq.*

[49] JFK's sexual activities have been extensively covered, see S. Hersh, *op. cit.* (note 5) and T. C. Reeves, *op. cit.* (note 3).

[50] See footnote 49.

enemies when it proved necessary to do so. It was the ruthless pragmatism learned from his father that eventually set in motion the forces that led directly to his assassination. From his early experiences with American politics through his tutoring by an aggressive and manipulative father, Kennedy was a totally pragmatic politician, and this pragmatism made him far more dangerous enemies than American organized crime or furious Cuban activists.

He crossed swords with, and greatly antagonized, the most powerful secret society in American history: the Central Intelligence Agency.

The CIA

The Central Intelligence Agency grew out of the wartime Office of Special Services (OSS) which was set up by William Donovan, a New York attorney, at the request of his friend, President Franklin D. Roosevelt.

The President, a firm supporter of Josef Stalin and a man of strong left wing politics, mandated the OSS to render as much logistical support to the Soviet Union as possible. The Roosevelt administration was packed with Soviet agents who dedicated their existence to the unqualified support of the Communist State.

Top presidential aide Harry Hopkins has been identified as a paid Soviet agent as were Harry Dexter White, top advisor to Secretary of the Treasury Henry Morgenthau, Jr., Alger Hiss, senior official of the Department of State, David K. Niles, senior presidential advisor, and many others.

The Vice President, Henry Wallace, was in complete sympathy with the aims of Stalin, and while he was not a paid agent, he was an agent of influence and worked closely with the head of Soviet intelligence in Washington throughout and after the war.

The OSS was filled with pro-Soviet agents who had been instructed by OSS chief William Donovan to cooperate fully with their counterparts in the NKVD.[51]

With the death of Roosevelt in April of 1945 and the elevation of Vice President Harry Truman to the presidency, the eager, unstinting, and certainly unquestioned cooperation between Stalin's agents and the United States came to an end. Unlike his predecessor, Truman was not enraptured with fuzzy dreams of a People's

---

[51] There is an excellent new book on this subject. Thomas Fleming, *The New Dealers' War*, Basic Books, New York, 2001.

Republic on the Potomac and almost immediately ordered the disbanding of the OSS.[52]

A number of its ultra-left wing former agents were posted to the U.S. Department of State to await a dignified separation from government service, untainted by accusations of being active Communists. There the matter stood until 1947 when Truman mandated the formation of a new intelligence-gathering agency.

This was to be called the Central Intelligence Agency, and its sole purpose was to keep the President and his top officials current with global political intelligence.[53]

Military intelligence was in the hands of the respective services, but Truman wished to prevent another Pearl Harbor from being launched on the United States. One of the training films shown to CIA recruits has this anti-Pearl Harbor message as its main theme.[54]

If the purpose of the CIA was to prevent future surprise attacks on the United States, the terrorist attacks on the United States on September 11, 2001, are overwhelming evidence that an astronomical amount of taxpayer's money was completely wasted.

The vast sums voted by Congress and not subject to accounting under any circumstances might have been far better spent on constructive national programs that *would* have been subject to strict accountability.[55]

Starting out as a small agency under the direction of Rear Admiral Roscoe Hillenkoetter, the CIA was filled with former OSS

---

[52] D. McCullough, *op. cit.* (note 47), *passim.*

[53] See footnote 39.

[54] This contention can be found on the CIA's web site, www.CIA.gov.

[55] An excellent, if often anecdotal, accounting of the misuse by the CIA of its funding and other pertinent material, can be found in the two volume work, *Müller Journals: The Washington Years, Vol. 1: 1948-1950*, by G. Douglas, San Jose: Bender, 1999 (vol. 2 in preparation). The Müller in question had once been the head of the German Gestapo who was recruited by the CIA after the war and worked in Washington from 1948 onwards under the control of Robert Crowley. For additional information on the CIA's use of Heinrich Müller, see Joseph Trento, *The Secret History of the CIA*, New York: Random House, 2001, p. 29 and notes. The former Gestapo chief worked with and was under the control of Robert Crowley, and this information can be found not only in the Douglas works but also in the Crowley Papers as noted by Trento.

personnel who certainly found their new role confusing. Instead of giving powerful assistance to the Soviet Union, their new agency rapidly grew into an anti-Soviet entity.

When Allen Welch Dulles joined the CIA in 1950, the agency was under the control of General Walter Bedell Smith, once Eisenhower's Chief of Staff and later U.S. Ambassador to the Soviet Union. Dulles had been the OSS Chief of Station in neutral Switzerland, and his officially praised activities there were nothing more than an intelligence disaster of the highest magnitude.

Dulles, who always entertained a very high opinion of himself, attempted to penetrate the defenses of the German *Reich* and actually believed that he had done so with brilliant success. In truth, German counterintelligence had easily penetrated his organization and filled the complaisant Dulles with an incredible amount of highly destructive disinformation.

The Dulles analysis of conditions inside the Greater German *Reich*, when read with hindsight, would be amusing in the extreme had not so many OSS agents been caught and executed because of the incompetence of the OSS chief of station, in many cases by the same man who later occupied a prominent position in the CIA.[56]

The Cold War was an engineered affair, and its chief architect was former German Army General Reinhard Gehlen, a former head of the Soviet military intelligence section of the *Wehrmacht*. In 1948, at the request of his superiors, Gehlen concocted a lengthy pseudo-informational report stating that 135 Soviet armored divisions were poised to strike into Central Europe.

This report was a complete fiction and was prepared solely to create a situation wherein the American military could legitimately increase its size, and American business, in a slump after the end of the boom years of World War II, would once again gear up for a highly profitable wartime economy.

The so-called *Gehlen Report* was brilliantly successful once it had been leaked to key members of Congress and the President. This was the starting gun of a Cold War that ran on for over forty

---

[56] Cf. G. Douglas, *ibid.*, Vol. 1, pp. 12, 18, 22n, 232.

years and lofted the CIA into a position of supreme power in the
ruling circles of the American government.[57]

At the time of his devastating essay into creative writing, former General Gehlen was a paid employee of the CIA.[58]

Because of what they convinced the American leadership was a
mortal danger to the security of the United States, the CIA grew
from an informational service to an enormous, bloated agency with
tens of thousands of employees and an annual budget running into
the billions.

They were, as they often pointed out to various occupants of
the Oval Office and Congress, the shield and buckler of American
freedom and, by extension, the freedom of the rest of the world.[59]
Or at least that part of the world that had the approval of the CIA
and, by inference, the American government.

After Truman came Eisenhower, a man who strongly supported
the CIA and cooperated in its empire building. From modest quar-
ters in a disused Washington hospital, the CIA later expanded into
an enormous office complex in Langley, Virginia. It now owns hundreds of "proprietary" businesses, including air and shipping lines,
publishing and weapons companies, think tanks, import and
export companies, and telecommunication networks. It also con-
trols hundreds, if not thousands, of voluntary sources scattered
throughout key elements of both the American and European private sectors.[60]

It was under Eisenhower that the CIA launched its clandestine
warfare against the Marxist Cuban regime of Fidel Castro, warfare that the Agency warmly believed would terminate in a suc-

---

[57] Christopher Simpson, *Blowback*, New York: Weidenfeld & Nicholson, 1988, pp.
60f.

[58] Gehlen initially worked for the United States Army until his group was given over
to the CIA in 1948. It was run out of Pullach, a Munich suburb, by Colonel James
Critchfield, an Army officer who worked for the CIA at that time. The CIA con-
trolled Gehlen until 1955-56, when his organization was taken over by the West
German Government as their equivalent of the CIA, the *Bundesnachrichtendienst*
(BND).

[59] An interesting work on the Bay of Pigs was prepared by some of its leading participants. Haynes Johnson *et al.*, *The Bay of Pigs*, New York: W. W. Norton, 1964.

[60] See Appendix.

cessful invasion of the Caribbean bastion of the world Communist movement.

If history can be said to be instructive, the CIA, like the Bourbons, obviously forgot nothing and learned nothing from their past errors.

In 1956, a CIA-instigated revolt broke out in Hungary, fueled by repeated CIA promises of immediate U.S. military assistance if the occupants of that nation rose up against their Soviet occupiers.[61] The revolt was an initial success, but President Eisenhower quite sensibly refused to support it with American military aid, and it died in a bloodbath of Soviet military repression. Better, Eisenhower reasoned, a few thousand dead Hungarians than hundreds of thousands of dead Americans.

The identical scenario was to be repeated in the so-called Bay of Pigs invasion in April of 1961. Kennedy, Eisenhower's successor, had only been partially briefed by the CIA and had given his conditional approval to the projected invasion *by Cuban nationals* of Castro's fortress.[62]

In order to prevent another Hungarian fiasco, the CIA had thoughtfully dispatched a boatload of Cuban rebels disguised as members of the regular Cuban armed forces to launch an attack on the U.S. naval base at Guantánamo Bay in Cuba.

In furtherance of strongly desired military attacks on Cuba, the U.S. Joint Chiefs of Staff (JCS) prepared Operation NORTH-WOODS. This plan was to deliberately provoke a war with Cuba by executing a series of assaults *on the United States by American special forces!* Boats full of Cuban refugees were to be sunk on the high seas, aircraft were to be hijacked, bombs detonated in American cities, an American military ship was to be blown up, and passenger aircraft destroyed in the air. All of these terrorist acts against American cities and its citizens, shockingly redolent of the

---

[61] Background information about the Hungarian revolt can be found in C. Simpson, *op. cit.* (note 57), pp. 254ff.

[62] It has tentatively been approved by Eisenhower and was under the supervision of his Vice President, Richard M. Nixon, prior to Kennedy's assumption of office in January of 1960; cf. P. Grose, *op. cit.* (note 32), p. 519; see also V. Marchetti, J. Marks, *op. cit.* (note 37), pp. 260-265; H. Johnson, *op. cit.* (note 59).

September 11, 2001, terrorist attacks on New York and Washington, were to be planned and executed by the American military, under orders of the Joint Chiefs of Staff, and conducted by American military and civilian personnel.

The attacks on shipping in Guantánamo Bay were part and parcel of Operation Northwoods:[63]

> 37. At that time, the FBI was involved, at the request of the Attorney General, ~~Robert Kennedy, in watching the clandestine~~ activities of the CIA and its ~~Alpha and Omega special commando groups, some~~ of whom were in training ~~in the New Orleans area.~~
>
> 38. The American President was greatly concerned that continued and fully unauthorized para-military action against Cuba might upset the balance he had achieved in seeking peace with the Soviet Union.
>
> 39. It is known from information inside the CIA and also from Cuban double agents that the CIA was, in conjunction with the highest American military leadership, to force an American invasion of Cuba.
>
> 40. These joint plans, which consisted of acts of extreme provocation by American units against American property and citizens, were unknown to Kennedy.
>
> 41. When the American President discovered that Cuban insurgents, under the control of the CIA and with the support of the highest military leadership, were embarked on a course of launching military action against American naval bases under the cover of being Cuban regular troops, he at once ordered a halt.
>
> -5-

Russian Intelligence Study, *Driscoll Report*, p. 5

The JCS anticipated that the U.S. forces at the base would naturally return fire and call for military assistance. This assistance, they reasoned, would guarantee full and official American military support of their venture.

They did *neither* anticipate that some unhelpful individual in their ranks would have informed Kennedy of their scheme to involve the United States in a massive invasion of Cuba, *nor* that the new President's immediate response to the Guantánamo diversion

---

[63] James Bamford, *Body of Secrets*, New York: Doubleday, 2001, pp. 82-91. Also see JCS, Top Secret/Special Handling/Noforn. Appendix to Enclosure A—"Pretexts to Justify US Military Intervention in Cuba, March 12, 1962," Assassinations Records Review Board.

was to not only recall the projected attackers but also refuse to support the CIA-organized landings at the Bay of Pigs.[64]

Instead of the Cuban people rising in joyous revolt against Castro, as the CIA pundits fondly believed, the evil Marxist dictator easily crushed the invasion and captured or killed all of the CIA's troops.

There was great and understandable unhappiness in the camps of Cuban rebels, and the CIA, with commendable forthrightness, shifted the blame for the disaster onto the new President.

This was one of the major building blocks of the conspiracy to remove John Kennedy from office.

When the President learned the full scope of the CIA's duplicity, he fired the beloved head of the CIA, Allen Welch Dulles, as well as General Charles P. Cabell and Richard E. Bissell, Jr., the CIA's Director of Clandestine Services. He also told Senator Mike Mansfield that he planned to "break up the CIA and scatter it to the winds."[65]

The leadership of the CIA, especially James Jesus Angleton, felt that Kennedy had sufficient knowledge of the Cuban *putsch* and that his sacking of their top officials and threats to disband them were merely designed to distance him from the debacle.[66]

This was another of the building blocks in the CIA's growing fear of the Kennedy presidency.

After the Bay of Pigs fiasco, the CIA continued their commando raids against Cuba and its ruler. It was during this time that Angleton approached the Chicago Mafia with an eye to assassinating Fidel Castro:[67]

---

47. The attempts of the CIA and the JCS to remove Castro by assassination are also part of the official record. These assassination plots, called RIFLE show the connections between the CIA and the Chicago branch of the Mafia.

---

[64]   V. Marchetti, J. Marks, *op. cit.* (note 37), p. 108; also H. Johnson, *op. cit.* (note 59).

[65]   R. Groden, H. Livingstone, *op. cit.* (note 11), p. 355. See also the Soviet Intelligence Study, *Driscoll Report*, p. 5, as reproduced on p. 76.

[66]   Bay of Pigs and the Dulles firing can be found in S. Hersh, *op. cit.* (note 5), pp. 202-221, P. Grose, *op. cit.* (note 32), 522-539.

[67]   Personal conversation with R. T. Crowley.

> **48.** This Mafia organization was paid nearly a quarter of a million dollars to effect the killing of Castro but apparently kept the money and did nothing.

Driscoll Report, p. 15

The mob was certainly eager to regain control of its lucrative Cuban casinos, and various conversations took place concerning the physical removal of the Cuban leader.

As has always been the case, the CIA demands plausible deniability on its part should one of their often-bizarre plots suddenly come to the public attention. In the case of Castro, the plans discussed bordered on the lunatic: he would be blown up by a booby trap cunningly disguised as a rare sea shell; his wet suit would be poisoned; and even more ludicrous, a drug would be put into his shoes to cause his trademark beard to fall out![68]

As the usual method of Mafia removal was to shoot their target and be done with it, one wonders if Sam Giancana was entertaining himself with the slapstick efforts of the shield of democracy.

The Soviet KGB learned of these plots, and Nikita Khrushchev became convinced that the United States planned to kill off one of his more prominent satellite leaders and invade his bastion of Western Hemisphere Marxism. In order to frustrate the United States in its ambitions and to protect his client, Khrushchev began to clandestinely move Soviet troops and missiles into the tropical paradise with an eye to balancing the scales.

The United States, after all, had placed its Jupiter missiles in Turkey, right on the Soviet border, and a *quid pro quo* appeared to be entirely in order:

> **74.** American, and most especially the CIA, attempts to destabilize a Communist state i.e., Cuba, could not be permitted by the Soviet leadership. Castro was a most valuable client in that he provided an excellent base of intelligence and political operations in the American hemisphere. As the CIA had been setting up its own ring of hostile states surrounding the Soviet Union, Cuba was viewed officially as a completely legitimate area of political expansion. Threats of invasion and physical actions against Cuba were viewed by the Chairman as threats against the Soviet Union itself.

Russian Intelligence Study, *Driscoll Report*, p. 9

---

[68] S. Hersh, *op. cit.* (note 5), pp. 185f., P. Grose, *op. cit.* (note 32), pp. 493f.

> **77.** Soviet attempts to gain a strategic foothold in close proximity to the United States and certainly well within missile range, was intolerable and had to be countered with equal force. At that time, the threat of a major war was not only imminent but anticipated. In retrospect, all out nuclear warfare between the United States and the Soviet Union was only barely averted and only at the last minute.

Driscoll Report, p. 18

The U.S. discovered the Soviet actions, and the Cuban Missile Crisis erupted in October of 1962. Kennedy ordered overflights of Cuba to verify Soviet missile positions, then blockaded the country and threatened to prevent further Soviet shipments of weaponry by force if necessary.

In the end, common sense on both sides prevailed, and the crisis ended peacefully. The Soviets agreed to withdraw their weapons, and the United States agreed to withdraw its Jupiter missiles from Turkey. Kennedy also agreed to halt armed commando raids against Cuba and abandon any attempt to physically invade Khrushchev's ally.

As this meant the cessation of the CIA attacks, the Agency was infuriated. The training and supply of these militant units was an excellent source of money that, again, did not need to be accounted for. The termination of funding for the Cuban adventurers meant a serious diminution of the flow of money that the CIA found so comforting and useful.[69]

As a result of his rapprochement with his opposite number in the Kremlin, Kennedy ordered all CIA incursions and commando activities against Cuba to cease.

The CIA paid no attention to the President's orders, and Kennedy then ordered the FBI to raid the CIA camps, seize weapons and paperwork, and arrest anyone found:[70]

> **43.** The American President, unsure of the depth of his influence with the leadership of the American military and the CIA, ordered the FBI to investigate these matters and ordered the Director, Hoover, to report <u>directly</u> to him on his findings.

Russian Intelligence Study, *Driscoll Report*, p. 6

---

[69] Personal conversation with R. T. Crowley.

[70] S. Hersh, *op. cit.* (note 5), pp. 380-383.

These actions merely confirmed to certain high elements in the CIA that Kennedy had to be silenced. He had, in fact, become a stone in their shoe.

What really convinced the CIA to remove their President had its roots in the Bay of Pigs episode and was viewed by Angleton, Crowley, and others as an imperative that both Kennedy and his brother Robert be removed from the levers of power as expeditiously as possible. Injured feelings and lost revenue aside, the leadership of the CIA did indeed have what could well be considered as a thoroughly legitimate reason for their actions.

The information about the CIA's activities on behalf of John F. Kennedy between summer 1962 and February 1963, as it is laid out in the rest of this chapter, mainly rest on conversations the author had with Robert T. Crowley. Where information could be corroborated with other sources, these are given in the footnotes. Documents of these events—if they ever existed—were probably destroyed. There exists, however, one document found in R. T. Crowley's papers which describes in a very brief way the CIA's actions between March 1963 and November 1963, the already mentioned "ZIPPER document." It will be referred to in detail in the following chapter.

The author is well aware of the somewhat unreliable nature of the oral evidence given by Crowley more than thirty years after the event, nevertheless, his witness accounts are reproduced here, since the events prior to March 1963 are not crucial to the understanding of what happened afterwards, and because they merely flesh out and corroborate the much more reliable documentary framework that exists for the time after 1963. Hence, if not indicated otherwise, the following information is taken from conversations the author had with R. T. Crowley.

One of the top Soviet intelligence agents in Washington at the time of the Bay of Pigs was Georgi N. Bolshakov. Ostensibly a reporter for the Soviet TASS news agency, Bolshakov was approached by Robert Kennedy's press secretary, Edwin Guthman, shortly after the disastrous Bay of Pigs. The President and his brother were, above all, political pragmatists. They had learned this from their practical and ruthless father. From April of 1961 onward, the President of the United States, through his brother, the Attorney General, was in direct contact with Soviet Premier Khrushchev, effectively bypassing not only his Department of State but the CIA as well.[71]

The Soviets bypassed their own ambassador in this, and the two leaders kept in constant contact. The purpose of this unofficial contact was to insure that neither party suffered from the actions of the other and that both men could be of mutual assistance to each other's political careers without the danger of serious confrontations and possible conflict.

In August of 1961, in order to prevent the flight of valuable East German professionals to the West, the German capital was bisected by the Berlin wall. In the West, this act was viewed as a terrible provocation, but serious confrontation between the two powers was quickly averted when Kennedy granted, through the offices of Bolshakov, that he would not make any serious move to contest the Soviet actions.

The Kennedy-Khrushchev contacts continued on a regular basis at the very least until January of 1963.[72]

In August of 1962, James Jesus Angleton, Chief of Counterintelligence for the CIA, was informed from a very reliable Soviet source that highly secret top-level American intelligence information was coming into the hands of the Soviet leadership on a regular basis. Angleton was given several specific items of an extraordinarily sensitive and accurate nature then circulating in Moscow.

A second report from the same source, via Sweden, in early September of 1962 thoroughly frightened Angleton and convinced him that there was a very high level mole somewhere in the upper levels of his own CIA.

Always inclined to a paranoid view of his profession,[73] the frantic Angleton started an intense search for the disastrous leak. The

---

[71] *Driscoll Report*, pp. 9, 18, as reproduced on p. 84, and S. Hersh, *op. cit.* (note 5), pp. 248ff., 254f., 261f.

[72] S. Hersh, *op. cit.* (note 5), pp. 346-350 *et seq.*

[73] James Jesus Angleton was an inherently suspicious person, bordering on paranoia. *Driscoll Report*, p. 18, no. 74 (see p. 54), and Tom Mangold, *Cold Warrior: James Jesus Angleton: The CIA's Master Spy Hunter*, New York: Simon and Schuster, 1991.

CIA was so large and those possessing knowledge of the secret material so diverse in number that he found himself frustrated in his efforts to pinpoint the mole in his agency.

Finally, Robert Crowley suggested a possible means by which the leak could be identified. He knew that the leaked information was all contained in the regular CIA reports that were circulated in official Washington. These reports were highly classified, and only a handful of top-level personnel were privy to their contents.

Crowley suggested that each report be prepared with a different additive. The basic reports, he said, should all be the same but each one should contain an entirely different subject. This inclusion should be of such a nature as to draw strong attention to itself but not detract from the thrust of the intelligence evaluations.

Desperate and frantic at his lack of success in tracking the leak and the leakers, Angleton followed Crowley's shrewd and very practical advice.

Subsequent top-level CIA briefing reports did indeed have the telltale additives included in them. In December of 1962, a report from the Soviet source contained an almost verbatim copy of a CIA report with an identifying marker included.

Angleton and his inner circle of counterintelligence staff were horrified to discover that the leak was coming from the CIA reports given to the President himself!

It was a well-known Washington secret that the President entertained a steady stream of Washington prostitutes, party girls, and other women of easy virtue in the White House whenever his wife was absent. There were nude swimming parties in the White House pool with Kennedy and some of his aides cavorting with his female visitors. Drugs were used, including marijuana, cocaine, and finally LSD.[74]

Kennedy, who liked three-way sex, had professional pictures taken of himself and his ladies. A number of these photographs, developed and printed (and often framed as presidential gifts) by a

---

[74] S. Hersh, *op. cit.* (note 5), pp. 10f. *et seq.*; T. C. Reeves, *op. cit.* (note 3), pp. 240ff., Nina Burleigh, *A Very Private Woman*, New York: Bantam Books, 1998, pp. 194ff.

well-known Washington photography gallery, came into the hands
of Robert Crowley at one point and ended up in his papers:[75]

> It
> is an absolute fact that both the American President, Kennedy, and his
> brother, the American Attorney General, were especially active in a sexual
> sense. A number of sexually explicit pictures of the President engaging in
> sexual acts are in the official files as are several pictures of the
> Attorney General, taken while on a visit to Moscow in 1961.
>
>   75. The President was aware that a number of these pictures were in
> Soviet hands and acted accordingly. In addition to a regular parade of
> whores into the White House, it was also reliably reported from several
> sources that the President was a heavy user of various kinds of illegal
> narcotics. It is also known from medical reports that the President
> suffered from a chronic venereal disease for which he was receiving
> medical treatment.

Russian Intelligence Study, *Driscoll Report*, p. 9

Angleton found it an extremely difficult prospect to investigate
the White House personnel to determine the source of the serious
leaks of the CIA's top briefing papers.

Kennedy's personal staff was noted for its loyalty to the President, and Angleton said repeatedly that any hint of his very active
suspicions of peculation in the White House might well backfire in
a fatal way if they became known.

Finally, in late December of 1962, a personal friend commented
in passing that Bobby Kennedy had developed a very close relationship with a top Soviet agent in Washington, and at this point
the entire secret backstairs diplomacy became a matter of growing
knowledge in the CIA.

Angleton had the technical section of the CIA tap the telephones of the Attorney General, both those in his private office and
the ones in his home in Virginia. It was only a matter of time before the CIA technicians successfully intercepted a call between
Bobby Kennedy and Bolshakov in February of 1963.[76]

---

[75] These professional and pornographic pictures, 8½"×11", black and white and color,
were prepared for the President by the Mickelson Gallery in Washington (S.
Hersh, *op. cit.* (note 5), p. 11). These are from the Crowley Papers but are not included in the present work. Kennedy gave these very explicit pictures to various
women who had participated in his group sex acts.

[76] Later, the Director of the National Security Agency, Lieutenant General Gordon
Blake, helped the CIA to gather more information on Kennedy's activities: ZIPPER

During the course of this taped conversation, it became very clear that the American President and the Soviet Premier had been in direct contact for some time through the medium of Bobby Kennedy and a senior KGB agent. A comment from the Russian about material that could only have come from the President's CIA briefing papers convinced Angleton that the Kennedys were engaging in treasonable activities and had severely compromised a number of important CIA agents and operations throughout the world:

> 76. In order to better cooperate with the Soviet Union, President Kennedy used to regularly keep in close, private communication with the Chairman. These contacts were kept private to prevent negative influences from the State Department and most certainly from the Central Intelligence Agency. The President said several times that he did not trust this agency who was bent on stirring up a war between the two nations. Through this personal contact, many matters that might have escalated due to the interference of others were peacefully settled.
>
> -9-

Russian Intelligence Study, *Driscoll Report*, p. 9

> 78. The President's highly unorthodox form of personal diplomacy vis a vis the Soviets created far more problems than it ever solved. When it came to light, both the DOS and the CIA were extremely concerned that sensitive intelligence matters might have been inadvertently passed to the Soviets.

Driscoll Report, p. 18

The fact that the President's brother, with his permission, was passing what the CIA considered highly secret material to their chief enemy had a terrible effect. Angleton, who knew the President and his family socially, was devastated. In a series of private meetings held between himself and several of his trusted associates, including Robert Crowley (who took notes), Angleton made a strong case against Kennedy.

He claimed that Kennedy himself had approved the Bay of Pigs action but dropped it at the last minute out of moral weakness. Angleton believed that Kennedy then deliberately attacked the leadership of the CIA, firing Allen Dulles among others and basically accusing the Agency of bad faith and duplicity. Angleton was

Document, 9 April (1:20pm), 5, 21, 28 May (11:34am), 3, 4, 6, 19 June (11:35am), 25 June, 4, 11, 16 July (10:45am).

positive that Kennedy had fully approved all of the CIA's actions in the Bay of Pigs mission but had blamed others to save his own reputation. The failure of the mission was, Angleton said, solely the result of Kennedy's cowardice.

His negotiations behind the back of responsible American government agencies with the head of the Soviet Union smacked of treason and certainly undermined all of the intense work the CIA was doing to thwart Soviet imperialism both in Europe and Latin America.

But far and away the gravest charge leveled against the President was his behavior in not striking militarily at the armed Soviet troops and their deadly missiles stationed only a few miles away from American soil. Not only had Kennedy allowed the Soviets to get away with their aggression, he further removed American missiles from Turkey and materially weakened the American military position in Europe. As far as the passing of highly sensitive material to the Soviets was concerned, a furious Angleton claimed that this was high treason and the President should be removed from his high office.

Kennedy was far too popular to institute impeachment proceedings against him in the Congress.[77] Leaking the information about the CIA reports being given to Khrushchev to the CIA's many friendly press sources was also ruled out. If made public, this information would not only damage Kennedy, it would also damage the reputation of the CIA and unduly alarm its many highly placed international sources.

Finally, after a series of heated meetings over the period of a month, the subject of physical removal was not only broached but also developed. After all, the CIA had been responsible for a significant number of high-level political assassinations in the past, albeit in other countries,[78] and they had not only the means but also the conditioning to assist their planning.

---

[77] See ZIPPER Document, no. 4.

[78] Patrice Lumumba, Rafael Trujillo, Salvatore Allende Goosens of Chile, President Diem of South Vietnam, plus many more, were all removed as the result of CIA orders. The leadership in Langley never pulled a trigger in its life but was very

In late February, the general outline of the plot was well set. Initial plans to blow up the presidential plane were scrapped. Secret Service and U.S. Air Force security were far too comprehensive to permit the clandestine placing of an explosive device on Air Force One.[79]

A second plan was to approach one of the President's physicians, Dr. Max Jacobson, with a view to convince the doctor, who supplied and injected the President with amphetamines, to put certain fatal additives in Kennedy's drugs. The CIA had a small but effective laboratory that specialized in rare poisons. This plan was rejected because it was felt Jacobson was unstable and associated with too many questionable individuals. Using his services would have necessitated removing the doctor as well, and Angleton was strongly against involving more untrustworthy people than necessary in his plot.

It was also suggested that since the President was known to sail in Massachusetts' coastal waters, an assassin could either shoot him at a distance or attach an explosive charge to the bottom of his boat.[80] This was generally rejected by everyone but Angleton, because the President's wife and children might well be on board, and this was found to be unacceptable.

It was finally decided to shoot the President when he was in the open rather than in a building that could easily be sealed off and immediately searched. The political trip to Dallas had not yet been planned, and there was a great deal of practical work to do before any assassination could be successfully attempted.

If the President was shot in public, the assassin stood a high risk of being captured. If this happened, there was an even worse risk that he could somehow be traced to the CIA. The CIA therefore realized that it had to get the support of the entire governmental apparatus to be able to implement such a radical solution

---

adept at getting its servitors to do this. All of this information stems directly from conversations with R. T. Crowley.

[79] See the entries about AF1 (Air Force One) on 24 May and 5 July of the ZIPPER Document as reproduced in the Appendix.

[80] See the entry about "sailboat plan" on 2 May (4:30pm) in the ZIPPER Document as reproduced in the Appendix.

to what it considered to be the most serious threat to U.S. security in decades.

...And Everybody Else

According to a document found in R. T. Crowley's papers, the officially organized assassination of John F. Kennedy by the CIA had the code name: "Operation ZIPPER." This document, which is entitled "OPERATION ZIPPER Conference Record," is reproduced in the appendix of this book, with this author's subsequent explanation of the abbreviations used in it.[81] In the following, the events unfolding between March and November 1963 are reconstructed using both this document and R. T. Crowley's comments to this author.

Early in March of 1963, the matter of the actual assassin became a pressing issue. Because of Crowley's connections with the mob in Chicago (his father had been an important Chicago politician, parks commissioner, in the Kelly-Nash machine), he received the task of personally contacting members of the Chicago Mafia for advice and possible assistance.[82]

Chicago mob leader Sam Giancana, who had assisted in locating persons to carry out the CIA's murder plots against Fidel Castro, loathed the Kennedy brothers but was far too shrewd to lend any of his identifiable men to cooperate in such a project. In two conferences in the Drake Hotel with Crowley, Giancana agreed to locate assassins who could be expected to perform in a professional manner. It was suggested that perhaps this recruitment might be better done outside of the United States. Rather than involve the

---

[81]   The document actually covers the period from March to November 1963. According to personal information received from R. T. Crowley, the choice of ZIPPER was his. He said that since Kennedy could not keep his zipper shut, the CIA would do it for him. Originally, he wanted to call the plot "Operation JANUS" after the two-faced Roman god (a reference to Kennedy's perceived duplicity) but decided that his co-workers were far too ill-educated to understand it.

[82]   See ZIPPER Document, 16, 19, 20 March, 4 April (3:35pm), 9 & 10 April (passim, about payments), 18 April (2:01pm, 2:25pm), 23 & 24 April, 2 May, 6 May (11:10am c.), 10 May, 19 June (1:45pm), 24 Oct. 1963.

Sicilian Mafia,[83] Giancana had one of his connections in that entity contact someone in the Corsican Mafia, the so-called *Unione Corse*, and it was from the ranks of this Marseille-based, well-knit, and very professional criminal organization that the assassins were found.[84]

The plotter's reasoning was that if the killers were somehow caught before the CIA could kill them first, they could only identify the Chicago Mafia as their employers, and the Mafia would never identify the CIA as the real moving force. If this question arose, the Mafia could much more easily be silenced than foreign killers could.

Before the Corsicans were finally brought on board, a co-worker suggested shopping in Beirut, Lebanon, then a center of assassination professionals. The argument against this was that Corsicans would have no problems blending in the background in race conscious Dallas. Darker complexioned Lebanese or Arab professionals would certainly attract unwelcome notice in the provincial southern city.

Cuban militants had been ruled out in the beginning as too volatile and inclined to emotional excesses.

It would be Marseilles, then, instead of Beirut, that would supply the killers.[85]

Early March 1963, the Director of Central Intelligence, John McCone, began a series of delicate contacts outside his immediate circle.

The first government agency contacted was the FBI. The first conferences with its director John Edgar Hoover and Deputy Director William Sullivan were held on March 4th. According to the ZIPPER Document, the head of the FBI was permanently kept informed about the CIA's actions by his top aide William Sullivan. Since Sullivan is described in the ZIPPER Document as a "partici-

---

[83] The Sicilian Mafia appears to have been the first option, see ZIPPER Document, 4 April 63 (3:35pm)

[84] See ZIPPER Document, 2 May (4:09pm), 10 May, 12 June (4:11pm), 16 July (1:45pm), 24 Oct., 14 Nov. 1963.

[85] For information on the *Unione Corse* and its connection with drugs and the CIA, see also J. Nutter, *op. cit.* (note 37), pp. 180f.

pant" in the entire plot, it must be assumed that the FBI as a government department was collaborating with the CIA to achieve the projected goal.[86]

On March 13 and 15, the next delicate contacts were made to Walter Jenkins and Abe Fortas, top aides of Vice President Lyndon B. Johnson. According to the ZIPPER Document, Jenkins and Fortas, and with them of course the Vice President, were also kept informed about the rising plot.[87]

Not a bold man, Johnson's concerns were entirely typical for him. He had forced himself on the 1960 Democratic ticket against Kennedy's wishes, and throughout the thousand days of the Kennedy presidency, Johnson was treated with contempt by Kennedy's people. Their favorite epithet was "Uncle Cornpone," and it became common knowledge that Kennedy was planning to replace Johnson on the 1964 ticket. To accomplish this, Bobby Kennedy was preparing criminal charges against Bobby Baker, one of Johnson's top aides.[88]

Johnson was aware that such charges would give the Kennedy faction the ability to force him off the ticket. Since Vice Presidents traditionally have run for the Presidency at the expiration of the mandatory two-term limit, any hope of gaining the White House would have been dashed. Johnson, therefore, became a willing if very timid participant in the ZIPPER project.

The two most important groups, the FBI and the future President of the United States, were hence quickly convinced to support the CIA:

---

[86] The FBI is listed as a "government department directly concerned," see ZIPPER Document, no. 8.b. Though Hoover himself was only a few times directly involved with operation ZIPPER (4 & 15 March, as well as no. 12), it is obvious that Hoover's assistant Sullivan was a permanent part of the plot, since his name is mentioned on many occasions as a participants during the preparation of Operation ZIPPER: no. 12; 4, 7, 12 (8:30am) & 29 March (2:35pm), 30 April, 2 & 10 May.

[87] See ZIPPER Document, 13, 14, 15, 18 March (9:30am) 25, 28 March (4:45, 4:55pm), 11 April (11:45am), 15 April (5:20pm), 30 April (9:31am), 6 May (11:10am a.), 31 May (1:35pm), 11, 12 June (5:30pm), 26 June (9:30am).

[88] See ZIPPER Document, 18 March (9:30am), which apparently refers to the handover of copies of files compiled by the attorney General Robert F. Kennedy regarding Bobby Baker; see also the more explicit entry on 5 May, no. 8.

"11. As both the Vice President and the Director of the Federal Bureau of Investigation has been slated for replacement by the Kennedy faction, their support for this project was practically guaranteed from the outset.

12. The Vice President came to believe that an attempt would be made on his life at the same time and was greatly concerned for his own safety.[89]

13. As the Vice President and the Director of the FBI were longtime neighbors and very friendly, the Director has repeatedly assured the [Vice] President that he was not considered a target and that no shots were fired at him in Dallas." [LBJ was riding two cars behind JFK.][90]

There was, of course, another power to be taken into consideration, which could successfully prevent or reverse the attempted *coup d'état*: the Armed Forces of the United States of America. To integrate the U.S. Army into their *putsch*, the Director of the CIA conferred on March 28 with James Jesus Angleton to coordinate the objectives of the Joint Chiefs of Staff of the U.S. Army with the CIA's objectives within Operation ZIPPER.

The fourth cautious contact was made on 9 April by James Jesus Angleton: Lt. Colonel Bevin Cass, United States Marine Corps, was a U.S. Military Attaché to the Dominican Republic and had been involved with the logistics of the Trujillo assassination.[91] Cass was later Commanding Officer of the Marine Corps infantry training center at Quantico, Virginia.

Cass obviously served as a liaison officer between the Joint Chiefs of Staff and the CIA, as an entry on 14 April 1963 indicates, according to which Cass was recommended by the Chairman of the JCS, General Lyman Lemnitzer. The fact that LtCol. Bevin Cass is listed as a "participant" in the ZIPPER Document, that the Chairman of the JCS was either directly[92] or via LtCol. Cass[93] in fre-

---

89 Compare this with Hoover's Memorandum, note 14, and R. T. Crowley's *Aide-Mémoire*, see Appendix.
90 ZIPPER Document, no. 11-13.
91 This information was gratefully obtained from a source inside the U.S. intelligence community, which cannot be revealed here for legal and privacy reasons.
92 ZIPPER Document, 14 April (9:35am), 25 May, 31 July (9:40am).

quent contact with the CIA regarding Kennedy's assassination, and finally because the JCS is expressly mentioned as a "government department directly concerned" in the ZIPPER document that had specific knowledge about the assassination, it must be concluded that the U.S. Armed Forces are the fourth big cornerstone of the assassination of John F. Kennedy and, hence, the overthrow of the democratically elected government of the people of the United States of America.[94]

In the middle of April, Chicago Mafia boss Sam Giancana advised Crowley that a team of Corsicans had been assembled. Their price for the job was one hundred thousand dollars per man, and there were four involved.

The immediate overseer of the execution of the plot was William King Harvey, former FBI agent and head of the Berlin operations base of the CIA.[95]

Harvey was responsible for the construction of the famous Berlin tunnel. Soviet intelligence was fully aware of this interdiction of their secure telephone lines in the Soviet sector of Berlin, and Harvey proudly garnered crates full of creative Soviet disinformation.

In addition to this, Angleton contacted Israeli intelligence for assistance.[96] The man he contacted was Amos Manor, then head of Israeli counterintelligence, the Shin Beth, and an old friend of Angleton.[97] Angleton had worked closely with Zionist organiza-

---

[93] ZIPPER Document, 9 April (8:31am), 14 April (2:35pm), 24 April (3:09pm), 5 May, 6 May (11:10am), 28 May (8:32am), 31 May (3:00pm), 12 June (12:30pm), 25, 26 June (11:30am).

[94] As a less important conspirator, we should mention Allen Dulles, the former head of the CIA, see ZIPPER Document, 19, 31 July (9:40am). He, too, had no problem with the concept of the removal of the man who had removed him as head of the CIA. In the event of the President's death, he fully expected to be called back to duty although he was not in particularly good health.

[95] See ZIPPER document: participants/recipients; no. 7.; 14, 16 March (3:32pm), 29 March (6:60pm[sic!]), 9 April (10:20am, 1:20pm), 10 April (4:40pm), 14 April (9:35am), 15 April (12:35pm), 10, 25 May, 24, 25 June, 5 July, 31 July (11:30 am): "transfer operation to WKH," 9, 16, 23, 30 August, 6, 12, 20, 27 Sept., 18 Oct., 1, 14 Nov.

[96] See ZIPPER document, 3 April.

[97] An excellent overview of the CIA/Israeli intelligence cooperation can be found in P. Grose, *op. cit.* (note 32), pp. 422-424.

tions in Italy during and after World War II and in 1951 had been
appointed to be the CIA's top liaison with both the Shin Beth and
the Mossad. Through Angleton's good offices, the CIA developed a
close working relationship with both Israeli agencies, and in order
to facilitate his plot against Kennedy, Angleton sought an Israeli
agent who would oversee the entire operation.

In actuality, the Israeli's sole reason for existence, as far as
Angleton was concerned, was to make entirely certain that the
Corsican assassins were removed as soon as possible after their
work was done.

The man sent to him was known as Binjamin Bauman who
came well recommended.[98] He had been one of the Stern Gang
members, a terrorist group controlled by Menachim Begin, later
Israeli Prime Minister, who had assisted in blowing up the King
David Hotel in Jerusalem in 1946 with heavy loss of life. Begin
was still wanted for murder in England, but Bauman had merely
changed his name and went to work for the new state in an official
capacity. This is a classical example of a terrorist becoming a freedom fighter.

John F. Kennedy was decidedly unpopular in Israel because of
his firm determination to prevent that state from developing
atomic weaponry.[99]

A safe house was to be set up in Maryland, and there the Corsicans were to be killed, their bodies dissected and put into crab
pots. The science of DNA had not yet been discovered, and what
the famous soft-shelled crabs could not eat was to be dumped back
into the water. Bones do not float.

In September of 1963, the visit by Kennedy to Dallas in November was announced, and the Angleton assassination plan now
had a specific time frame and geographical location with which to
work.

The Corsicans would be flown to Canada at the end of October,
met by members of the Mafia, and driven into the United States
over the Windsor, Ontario, International Bridge. They would re-

---

[98] See ZIPPER document, 3, 4, 16 July (1:45pm), 17 July.
[99] See *Foreign Relations of the United States, 1961-1963*, Vol. XVII, Washington,
      D.C.: U.S. Government Printing Office, 1994.

main in a Mafia safe house in the Detroit area and then be flown in a private aircraft to the Dallas-Ft. Worth area:

---

52. French intelligence sources have indicated that a recruitment was made among members of the Corsican Mafia in Marseilles in mid-1963.

53. French intelligence sources have also indicated that they informed U.S. authorities in the American Embassy on two occasions about the recruitment of French underworld operatives for a political assassination in the United States.

54. It is not known if these reports were accepted at the Embassy or passed on to Washington.

55. In the event, the Corsicans were sent to Canada where they blended in more easily with the French-speaking Quebec population.

Driscoll Report, p. 16

The Corsicans were under no circumstances to be told of the role of the CIA in their project. They always considered that they were working solely for the American Mafia and no-one else.

Weapons for the assassination were procured from Sam Cummings, CIA agent and head of INTERARMCO, a "proprietary" branch of the Agency.[100] This company, run by a British expert living in Warrentown, Virginia,[101] specialized in gun running for the CIA. It was an easy matter for Cummings to procure two silenced .38-caliber pistols, two 7.65-mm surplus Argentine army Mausers, and a specially constructed .223-caliber rifle, which was cut down and modified from a standard NATO weapon. Special bullets for the latter weapon, filled with mercury and designed to explode when entering a body, were manufactured and accompanied the weapon.

A check of CIA records located the names of several persons of interest to the Agency in the Dallas area. One was Lee Harvey Oswald, the returned defector, and the other was a man with whom the CIA had extensive and documented dealings. This was the Baltic aristocrat George De Mohrenschildt. Born into the

---

[100] See ZIPPER document, no. 9.d.; 18 March (8:44am), 13, 15 April (12:35), 18 April (1:23pm), 6 May (11:10am d.), 14 May, 24 June, 17 July (9:45am). A full listing of CIA proprietary businesses were in the Crowley Papers but are not included in this work.

[101] A number of important CIA agents and sources lived in Warrenton, including Heinrich Müller, former Gestapo Chief, see note 47 and Crowley Papers.

lesser Russian nobility, De Mohrenschildt had served in a Polish cavalry unit, the Promorski Brigade. After the Russian revolution, he immigrated to the United States and acquired a degree in petroleum geology. He traveled in establishment social circles, spent a good deal of time out of the country, and certainly worked for the CIA. He had encountered Oswald quite by accident through his connection with the Russian community in Dallas and became his mentor and, according to a later CIA classified report, his lover.

When De Mohrenschildt passed on the information that Oswald had been hired at the Texas School Book Depository on October 16, it was later realized that this building immediately overlooked the route that Kennedy would take on his November 22 visit to Dallas. Oswald was now viewed as the perfect foil:

14. Oswald was also intimately connected with De Mohrenschildt who was certainly known to be a CIA operative. Oswald's connections with this man were such as to guarantee that the CIA was aware of Oswald's movements throughout his residence in the Dallas area.

15. When Oswald secured employment at the Texas Book Depository, De Mohrenschildt, according to an FBI report, reported this to the CIA.

Driscoll Report, p. 12

77. The pseudo-defector, Oswald, became then important to the furtherance of the plan to kill the American President. He had strong connections with the Soviet Union; he had married a Soviet citizen; he had been noticed in public advocating support of Fidel Castro. His position in a tall building overlooking the parade route was a stroke of great good fortune to the plotters.

Russian Intelligence Study, *Driscoll Report*, p. 10

In the first week of November, the assassination team had been flown to Dallas and spent two weeks in reconnaissance of the entire presidential route. It had initially been felt by the Corsican team leader that the shooting could be done as the cavalcade turned from Houston to Elm Streets. The presidential car would be moving very slowly as it negotiated the right angle turn and would present an excellent target. A shooting blind could be constructed on the top of the Dallas County Records Building on Houston Street that had an excellent line of sight to the Elm Street corner, but flanking buildings were higher and could provide an undesired observer a clear view of the shooters.

It was finally decided to use the Book Depository as one base. The railroad overpass was considered another excellent position but eventually ruled out because it was sure to be guarded. To its right, however, the heavy bushes and fences of the elevated "grassy knoll" proved to be irresistible. The official car with the President would be moving slowly past the spot and would permit a slightly downhill shot at very close range. Also, the extensive railroad yards behind this position gave ample room for an unobserved escape.

The final disposition of the assassination team was:

– A shooter in the Texas Book Depository, sixth floor;
– A shooter in the ornamental bushes just before the underpass;
– Two English-speaking personnel in suits and equipped with false law enforcement identification in the railroad yard behind the second shooter.

It was later reported that if anyone tried to investigate or interfere with the escape of the shooter, the two *faux* law enforcement agents would be able to display their identification and deflect pursuit.

Through his friendship with Oswald, De Mohrenschildt was aware that Oswald had bought a rifle from Klein's Sporting Goods through the mail in March of that year. Both Oswald and his wife had mentioned this rifle to De Mohrenschildt, and he also learned where the weapon was kept.

> 16. The existence and location of Oswald's mail order Mannlicher-Carcano rifle in the garage of his wife's friend, Ruth Paine, was also known to De Mohrenschildt at least one week prior to the assassination.

Driscoll Report, p. 12

Oswald was a bad shot with a rifle, the Warren Commission Report to the contrary, and had never even test shot this surplus Mannlicher-Carcano Italian army weapon.[102] Stories about him going to Dallas rifle ranges with others and firing the Carcano were total fabrications as was an accepted tale of him driving a

---

[102] Oswald's Marine Corps Personnel Records indicate that he barely qualified as a rifle man.

car. Oswald had never shot the purported murder weapon, possessed no driver's license, and did not know how to drive any kind of a car.[103]

On September 26, Oswald went to Mexico City by bus. He returned to Dallas on October 3. During this period, the official story is that Oswald went to the Soviet and Cuban embassies and made very vocal attempts to secure visas for trips to Russia via Cuba.[104] He was told, the official version explains, that a visa to go to Soviet Russia would take four months to process and the Cubans would not grant a visa for Cuba without a Soviet visa.

After the assassination, the CIA sent out a number of reports to various American agencies containing *their* version of the Oswald visit to include physical descriptions and photographs. All of this material was totally incorrect, and the person depicted was very obviously not Lee Harvey Oswald. What Oswald did while in Mexico is not known, but a CIA report of his dramatic visits to the two embassies is a deliberate falsehood:

> 78. Oswald was then reported by the CIA to have gone to Mexico City on 26 September, 1963 and while there, drew considerable attention to his presence in both the Soviet and Cuban embassies. What Oswald might have done in the Cuban embassy is not known for certain but there is no record of his ever having visited the Soviet embassy in Mexico at that time. CIA physical descriptions as well as photographs show that Oswald was not the man depicted. This appears to be a poor attempt on the part of the CIA to embroil both the Soviet Union and Cuba in their affairs.

Russian Intelligence Study, Driscoll Report, p. 10

> 79. Reports from the CIA concerning Oswald's September/October visit to Mexico City are totally unreliable and were rejected by the FBI as being "in serious error." The reasons for Oswald's visit to Mexico are completely obscure at this writing but the individual allegedly photographed by CIA surveillance in Mexico is to a certainty not Lee Oswald. As the CIA had pictures of the real Oswald, their reasons for producing such an obvious falsity are not easy to ascertain at this remove.

Driscoll Report, p. 18

The famous Mexican trip was a typical official red herring deliberately dragged across the investigative trail. In point of fact, it matters not what Oswald did while in Mexico because this trip had

---

[103] See Warren Report, *op. cit.* (note 1) for stories about the Oswald public appearances with the Carcano, e.g., on the license, p. 266.

[104] Warren Report, *op. cit.* (note 1), pp. 301ff.; G. Posner, *op. cit.* (note 6), pp. 170-176, 211-212.

no possible bearing on the allegations of assassination heaped onto a dead Oswald.

The patently obvious disinformation put out by the CIA about Oswald's visit either indicates a frantic desire to be current with intelligence matters or, in a more sinister interpretation, a crude attempt to somehow link the assassination to the Soviet Union and Cuba via the predetermined assassin, Lee Harvey Oswald.

Had this course been followed during the sittings of the Warren Commission, it might well have forced the timid new President to make accusations against both Russia and Cuba that could quite conceivably lead to armed conflict. Since this is the one thing that Johnson frantically wished to avoid, the Mexico City visitation was relegated to the oblivion of the Warren Commission Report without official attention, but certainly deserving of the subsequent sarcasm from a legion of anti-establishment historians.

- Kennedy was shot on Friday, November 22, 1963.
- Oswald was shot on Sunday, November 24, 1963.
- Chicago Mafia leader, Sam Giancana, was shot to death in the basement of his home in June of 1975, prior to when he was supposed to appear before a Congressional committee.
- Oswald's CIA connection in Dallas, George De Mohrenschildt, is alleged to have shot himself just prior to his scheduled appearance before a Congressional committee in March of 1977.

Arranging a murder is relatively simple, but arranging a suicide is much more difficult.

The Warren Commission was instituted shortly after the Dallas murders, evidence was gathered and presented to the Commission, and a final report was duly released. Predictably, it named Lee Harvey Oswald as the sole assassin and, further, carefully played down the strong connections his killer, Jack Rubenstein, had with the Chicago mob.

Historians have discussed the number of witnesses who died in the following months and years. The number tends to raise suspicions of foul play, but so far no hard evidence of a concerted effort to silence witnesses has been produced. However, considering the vast extent of the conspiracy to assassinate Kennedy and overthrow his administration, the conclusions are more than obvious.

The Warren Report included a number of issues intended to bolster the Commission's case against Oswald. One was the attempt to shoot General Edwin Walker, a retired right wing professional Army officer resident in Dallas, on April 12, 1963. That Oswald had nothing to do with this incident is obvious from examining the published evidence and investigative reports. The General was shot at by a .30-06 rifle. Eyewitnesses all agreed that two dark complexioned men were seen driving away from the scene. Oswald did not own such a gun, was not dark complexioned, and did not drive. The Walker story was supplied by Oswald's terrified widow who desperately was attempting to avoid being sent back to Russia. She spoke no English and did in general what she was told.[105] Her story of the Walker incident has no value whatsoever and could never have been used in a court of law.

Of the four Corsicans, three vanished from the face of the earth after being escorted to a private plane at a Dallas area airfield about 2:30 on the afternoon of November 22. They were accompanied by Mr. Bauman and were informed they would be flown first to New Orleans, where the pilot, David Ferrie, was based, and thence to a safe house in Maryland. From the moment they climbed into the two-engined aircraft, they were never seen again.

One of the assassins, the man who fired at Kennedy from nearly point blank range and blew out the presidential brains, decided to work his way back to Marseilles on his own. For some unknown reason, he took a commercial bus to Mexico, and from there he ended up in Barcelona, Spain. All that is known of him is the name he used on his passport: Guidobaldo Fini.

```
                                              It is understood
that the actual assassins were subsequently removed in a wet action but that
one apparently escaped and has been the object of intense searches in France
and Italy by elements of the CIA.
```

Russian Intelligence Study, *Driscoll Report*, p. 10

```
80. The hit team was flown away in an aircraft piloted by a CIA contract
```

-18-

---

[105] Hoover Memorandum, note 14., p. 4.

> pilot named David Ferrie from New Orleans. They subsequently vanished without a trace. Rumors of the survival of one of the team are persistent but not proven.

Driscoll Report, p. 18f.

There was one other murder that bears directly on the Kennedy assassination. On October 12, 1964, shortly after noon, Mary Pinchot Meyer, 44, former wife of Cord Meyer, Jr., a senior CIA official, was found shot to death in a wooded area near her Georgetown studio. She had been shot once in the head and once in the upper body, a professional technique of assassination.

A dazed black day-laborer was found in the vicinity by police and, although not matching the description of an eyewitness, was arrested and put on trial for murder. The suspect, Ray Crump, had no coherent statement for the police at the time of his arrest, and an intensive search of the area failed to locate the handgun used in the killing. This, in spite of the fact that the suspect was apprehended in the immediate area of the killing.[106]

Period press reports indicate that a large number of CIA personnel were present immediately after the discovery of the body.[107]

Crump was acquitted at his subsequent trial.[108] The prosecution depicted him as a rapist, but he had no record of such offenses. He had been seen waiting on a Washington street corner for day labor prior to being found in a dazed condition on the towpath near Mary Meyer's body.[109]

Her husband, Cord Meyer, Jr., was a close personal friend of James Angleton and a very bitter enemy of John Kennedy. Meyer's intense hatred of Kennedy was due to the attentions that Kennedy had once paid to his ex-wife. In point of fact, Mary Pinchot Meyer had been Kennedy's long-term mistress subsequent to her divorce

---

[106] N. Burleigh, *op. cit.* (note 74), pp. 234ff.

[107] N. Burleigh, *op. cit.* (note 74), makes references to mysterious "men in suits" at the murder scene and the fact that newsmen were kept at a distance during the investigation. Plates following p. 182 and comments in the text.

[108] *Ibid.,* pp. 273ff.

[109] *Ibid.,* pp. 209ff.; T. C. Reeves, *op. cit.* (note 3), pp. 240f.

from her husband. Mrs. Meyer had introduced LSD to the President during her many visits to the White House.[110]

Immediately after her murder, Crowley associate James Angleton was caught in her Georgetown studio going through her papers. He later removed her diary and kept it. Robert Crowley, who saw it, stated that it contained a significant number of references to her connection with Kennedy, the use of drugs at White House sex parties, and some very bitter comments about the role of her former husband's agency in the death of her lover the year before.

Mary Meyer had made angry and indiscreet comments about her views on her suspicions of CIA involvement in the Kennedy killing to a number of her neighbors, a significant number of whom had husbands that were senior CIA officials.

This murder is still listed as unsolved, and the police records have disappeared. Shortly after her murder, her bitter former husband painted "Tough luck, Mary" on the Key Bridge near the site of her death.[111]

John Kennedy may have been a charismatic man, but neither he nor his family could be considered either ethical or moral. The President and his brother, the Attorney General of the United States, repeatedly betrayed their wives, their criminal associates, their loyal Cuban supporters, and many others with alacrity when it suited them to do so.

According to the CIA, the FBI, the Vice President, and the Joint Chiefs of Staff, they also betrayed important intelligence secrets to the Soviet Union for political gain. Hence, John F. Kennedy had to die:

> "6. This removal [of JFK] is the result of a consensus between the various concerned official agencies."[112]

---

[110] T. C. Reeves, *ibid.*, N. Burleigh, *op. cit.* (note 74), pp. 193 *et seq.*

[111] R. T. Crowley, private communication to the author, and N. Burleigh, *op. cit.* (note 74), p. 282.

[112] ZIPPER Document, no. 6.

79. From this brief study, it may be seen that the American President was certainly killed by orders of high officials in the CIA, working in close conjunction with very high American military leaders. It was the CIA belief that Kennedy was not only circumventing their own mapped-out destruction of Fidel Castro by assassination and invasion but actively engaged in contacts with the Soviet Union to betray the CIA actions.

80. The American military leaders (known as the Joint Chiefs of Staff) were also determined upon the same goals, hence both of them worked together to ensure the removal of a President who acted against their best interests and to have him replaced with a weaker man whom they believed they could better control.

81. President Johnson, Kennedy's successor, was very much under the control of the military and CIA during his term in office and permitted enormous escalation in Southeast Asia. The destruction of the Communist movement in that area was of paramount importance to both groups.

Russian Intelligence Study, *Driscoll Report*, p. 10

ANALYSIS OF THE SOVIET INTELLIGENCE REPORT

1. The Soviet analysis of the assassination of President John F. Kennedy contains material gleaned from American sources both official and unofficial i.e., media coverage, etc. Some of this material obviously stems from sources located inside various agencies. To date, none of these have been identified.

81. A study of the Soviet report indicates very clearly that the Russians have significant and very high level sources within both the Central Intelligence Agency and the Federal Bureau of Investigation. Their possession of material relating to certain highly classified American military papers has been referred to the CIC for investigation and action.

Driscoll Report, p. 11, 19.

Aftermath

The chapter "The Official Cover Up" already addresses briefly what happened after the actual assassination. The ZIPPER Document contains more interesting pieces of information that make it understandable how the cover up was implemented and why it could be so successful.

There is, of course, the most important fact: that the FBI itself, which was in charge of all investigations, was a participant in the assassination. The FBI gave James Jesus Angleton, the main plotter, complete control of the evidence:

> "10. Following the removal of the President, the new President, who had been fully briefed prior to the act, agreed 'in the interest of national concerns' to appoint a special Commission chaired by the Chief Justice, for the purpose of 'setting public concerns to rest.' Mr. Angleton was in complete control of all evidence presented to this Committee and worked closely in conjunction with Mr. Sullivan of the FBI to ensure that nothing was brought before the Committee that it did not wish to acknowledge."

It is also interesting that Gerald Ford, who became President of the United States of America in 1974, helped FBI Director J. E. Hoover, and it is hard to believe that by so doing, he did not know that he actively participated in the cover-up of the *putsch*:

> "16. Representative Ford, R, of Michigan, a member of the Commission, is working closely with Director Hoover and reports all incoming information directly to him."

The CIA's many supporters within the media did their best to hide and distort the truth:

> "17. Full cooperation with friendly media sources has ensured that the public attention has been drawn to Oswald as the sole killer. [...]

32. In the matter of the public perception of the Dallas action, extensive use has been made of Agency connections with major American media organs, i.e., the New York Times and the Washington Post. The Times is strongly supporting the Commission and its findings and we are assured that they will continue to do so. The same attitude has been clearly and strongly expressed by the Post."

A very interesting effect on U.S. foreign policy had the fact that the French Intelligence Services, due to their informants in the *Unione Corse*, had knowledge about the real assassins of JFK and threatened the United States if they would not make certain concessions:

"25. The [French President] General [Charles DeGaulle] also stated that he was aware through French intelligence reports, that the assassins of the President were French citizens."

The knowledge of the French government at the highest level about some kind of high level political assassination was apparently passed on to the U.S. Embassy in Paris, but there is no record of any of these warnings having been passed on to Washington. If, in fact, these warnings were passed, there was obviously no heed paid to them.

"26. Because it is viewed as vital that the French become involved in NATO and to assuage the concerns of the General, guarantees were given both by the [U.S.] President and the DCI [Director of Central Intelligence...] that the United States would actively support French commercial interests in French Indo China in return for French cooperation with NATO."

There were extensive French rubber plantations in Vietnam as well as significant off-shore oil deposits.

"27. The French President agreed to this but made several oblique threats to the President about his reactions in the event of future Agency "meddling" in French domestic and foreign policy.

28. The General was reassured repeatedly on these points and is now apparently in agreement with United

States aims in Southeast Asia. He made several remarks about the trade in opium in that area being extremely lucrative and stated that he had his own problems with narcotics traffic in the Mediterranean area.

29. It is not believed, and electronic surveillance of the President's lines of communication while in the United States does not support, the possibility that he might have actual knowledge of any American involvement, or projected involvement, in this sensitive area.

30. Both the Agency and the President feel that the French President has 'fired a shot across our bows' but that these issues have now become resolved. The President feels, however, that the French will have to be watched carefully in the future and that if American interests become established in French Indo China, we had best consider our own interests at that time."

Considering that the U.S. Joint Chiefs of Staff had been more than eager to start a war against Cuba, it might not be surprising that they were quite open to the French "request" for help in French Indo China, which could be more appropriately called "blackmailing America into war." In fact, the Tonkin incident in 1964, which triggered America's involvement in the Vietnam War, reads like an implementation of what the U.S. Army had unsuccessfully planned only a few years earlier for Cuba, as James Bamford correctly noticed.[113]

With increasing American military involvement in Vietnam and Laos, the increase in opium smuggling was highly significant and has not stopped to this day. It is a published fact that much of the movement of raw opium from the so-called Golden Triangle was effected by the CIA and its Air America private airforce. The CIA's own statement about "American involvement" in the "trade in opium" in Indochina is a topic that will be dealt with in a subsequent book, offering much more secret documentation on the U.S. government as one of the major drug traffickers of the world.

---

[113] See footnote 63.

The Crowley Papers

In 1963, the author met a German *Luftwaffe* officer who lived in Palo Alto, California. His name was Frederick Laegel, and he was employed in the medical department of Stanford University. During lengthy conversations Laegel admitted that he had been a German *Sicherheitsdienst* (security service) officer, attached to Hitler's military headquarters, as well as being attached to the *Führer-Kurierstaffel* (courier squadron). He said, and showed documents in proof of his statements, that he had worked for the CIA after the war.

At one point, Laegel indicated that he had a friend who knew even more about the period than himself, and eventually the author came into contact with Heinrich Müller, then a resident of Piedmont, California. These ongoing contacts and interviews with the former head of the Gestapo led to the books based on Müller's papers and eventually to an approach by Robert Crowley, a retired high-level CIA official, in 1993.

Crowley was working with British author John Costello, and in return for papers concerning British surveillance of Ambassador Joseph Kennedy in 1939, Crowley and Costello supplied the author with official documentation on Müller's postwar employment by the American intelligence community.

In 1994, the author published the first of his series on the papers of Heinrich Müller, once Chief of the German Gestapo. The first work appeared in Germany and was subsequently printed in English in 1995 by Bender Publishing. When these appeared, there was considerable official, but very private, concern expressed in CIA circles due to the inflammatory issues raised.

The author was then contacted by Dr. William Corson of Potomac, Maryland, regarding the name of the CIA official who interrogated Müller in Switzerland in 1948. Corson, an intelligence specialist and published author, informed the writer that the unidentified interrogator was one James Speyer Kronthal, in 1948 CIA station chief in Bern, Switzerland.

Subsequent to the publication of the first book, the author rapidly developed his friendship with Robert Crowley. Crowley, a courtly and extremely well-informed man who had formerly held a very high position in the CIA, proved to be more than cooperative and informative regarding the CIA's use of Müller. Crowley stated to the author and to others in Washington that *he* was the man who had worked with Müller when the former Gestapo chief arrived in Washington in 1948.

More than once, Crowley informed the author that various official American agencies had been in touch with him regarding the author and his works, attempting to discover whatever they could to discredit the thesis that Müller had been in the employ of the CIA. Crowley put the author in touch with former CIA officials who were well aware of Müller's American employment. However, since none of these retirees would either admit or deny the Müller employment, this action was more in the way of annoying his former colleagues, on Crowley's part, than in supplying sources for the writer.

Robert Crowley was a very intelligent, courteous, and generous person. The author used to speak with him over the telephone at least twice a week. Crowley was in retirement, and none of his old associates bothered to contact him. As a man who once wielded considerable power, his retirement plunged him into a lonely void. Eventually, he became more and more confidential in his anecdotes to the author, whom he felt was both a sympathetic listener and fellow-historian.

Finally, in 1996, Crowley was asked by his concerned family to undergo exploratory lung surgery. Cancer was suspected, since Crowley was a heavy cigarette smoker. Before he went into the hospital, Crowley became very depressed. He was, he said, an old man and might well die on the operating table. In the years preceding this operation, a reflective Crowley had often expressed his desire to help others understand the many historical events that he was party to. For these reasons, he told the author, he would send to him a number of papers from his personal files.

For example, the author had been bombarded with obviously specious requests from members of the media for specific information on Müller's postwar persona. When the author made sarcastic comments about repeated visitations from *Time* magazine and others, Crowley sent him a thick computer printout containing the names of thousands of individuals who were either CIA operatives or were sympathetic to their operations. The purpose of sending this list was that the author could easily check the names of suspicious callers against it. In the sense Crowley intended it, the list proved to be invaluable and has been included in this work.

Other material from Crowley's files covered a number of CIA clandestine operations, both national and international, from 1948 through 1982. For instance, among papers in the Crowley archives there is, aside from the explosive signed report concerning the underlying facts of the assassination of President John Kennedy, other material on such controversial issues as Operation *Phoenix*, the MK-ULTRA program, Operations *Condor* and *Applepie*, and even an in-house budget for the 1996-97 fiscal years. Details of these operations will be published in subsequent books.

The papers sent to the author were embargoed by Crowley. They were not to be used or attributed during his lifetime. When he died in October of 2000, the embargo was lifted.

The CIA (and in fact the government itself), may well find the publication of a selection of Robert Crowley's large personal files a disaster, but the American public, who pays their salaries, might have a different view.

During the author's relationship with Crowley, the former CIA official began to express extreme annoyance with his former colleagues at Langley. The focus of his anger was directed at their ouster of his good friend, James Angleton, once head of CIA Counterintelligence.

Crowley felt that Angleton was a "great patriot" who had been forced out of his position by younger men who saw in Angleton's constant searches for moles in the CIA a disruptive and nonproductive nuisance. Angleton had been correct in his assumptions, and at least one Russian agent, Aldrich Ames, was discovered after Angleton's death, when it was too late for an apology.

When defending Angleton's actions, Crowley began to speak of the Kennedy assassination and why it had proved to be necessary. Because the author was obviously skeptical, Crowley, defending his position, began to send papers to support his thesis that Kennedy had been practicing treason and endangering the American public by his reckless and ill-informed ventures into brinkmanship.

The basis for this work was found in the two large boxes of files the author received in 1996. By releasing these documents and others, Crowley placed himself squarely in the middle of the conspiracy, but in his eyes, at least, he felt that he and his fellow plotters and assassins were entirely justified in their actions.

Whether they were so justified is a matter for the reader to determine upon careful reflection.

Morals and ethics are excellent norms but hardly effective motivating factors in any intelligence community.

The Mighty Wurlitzer

"For a quarter of a century the CIA has been repeatedly wrong about every major political and economic question entrusted to its analysis."

Senator Daniel Patrick Moynihan, *New York Times*, 1991

"The Central Intelligence Agency is now using several hundred American academics, who in addition to providing leads and occasionally making introductions for intelligence purposes, occasionally write books and other materials to be used for propaganda purposes abroad. [...] These academics are located in over 100 American universities, colleges, and related institutes.

Prior to 1967, the Central Intelligence Agency sponsored, subsidized, or produced over 1,000 books. [...] For example, a book written for an English-speaking audience by one CIA operative was reviewed favorably by another CIA agent in the New York Times.

Until February 1976, when it announced a new policy towards U.S. media personnel, the CIA maintained covert relationships with about 50 American journalists or employees of U.S. media organizations. They are part of a network of several hundred foreign individuals around the world who provide intelligence for the CIA and at times attempt to influence foreign opinion through the use of covert propaganda."[114]

---

[114] U.S. Senate, *Final Report of the Select Committee to Study Government Operations With Respect to Intelligence Activities. Book 1: Foreign and Military Intelligence.* 94th Congress. 2nd Session, Washington, D.C.: U.S. Government Printing Office, 1976, pp. 452ff.; also known as "Church Committee Final Report".

Frank Gardiner Wisner, head of the CIA's clandestine operations directorate, liked to boast of his powerful connections with
the American media. Claiming that he could plant any kind of a
story he wanted in the major American newspapers, he also
claimed that he could prevent the publication of any article or book
that he felt reflected negatively on the CIA.

Wisner called this his "mighty Wurlitzer" after both the massive and very loud organs found in most large movie houses in the
1930s as well as the large garish juke boxes found in dance halls
and cheap restaurants in the 1940s.

By a judicious mixture of bribery, special favors, and outright
payments of cash, Wisner and his associates could powerfully influence American perceptions and completely silence any media
opposition. Prominent academics, revered newspaper columnists,
historical writers, newspaper and magazine editors, book publish-
ers, and, later, television executives all gorged at the CIA pig
trough, and when one died, there were many eager to take his
place.

In the 1996 list received from Robert Crowley, one of Wisner's
senior executives, a number of names of such individuals can be
found who are politely termed CIA "sources." These published
names include: Tim Golden and Ivar Peterson of the *New York
Times*, Howard Kurz and Walter Pincus of the *Washington Post*,
Doyle McManus of the *Los Angeles Times*, Ted Koppel of the
Nightline television program, Professor Timothy Naftali of Yale
University, and a significant number of other members of the media, the business world, and academia.[115]

There is a very illustrative book that covers an example of the
methods the CIA uses to either plant stories favorable to it or to
destroy the reputations of those who produce material unfavorable
to it.

In *Whiteout* by Alexander Cockburn and Jeffery St. Clair, published in 1998 by Verso in London, there is considerable space
given to the trials and tribulations of one Gary Webb. Webb was
an investigative reporter for the San Jose, California, *Mercury-*

---

[115] See Appendix for a full copy of the Crowley data base list.

News, and his investigations into the often-rumored drug dealings of the CIA dredged up sufficient evidence that the agency was indeed heavily involved in American drug traffic. His articles on the subject, published in August of 1996, initially alarmed and then infuriated the heads of the CIA.

This agency has a standing policy of completely ignoring any criticism of their actions or purported actions. It has always been their favorite method of attacking their enemies to do so through their many surrogates and avid supporters in the American and foreign media.[116]

After the publication of Webb's charges, friendly members of the media began an assault on his story, bringing the well-researched work into question and, in the main, denigrating and trivializing his articles. His editor quickly and publicly disavowed him, and the issue was considered negated.

The CIA almost never engages in disputes with someone who questions its actions. They are able to activate the Wisner media Wurlizer to considerable effect. The "Company" (as it is called by its initiates) is then always able to claim plausible denial in the event that some manner of irrefutable proof surfaces.

Insofar as the Webb charges of CIA drug dealing is concerned, it might be instructive to note that a thorough investigation of these charges was made by a very reputable and unbiased Federal official. It is pleasant to note that his report completely and thoroughly exonerated the Central Intelligence Agency from any possible connection with these heinous and destructive allegations. It was a most definitive and decisive report.

It was written by the Inspector General of the CIA himself.[117]

---

[116] A. Cockburn, J. St. Clair, *op. cit.* (note 38), pp. 1-59, gives an excellent well-researched example of these methods.

[117] The accusations of CIA drug trafficking are numerous and the Webb case is well covered in A. Cockburn, J. St. Clair, *op. cit.* (note 38), pp 54ff.; George Tenant, *Statement on Release of Inspector General's Report,* USCIA Public Affairs Office, January 29, 1998; U.S. Central Intelligence Agency. Office of Inspector General, *Report of Investigation Concerning Allegations Between CIA and the Contras in Trafficking Cocaine to the United States,* USCIA Inspector General's Office, January 29, 1998.

When a work appears in public that the CIA finds unsettling, revealing, or damaging, how does it react? It is one thing for them to sponsor laudatory and self-serving films and television shows and to have their media friends plant useful articles in the media for or against a topic of interest to them, but quite another to respond to substantive attacks.

Since the CIA and other American intelligence agencies have become ossified and ponderously bureaucratic over the years since their inceptions, their responses have become entirely and very often humorously predictable. For example, let the reader consider a work such as the present one.

The CIA personnel, whose task it is to review published material that might be of interest to it, will of course read it. That is, provided that they or a friendly media member can get the publisher to give them a free "review" copy. There will be no immediate response on their part because the work has to filter, at the very least, through a study group or, if it is considered a serious public relations menace, a committee. Several months will elapse, and the study group or committee will then make its report to senior levels of internal influence.

During this period of investigative gestation, no public comments will be forthcoming other than frantic requests to friends in the media to ignore the work and make no comment of any kind on either the work or its author. If the work in question contains serious allegations backed with documentary evidence, a determination will be made as to the potential damage that could be created if the work gained significant circulation.

The first step in CIA damage control is to beckon to an eager media friend to prepare another book that would completely demolish the thesis of the first unacceptable work. Once this literary antidote was in progress, supportive documents for it would either be located in official archives and deliberately misinterpreted or simply forged, and a media campaign of ridicule launched against the offending author, not his work. The work must never be reviewed lest someone might read it.

If the author had ever been ticketed for crossing a street against a light, this would be reported as "endangering motorists."

Overdue library books would translate into "attempted theft" and "conversion of government property." The unfortunate author would be accused of having sexual relations with the mother of his own children, his wife would be accused of being a practicing thespian and a maternal uncle smeared as a man who practiced nepotism with members of his own family.

Retail book outlets would be spoken to and asked not to stock a book that would never receive a positive media review. Sunday talk show hosts would conduct highly negative interviews with seedy academics and minor historians who haven't published anything since their 1963 seminal work on the Newfoundland Fisheries issue.

In all probability, there will never be an *official* CIA response because it is generally felt by the American public that a controversial issue is not considered proven until it is officially denied in Washington.

Envoy

In matters as prolix and entangled as the Kennedy assassination, there can never be an actual closure. There can, however, be a final word on the subject, and the clearest one can be found in John Jacob Nutter's excellent study, *The CIA's Black Ops: Covert Action, Foreign Policy, and Democracy*.[118] The author lists a number of the more important delinquencies of the Central Intelligence Agency, which cannot be improved upon:

"–spying on Americans for their political beliefs;

– opening the mail of Americans not suspected of any crime;

– harassing and disrupting legal American political groups simply for their dissenting views;

– testing neurochemical and biological agents (such as LSD) and toxins on American citizens without their consent or knowledge, covering up these activities, and destroying evidence of them;

– engaging in secret wars with neither the consent nor knowledge of Congress;

– engaging in acts of war or acts that created a high probability of war without the consent or knowledge of Congress;

– purposely concealing these acts or intentionally misleading members of the government who have a right to know about such activities;

– employing the policies and resources of intelligence agencies to further the goals of private corporations and political groups;

– subverting democratic processes and sponsoring the functional equivalents of coups d'etat in friendly and allied countries;

---

[118] J. Nutter, *op. cit.* (note 37), p. 300.

- creating private, off-the-books intelligence and operations organizations in deliberate attempts to evade U.S. law;
- negotiating with terrorists and paying ransom for hostages; and
- arming insurgent and terrorist organizations with modern weapons in spite of their anti-American positions."

Bibliography

Bamford, James, *Body of Secrets*, New York: Doubleday, 2001

Bernstein, Carl, "The CIA and the Media," *Rolling Stone*, October 20, 1977

Beschloss, Michael, *Kennedy and Roosevelt,* New York: W. W. Norton, 1980

Blakey, G. Robert, and Richard Billings, *The Plot to Kill the President: Organized Crime Assassinated JFK.* New York: Times Books, 1981

Brown, David G., *The Last Log of the Titanic*, Camden, Me.: International Marine/McGraw-Hill, 2001

Burleigh, Nina, *A Very Private Woman: The Life and Unsolved Murder of Presidential Mistress Mary Meyer,* New York: Bantam Books, 1998

Cockburn, Alexander, and Jeffrey St. Clair, *Whiteout: The CIA, Drugs, and the Press*, London; New York: Verso, 1998

Corson, William R., and Robert T. Crowley, *The New KGB. Engine of Soviet Power*, New York: Morrow, 1985

Crowley, Robert T., unpublished documents and manuscripts

Douglas, Gregory, *Gestapo Chief: The 1948 Interrogation of Heinrich Müller*, vols. 1-3, San Jose: Bender, 1995

Douglas, Gregory, *Müller Journals: The Washington Years, Vol. 1: 1948-1950*, San Jose: Bender, 1999

Fleming, Thomas, *The New Dealers' War,* New York: Basic Books, 2001

Foreign Relations of the United States, 1961-1963, Vol. XVII, Washington, D.C.: U.S. Government Printing Office, 1994

Gander, Terry, and Peter Chamberlain, *Weapons of the Third Reich,* New York: Doubleday, 1979

Groden, Robert J., and Harrison E. Livingstone, *High Treason,* New York: Conservatory Press, 1989

Grose, Peter, *Gentleman Spy: The Life of Allen Dulles,* Amherst: University of Massachusetts Press, 1994

Heilbrunn, Otto, *The Soviet Secret Services,* New York: Praeger, 1956

Hersh, Seymour, *The Dark Side of Camelot,* New York: Brown, 1998 (pb. edition)

House Select Committee on Assassinations, HSCA 567, 3. Vol., Washington, D.C.: U.S. Government Printing Office, 1976.

Johnson, Haynes, *The Bay of Pigs: The Leaders' Story of Brigade 2506,* New York: W. W. Norton, 1964

Lane, Mark, *Rush to Judgment: A Critique of the Warren Commission's Inquiry into the Murders of President John F. Kennedy, Officer J. D. Tippet, and Lee Harvey Oswald,* New York: Holt Reinhart Winston, 1966

Lane, Mark, *Plausible Denial: Was the CIA Involved in the Assassination of JFK?,* New York: Thunder's Mouth Press, 1991

Lifton, David S., *Best Evidence: Disguise and Deception in the Assassination of John F. Kennedy,* New York: Carroll & Graf, 1980

Mangold, Tom, *Cold Warrior: James Jesus Angleton: The CIA's Master Spy Hunter,* New York: Simon & Schuster, 1991

Marchetti, Victor, and John D. Marks, *The CIA and the Cult of Intelligence,* New York: Alfred Knopf, 1983

McCullough, David, *Truman,* New York: Simon & Schuster, 1992

Nutter, John Jacob, *The CIA's Black Ops: Covert Action, Foreign Policy and Democracy,* Amherst: Promethus Books, 2000

Oglesby, Carl, *Who Killed JFK?,* Berkeley: Odonian Press, 1992

Piper, Michael Collins, *Final Judgment: The Missing Link in the JFK Assassination,* Washington, D.C.: The Center for Historical Review, 1998.

Posner, Gerald, *Case Closed: Lee Harvey Oswald and the Assassination of JFK,* New York: Doubleday, 1993

Prados, John, *Presidents' Secret Wars: CIA and Pentagon Covert Operations Since World War II,* New York: William Morrow, 1986

Reeves, Thomas C., *A Question of Character: A Life of John F. Kennedy*, New York: Macmillan, 1991

Scott, Peter Dale, *Deep Politics and the Death of JFK*, Berkeley: University of California Press, 1993

Simpson, Christopher, *Blowback*, New York: Weidenfeld & Nicholson, 1988

Sullivan, William, *The Bureau: My Thirty Years in Hoover's FBI*, New York: Norton, 1979

Summers, Anthony, *Conspiracy*, New York: McGraw-Hill, 1980

Tenant, George, *Statement on Release of Inspector General's Report*, USCIA Public Affairs Office, January 29, 1998

Trento, Joseph, *The Secret History of the CIA*, New York: Random House, 2001

U.S. Central Intelligence Agency, Office of Inspector General, *Report of Investigation Concerning Allegations Between CIA and the Contras in Trafficking Cocaine to the United States*, USCIA Inspector General's Office, January 29, 1998

U.S. Senate, *Final Report of the Select Committee to Study Government Operations With Respect to Intelligence Activities.* Book 1: *Foreign and Military Intelligence.* 94th Congress, 2nd Session, Washington, D.C.: U.S. Government Printing Office, 1976. (Church Committee Final Report)

U.S. Senate, *Final Report of the Select Committee to Study Government Operations With Respect to Intelligence Activities.* Book 6: *Supplementary Reports on Intelligence Activities.* 94th Congress, 2nd Session, Washington, D.C.: U.S. Government Printing Office, 1976.

Warren Commission Report U.S. Government Printing Office, Vol. 1 and *Hearings*, 26 vols. [pb. edition, New York: St. Martin's Press, no year, ISBN 0-312-08257-6]

Appendix

Alphabetical Listing of CIA and Other Intelligence Sources

This is a reproduction of a list of intelligence sources of the CIA found in the papers of Robert Crowley, most likely compiled in the mid-1990s. It was, of course, neither possible to check whether the data given in it is correct nor to which degree and for which purpose the persons listed were—or still are—involved in any CIA intelligence activities. The list was digitized with OCR techniques and might therefore include typographical errors not included in the original.

– A –

Abbott, Alfred, P.O. Box 10205, Albuquerque, NM 87184
Abbott, Dr. Preston S., 1305 Namassin Rd., Alexandria, VA 22308
Abernathy, John W., 7601 W. Charleston Blvd., No. 60, Las Vegas, NV 89117
Abernathy, Thomas B., 1815 Beulah Rd., Vienna, VA 22180
Absher, Kenneth M., P.O. Box 6150, San Antonio, TX 78209
Achilles, Barbara H., 1014 Aponi Rd., SE, Vienna, VA 22180
Adams, Fred H., 509 Fourth Ave., New Kensington, PA 15068
Adams, Nathan M., 321 S. Piff St., Alexandria, VA 22314
Adams, Capt Robert E., USN 5127 North 37th Rd., Arlington, VA 22207
Addicott, Kenneth F., General Delivery, Carmel, CA 93921
Adkisson, Capt Hubert, USN 840 North Atlantic Ave., No C 402, Cocoa Beach, FL 32931
Adler, David B., 2300 Old Spanish Trail, No 2014, Houston, TX 77054
Adnet, Jacques J., 4515 Diamondback Dr., Colorado Springs, CO 80921
Aiello, Ms. Phyllis, 2207 Wagner Ave., Erie, PA 16510
Albers, Capt Steven C., USN 8340 Greensboro Dr., No 707, McLean, VA 22102 A
Albert, Garret L., 9002 Glenbrook Rd., Fairfax, VA 22031
Albertson, John P., 367 Main St., Old Saybrook, CT 06475
Albitz, Ben F., 7924 Inverness Ridge Rd., Potomac, MD 20854
Albrecht, LtCol Walter, USAF 15 Gardens Corner Ct., Charleston, SC 29407
Alden, Sygmund, P.O. Box 611374, Miami, FL 33161
Alderman, Col Nathaniel, USA P.O. Box 20772, St. Petersburg, FL 33742
Algrant, James J., P.O. Box 1047, Camden, ME 04843
Alkek, Lt James, USA 4107 Solway, Houston, TX 77025
Allen, Andrew E., 122 Pepper Ave, Larkspur, CA 94939
Allen, Charles J., 50 Holden St., Shrewsbury, MA 01545

Allen, George W., 5520 N. 23rd St., Arlington, VA 22205
Allen, Herbert L., P.O. Box 1291, Dunedin, FL 34697
Allen, John K., 3339 Military Rd., NW, Washington. DC 20015
Allen, LtCdr Scott, USN 1457 Aunsuna St., Kailua, HI 96734
Allison, Ms. E.T. Flandro Grossmont Gardens, 5480 Maringo Ave., La Mesa, CA 91942
Allner, Frederick A. Jr., 5225 Pooks Hill Rd., No. 1016 South, Bethesda, MD 20814
Althausen, William, 1305 Marlin Dr., Naples, FL 33962
Altobelli, Louis U., 1680 NW 133rd St., Miami, FL 33167
Altomare, Gasper R., 600 Amherst Dr., SE, Albuquerque, NM 87106
Amargo, Carlos A., 8802 SW 52nd Ct., Ocala, FL 34476
Amato, Joseph, 3716 Ramsgate Dr., Annapolis, MD 21403
Amazeen, Col Charles P., 2108 Penfield Ln., Bowie, MD 20716
Ames, Aldrich, 2512 N. Randolph St., N. Arlington, VA 22207
Anderegg, Richard, 103 G St.,SW, No. B 203, Washington, DC 20024
Anderson, Bruce, 900 Allied Bank Plaza, Houston, TX 77002
Anderson, David, 5703 West Hearn Rd., Glendale, AZ 85306
Anderson, Lt Douglas, USNR 27 Meadow Wood Dr., Greenwich, CT 06830
Anderson, Dwayne S., 2637 DePaul Dr., Vienna, VA 22180
Anderson, James A., 4400 East West Hiway, No. 903, Bethesda, MD 20814
Anderson, Major Karl, USAF 5886 Scripps St., San Diego, CA 92122
Anderson, Ms. Mary Louise, 26 Anchorage Rd., Sausalito, CA 94965
Anderson, Robert C., 2 Fenway, Derry, NH 03038
Anderson, Mrs. Sally, 7 Lexington Ave., No 7A, New York, NY 10010
Anderson, Thomas D., 3925 Del Monte, Houston, TX 77019
Anderson, Dr. William H., 34 Coolidge Hill Rd., Cambridge, MA 02138
Andraitis, LtCol Arthur, USAF11707 Flemish Miff Ct., Oakton, VA 22124
Anhalt, Dr. Edward B., 500 Amalfi Dr., Pacific Palisades, CA 90272
Ansley, Norman, 35 Cedar Rd., Severna Prk, MD 21146
Anthony, Michael, 17 Lockwood Rd., Bradford, MA 1830
Applegate, Col Rex, USA32956 State Hiway,39\8, Scottsburg, OR 97473
Aquino, Dr. Michael, P.O. Box 470307, San Francisco, CA 94147
Arenberg, Gerald S., 3801 Biscayne Blvd., Miami, FL 33137
Armstrong, Mrs. Marguerite, 7 Deborah Dr., South Burlington, VT 05403
Armstrong, Nicles, 815 Madison Ave., St. Charles, IL 60174
Armstrong, Major William, USAF1 North Federal St., No 225, New Market, MD 21774
Arnhym, Robert, P.O. Box 293, San Diego, CA 92112
Arnold, Daniel, P.O. Box 310, Cafferty Rd., Point Pleasant, PA 18950
Arnold, Peter, P.O. Box 477A, Kennebunkport, ME 04046
Arsenault, Paul A., 11743 Birch St., Palm Beach Gardens, FL 33410
Arvidson, Major John, AUSP.O. Box 7067, City of Industry, CA 91774
Asaoka, Kiko, 201 Vanderpool, Houston, TX 77024
Ash, Mrs. Dorothy, 2828 N. Atlantic Ave., No 704, Daytona Beach, FL 32118
Aster, Czapt George, USNR120 Baltimore Ave., Larkspur, CA 94939
Aston, Richard, 1712 Noe St., San Francisco, CA 94131
Atkeson, MajGen Edward, USA202 Vassar Pl., Alexandria, VA 22314
Atkinson, Capt James, USAF1D Sandy Bay Terrace, Rockport, MA 01966
Atkinson, Roderick, D.10849 Split Oak Ln., Burke, VA 22015
Atkinson, William, 8209 Jeb Stuart Rd., Potomac, MD 20854
Atwell, Joan D., 918 Siskiyou Dr., Menlo Park, CA 94025
Atwood, LtCol James P., USA5104 Pineland Dr., Savannah, GA 31405
Atwood, Walter, 3105 Gumwood Dr., Hyattsville, MD 20783
Aulenbacher, George, 2711 Grove Manor Dr., Kingwood, TX 77345
Avrakotos, Gust L., 1027 Whisperiing Woods Dr., Coraopolis, PA 15109
Aylesbury, Charles, 2 Middleridge Ln., Rolling Hills, CA 90274

– B –

Babbitt, Capt Franklin, USN10713 Miller Rd., Oakton, VA 22124
Babcock, Fenton, 106 Elderberry Dr., Winchester, VA 22603
Babcock, James H., 11500 Fairway Dr., No 307, Reston, VA 22090
Bachman, Lawrence, W.3419 Valewood Dr. Oakton, VA 22124
Baclawski, Dr. Joseph A., 11226 Mitscher St., Kensington, MD 20895
Bacot, John C., Bank of New York Co., New York, NY
Baczynski, John L., 4 Romero Ct., Novato, CA 94945
Baer, Richard T., 12104 Foxhill Ln., Bowie, MD 20715

Bailey, LtCdr George, USN1028 Isabella, No A, Coronado, CA 92118
Bailey, Paul L., 3640 Windjammer Dr., Colorado Springs, CO 30920
Bailey, Cdr William B., USN3802 Kendale Rd., Annandale, VA 22003
Baird, Dane E., 9 Park Ave., Belmont, MA 02178
Baker, Ms Margaret E., 4100 Massachusetts, Ave., NW, No 806, Washington, DC 20016
Baker, LtCol Paul D., AUSP.O. Box 83, Rockridge Baths, VA 24473
Balaban, Rudolph J., 522 Charles Ave., New Kensington, PA 15068
Balch, John W., 178 Thomas Johnson Dr., No 200, Frederick, MD 21701
Baldwin, Thomas, 202 SE 1st St., Evansville, IN 47713
Ball, Ms Virginia J., 1101 New Hampshire Ave., NW, No 821, Washington, DC 20037
Ballew, Frank B., P.O. Box 7641, St. Thomas, VI 00801
Ballow, CW4 Jearl E., USA83 Roundtable Rd., Springfield, IL 62704
Balserio, Aldo E., 1216 Kennedy Blvd., Union City, NJ 07087
Bane, Howard T., 10232 Confederate Lane, Fairfax, VA 22030
Bangs, Lawrence C., 4725 San Pedro Dr., NE, No. 16, Albuquerque, NM 87109
Bannerman, Robert L., P.O. Box 1132, Santa Rosa Beach, FL 32459
Barber, Hubert H. Jr., 913 Allegro Ln., Apollo Beach, FL 33572
Barber, William H., 19504 Gallitin Ct., Gaithersburg, MD 20879
Barclay, John G. L., Virgin Del Pilar 8, Cabrils, Spain
Barker, LtCol Wayne G, USA23995 Carrillo Dr., Mission Viejo, CA 92691
Barlow, William J., 11402 Chapel Rd., Clifton, VA 22024
Barndt, Walter D. Jr., P.O. Box 1155, Grantham, NH 03753
Barnhart, James M., 3310 Baltimore, Lawton, OK 73505
Barnwell, Michael J., P.O. Box 914, Union Lake, MI 48387
Barrett, Col Frederick T., USA4936 N. 33rd Rd., Arlington, VA 22207
Barrios, LtCol Jose Alberto, 1140 NE 110 Terrace, Miami, FL 33161
Barrow, Lonnie M., 12401 North 22nd St., No. F 706, Tampa, FL 33612
Barry, John J., 2300 Pimmit Dr., No 614, Falls Church, VA 22043
Barton, Donald E., 46-075 Meheanu Pl., No 3331, Kaneohe, HI 96744
Bartreau, William L., 4402 Wind River Ln., Garland, TX 75042
Basher, William E., 12504 Buckley Dr., Silver Spring, MD 20904
Basil, William, 41-48 171st, Flushing, NY 11358
Bass, W. Streeter, 3005 Willow Springs Ct., Williamsburg, VA 23185
Batcho, David G., 5611 Desert Star, Las Cruces, NM 88005
Bates, Mrs. Constance, N.660 S. Jefferson St., Arlington, VA 22204
Bath, Capt Alan H., USN2502 Watts, Houston, TX 77030
Bathke, Burton C., 4909 Piedra Rosa NE, Albuquerque, NM 87111
Bauer, Clyde W., 1652 North Oriole Place, Orange, CA 92667
Beach, Jenny L., 3906 Walt-Ann Dr., Ellicot City, MD 212042
Bean, Harold, 3820 N. Chesterbrook Rd. Arlington, VA 22207
Beasey, Mrs. Anita, H.9737 Ashbourn Dr., Burke, VA 22015
Beasley, Robert S., 17911 Pond Rd., Ashton, MD 20816
Bechtel, George, 14070 Sandy Hook Rd., NE, Poulsbo, WA 98370
Beck, Capt Donald A, USN5770 Arbolada Dr., Lake Don Pedro, La Grange, CA 95329
Beckman, Charles J., 10412 El Capitan Circle, Sun City, AZ 85351
Beed, Douglas K., 9081 Ocean Pines, Berlin, MD 21811
Beidleman, Edward B., 937 Kului Pl., Honolulu, HI 96821
Belferman, Herman, 9508 Milstead Dr., Bethesda, MD 20817
Bell, Maj James R, USA1929 Clubhouse Way, No. 1, Billings, MT 59105
Bell, Jean S., 1104 Cresthaven Dr., Silver Spring, MD 20903
Bellak, LtCdr Theodore, USN21 Craigside Pl No 8D, Honolulu, HI 96817
Bello, Roberto, 8701 Bergenline Ave., No. B8, North Bergen, NJ 07047
Belt, Charles V., 3330 N. Leisure World Blvd., No. 530, Silver Spring, MD 20906
Belt, William G., 330 Riola Pl., Pensacola, FL 32506
Bembry, Al G., RR1, Box 216C, Whittier, NC 28789
Benchea, Hortenziu, 3543 Tanglewood Trail, Palm Harbour, FL 34586
Benjamin, Capt Albert, USNR40 Old Farm Rd., Bellair, Charlottsville, VA 22903
Bennett, Robert S., 9521 Purcell Dr., Potomac, MD 20854
Bennett, Ms. Shelly Lea, 75-B Pelham St., Newport, RI 02840
Bennett, William, P.O. Box 4264, Civic Centre, San Rafael, CA 94913
Benson, Howard F. Jr., 8086 S. Niagara Way, Englewood, CO 80112
Beran, Miles, P.O. Box 40282, Bay Village, OH 44140
Bercovitz, George E., 195-40F Peck Ave., Fresh Meadows, NY, 11365
Berejkoff, George R., 3715 Wood Plaza Way, Kelseyville, CA 95451

Berent, LtCol Mark E., USAFRR1, Box 25, Remington, VA 227334
Berger, Col George C., USAF9713 Rhapsody Dr., Vienna, VA 22181
Berglund, Mrs. Ruth L., 319 Rolling Mountain Rd., Bentonville, VA 22610
Berkaw, Ernest de Mun Jr., Southporte 103, 3322 Casseekey Island, Jupiter, FL 33477
Berkeley, Roy G., RR1, Box 318, Shaftsbury, VT 05262
Berlin, Capt Richard G., AUS690 55th Ave., NE, St. Petersburg, FL 33703
Berman, Dr. Stanley J., 1575 Soquel Dr., Santa Cruz, CA 95065
Bernabel, Anthony A., 512 Main St., No 1011, Ft. Worth, TX 76102
Bernard, Richard L., 10009 Renfrew Rd., Silver Spring, MD 20901
Berrey, Michael D., 37340 Clubland Dr., Marietta, GA 30067
Berry, LtCol Clyde M., USA13505 Kingscross Ct., Midlothian, VA 23113
Bessac, Frank B., 1826 Traynor, Missoula, MT 59802
Bessette, LtCol Carol S., USAF8351 Taunton Pl., Springfield, VA 22152
Betts, John, 5416 Canterbury Rd., Fairway, KS 66205
Betts, Capt Roger S., USN110 Gulfview Rd., Punta Gorda, FL 33950
Beya, BGen Richard S., USAF7831 Lee Ave., Alexandria, VA 22308
Beyrle, Joseph R., 1782 Columbus Ave., Norton Shores, MI 49441
Biddle, Delbert W., P.O. Box 860, Sausalito, CA 94966
Bidwell, Richard F., 204 Needlewood Dr., Rt. 1, Huddleston, VA 24104
Biggs, Sgt Darryl G., USAP.O. Box 578, Newton, AL 36352
Billings, John M., 4101 Nellie Custis Ct., Alexandria, VA 22309
Billingsley, RAdm Edward, USN12401 N. 22nd St.,No A-510, Tampt, FL 33612
Birnbaum, Cdr P.O., USN1621 Inlet Ct., Reston, VA 22090
Bishop, Maj Lynn R., USA209 Alder St., Liverpool, NY 13088
Bishop, Maurice, 102 Bear Gulch Rd., Woodside, CA 94062
Bizic, Peter Jr., 7786 Turlock Rd., Springfield, VA 22135
Blackwood, Anna, M.13 Largo Vista Pl., Palm Coast, FL 32164
Blair, Joseph W., 3404 American Dr., No 3204, Lago Vista, TX 78645
Blake, Cochran, 1500 S. Fern St., No 618, Arlington, VA 22202
Blanche, James A., 405 Calavaras Ct., Las Vegas, NV 89110
Blank, LtCol Donald, USAF4500 W. 210th St., Fairview Park, OH 44126
Blank, William D., 1830 Avenieda Del Mundo, No 510, Coronado, CA 92118
Blas, Raymond H., 4789 E. Monticeto Ave., Fresno, CA 93702
Blaufarb, Douglas S., 601 Green St., Winchester, VA 22601
Blaylock, LtCol Norman R., USA7305 Lake Tree Dr., Fairfax Station, VA 22039
Block, Ralph D., 707 Holy Rood Ln., Houston, TX 77024
Bly, Herman O., 5315 Shalley Circle, Ft. Meyers, FL 33919
Boak, David G., RR2, Box 125, Vineyard Haven, MA 02568
Boardman, Col William, USAP.O. Box 445, Monument, CO 80132
Bock, Col Charles, USAF21 North Edison St., Arlington, VA 22203
Bodroghy, Col Robert, AUS131 Kingsley Rd., SW, Vienna, VA 22180
Boginis, James W., P.O. Box 1167, Purceville, VA 22132
Boland, Arthur F., 6415 Wilcox Ct., Alexandria, VA 22310
Boland, Mira L., 714 St. Johns Rd., Baltimore, MD 21210
Bolson, Mrs. Elizabeth B., 43155 Portola Ave., SP 73, Palm Desert, CA 92260
Bon, Michel, Agence Nationale pour l'Emploi, Paris, France
Boner, William C., Jr.8504 Quaint Ln., Vienna, VA 22180
Bonin, Mrs. Mildred A., 711 N. Church St., Hazleton, PA 18201
Bonner, Col William, USAF101 Londonderry Rd., Gooze Circle, SC 29445
Borel, Paul A., 188 Hunter Trail, Southern Pines, NC 28387
Borland, Ms Harriet, 3900 Watson Pl NW, No. 8 CA, Washington, DC 20016
Borrego, Eugene T., 6608 Seneca Farm Rd., Columbia, MD 21046
Borrmann, Donald A., 10154 Sterling Terrace, Rockville, MD 20850
Bort, Col Edward H., USARR1, Box 2085, Manchester Center, VT 05255
Boss, Hollis J., 444 Via Colinas, Thousand Oaks, CA 91632
Boswell, Dale E., 31 Karen Lee Lane, Manitou Springs, CO 80825
Botsford, LtCol Norman, USA15107 Interlachen Dr., No. 412, Silver Spring, MD 20906
Bottom, Dr. Norman R., P.O. Box 164509, Miami, FL 33116
Boublik, Mrs. Irene U., 8470 Greensboro Dr., No. 522, McLean, VA 22102
Boushee, Capt. Frank L., USN1937 Brookhaven Rd., Wilmington, NC 28403
Bowen, James R., 12502 Millstream Sr., Bowie, MD 20715
Bowers, Hollis, 116A Windsor Knot Rd., Edinburgh, VA 22824
Bowie, LtCol W. Russell, 8330 Loveland Dr., Omaha, NE 68124
Bowman, Harold W., 531-A West Alton Ave., Santa Ana, CA 92707

Bowman, Capt Marion E., USN10314 Royal Rd., Silver Spring, MD 20903
Boyd, Fredrick H., 19683 Spencer, Detroit, MI 48234
Boyd, Robert N., 8 Wild Turkey Run, Hilton Head Island, SC 29928
Boyer, Maj Charles R., DMASCPSC 821, Box 117, FPO, AE 09421
Boyes, Dr. Joseph H., 220 Coast Boulevard, La Jolla, CA 92037
Boyes, William W. Jr., 2214 McAuliffe Dr., Rockville, MD 20815
Boyle, Mrs. Barbara, 5101 River Rd., No 707, Bethesda, MD 20816
Boyle, Raymond E., 326 Markley Ct., Indian Harbour Beach, FL 32937
Boyles, Bruce, 871 Hunt St., Akron, OH 44306
Brackett, Dewey, 853 Armada Way, West Union, SC 29696
Bradish, Warren A., 4841 Foxshire Circle, Tampa, FL 33624
Braeuninger, A. Dale, 7 Northport Ave., Belfast ME 04915
Brandner, Robert T., 6475 Cedarbrook Dr., New Albany, OH 43054
Brandon, Harry B., 227 Forest Dr., Falls Church, VA 22046
Brandstetter, Col Frank, USALas Brisas, Box 1807, Acapulco, Mexico
Brandt, Dr. John H., P.O. Box 5003, Alamosa, CO 81101
Brannan, Ms. Mildred S., 6380 Lakewood Dr., Falls Church, VA 22041
Brass, Robin B., 242 Lake Plymouth Blvd, Plymouth, CT 06782
Bratcher, Steven K., 1390 Chain Bridge Rd., McLean, VA 22101
Bray, Wayne D., 250 E. Alameda, No 307, Santa Fe, NM 87501
Brazas, Edward S., 7726 Lisle Ave., Falls Church, VA 22043
Breaw, Richard, 1053 Jeff Ryan Dr., Herndon, VA 22070
Breckinridge, Scott D., 395 Redding Rd., No. 13, Lexington, KY 40517
Breitweiser, Paul B., 25042 Shaver Lake Circle, Lake Forest, CA 93630
Breitweiser, LtGen R., USAFP.O. Box 2454, New Bern, NC 28560
Brennan, Ms. Elinor L., 3154 Siron St., Falls Church, VA 22042
Brennan, Raymond J., 2129 W, New Haven Ave., No. 124, W. Melbourne, FL 32940
Brent, I. D'Arcy, 16 Monocan Dr., Nellysford, VA 22958
Brewer, Charles V., 8912 Ridge Pl., Bethesda, MD 20817
Brewer, Joseph G., 36 Pine Ln., Douglassville, PA 19518
Brewer, Mary O., 8912 Ridge Pl., Bethesda, MD 29817
Briggs, Charles A., 1752 Brookside Ln., Vienna, VA 22182
Briggs, Ms. Katherine, 8102 Highwood Dr., Bloomington, MN 55438
Briggs, Ralph T., 5224 D. Annie Oakley Dr., Las Vegas, NV 89120
Bright, Maj George, USAP.O. Box 47, Keene Valley, NY 12943
Brinegar, LtCol Maurine, USA98-351 Koauka LP, No. 1908, Alea, HI 96701
Britton, Theodore R., 310 Somerlane Pl., Avondale Estates, GA 30002
Brockwell, Dr. Robert L., 150 E. Hartsdale Ave., No. 4D, Hartsdale, NY 10530
Broder, James, 245 W. Bonita Ave., San Dimas, CA 91773
Brodie, Earl D., 4031 Happy Valley Rd., Lafayette, CA 94549
Broe, William V., 111 Indian Trail, North Scituate, MA 12060
Bronson, Col Howard, USAF5034 New Forest Dr., No. 5309, San Antonio, TX 78229
Bronson, Lynwood F., P.O. Box 1801, Carmel, CA 93921
Brooke, MajGen James, USA32 Bark Mill Terrace, Montville, NJ 07045
Brooks, RAdm Thomas, USN7125 Game Lord Dr., Springfield, VA 22153
Brophy, Gilbert T., 810 Saturn St., No 15, Jupiter, FL 33458
Browitt, James W., 1128 Old Chisholm Trail, Dewey, AZ 86327
Brown, A. Freeborn, 114 Glenwood Rd., Bel Air, MD 21014
Brown, F. Reese, P.O. Box 411, New York, NY 10021
Brown, Fravel S., 836 Kennebeck Ct., San Diego, CA 92109
Brown, Frederick, 6427 Pima St., Alexanddria, VA 22312
Brown, Capt Jeffery, USAR315 First St., Ste U-82, Encinitas, CA 92024
Brown, Cdr Lyle C., USNRRR2, Box 97, Waco, TX 76708
Brown, Marcus, 270 Matterhorn Dr., Sautee-Nacoochee, GA 30571
Brown, Ralph, 11911 Lomica Dr., San Diego, CA 92128
Brown, Robert, K.P.O. Box 693, Boulder, CO 80306
Brown, Cdr Ronald, USN10926 Middlegate Dr., Fairfax, VA 22032
Brown, Susanne, 208 Main St., No 45, Medford, MA 02155
Brown, Ted F., P.O. Box 26508, Albuquerque, NM 87125
Brown, Thomas R., 9519 Center St., Vienna, VA 22180
Brown, Mrs. Virginia, 1330 Torrance St., San Diego, CA 92103
Brown, William T., 2502 Rocky Branch Rd., Vienna VA 22181
Browne, Mrs. Jane, 3921 Palo Verde Ave., Bonita, CA 92002
Breummer, Russell, 4024 N. 40th St., Arlington, VA 22207

Brugioni, Dino, 301 Storck Rd., Hartwood, VA 22405
Brumbaugh, Granville, RR 1, Box 301, Waitsfield, VT 05673
Brumfiel, LtCol Robert, USAF12212 St. James Rd., Potomac, MD 20854
Brumm, Maj Steven, USAF5002 Ivy Rd., Panama City, FL 32405
Brune, Louis J., 12516 Over Ridge Rd., Potomac, MD 20854
Brunelle, Crd William T., USN4325 Willow Woods Dr., Annandale, VA 22003
Brunson, LtCol Jack, USA5604 Farmwood Ct., Alexandria, VA 22310
Brustolon, Mark, 3 Riversedge, Ivoryton, CT 06442
Buchanan, LtCol Charles, AUSHoward Ct., RD No 3, Pottsville, PA 17901
Buchanan, Edwin A., 3400 N. Venice St., Arlington, VA 22207
Buchanan. Phillip G., 3861 Gals Island Ave., St. James City, FL 33956
Buck, Frederick, 6441 Rainbow Heights Rd., Fallbrook, CA 92028
Buckelew, Alvin, 2742 Las Gallinas Ave., San Rafael, CA 94903
Buddenbaum Dennis, 8923 Hendon Ln., Houston, TX 77036
Budenbach, Mrs Mary, 21 Calibogue Cay Rd., Hilton Head, SC 29928
Buffham, Benson K., 3750 Galt Ocean Dr., No 1505, Ft. Lauderdale, FL 33308
Buford, William N., 6355 Moccasin Pass Ct., Colorado Spings, CO 80919
Bugliarello, George, Polytechnical University, Brooklyn, NY
Bullock, Roy E., 3674 16th St., No. 5, San Francisco, CA 94114
Bunton, Gerald P., 2088 Gillen Ln., Falls Church, VA 22043
Burbach, Robert T., 2673 Barnstone Ln., Laguna Hills, CA 92653
Burdick, Dr. Charles, P.O. Box 205, Ferndale, CA 95536
Burhans, LtCol William, USAFP.O. Box 225, Marshall, TX 75671
Burke, Gerard P., 1117 Spotswood Dr., Silver Spring, MD 20904
Burke, John M., 1522 Sudden Valley, Belllingham, WA 98226
Burke, Dr. Robert L., 2409 NE 37th St., Ft. Lauderdale, FL 33308
Burkhalter, Col Michael, USAF401 100th Ave., NE, Bellevue, WA 98004
Burks, A. Roy, 57 Flints Grove Dr., Gaithersburg, MD 20878
Burks, Martin, P.O. Box 8932, Horseshoe Bay, TX 78564
Burmeister, Mrs. Josephine, 652 Doral Ln., Melbourne, FL 323940
Burnham, William, 1005 Main St., Murray, KY 42071
Burnette, Capt Oliver, USN4004 Moss Pl., Alexandria, VA 22304
Burns, Robert F., 5463 Fox Hollow Dr., Naples, FL 33942
Burt, LtCol Joseph, USAF4534 N, 15th St., Arlington, VA 22207
Busch, Richard, 34 Remsen St., Brooklyn Heights, NY 11201
Bush, George H.W., P.O. Box 79798, Houston, TX 77297
Bush, Col James O., USAF8420 Masters Ct., Alexandria, VA 22308
Bush, Lester E., 2004 Michigan Ave., NE, St. Petersburg, FL 33703
Busic, Merle, 225 Bowie Trail, Lusby, MD 20657
Bussey, Col Donald, AUS350 Graham St., Carlisle, PA 17013
Bussey, Col Henry M., USAF2610 Chestnut Bend, San Antonio, TX 78232
Butcher, Clifton, 810 Hendrickson St., Clinton, TN 37716
Buterbaugh, Brian, 2321 Old Trail Dr., Reston, VA 22091
Buttleman, Col Leslie, USA1812 Birch Rd., McLean, VA 22101
Butts, RAdm John, USN20 Manor Dr. Pensacola, FL 32507
Byrne, James, 7229 Timber Ln., Falls Church, VA 22046
Byrom, Cecil L., 1101 Edgewood Dr., Greenville, TX 75401
    – **C** –
Cacioppo, Anthony J., 20 Tantara Circle, Springboro, OH 45066
Cahill, Edward, 8433 Hollins Ln., Vienna, VA 22182
Cahill, Capt William, USN3039 Dick Wilson Dr., Sarasota, FL 34240
Cake, Ms. Patricia A., 3242 Atlanta St., Fairfax, VA 22030
Calder, James D., 13330 Blanco Rd., No 1113, San Antonio, TX 78216
Calderon, Mrs. Priscilla, 2506 Vancouver Ave., San Diego, CA 92104
Calese, Donald J., 22015 N. Morage Ln., Sun City West, AZ 85375
Callaghan, Richard, 173 Pascack Ave., Emerson, NJ 07630
Callahan, Maj Harold, USA508 Apple Grove Rd., Silver Spring, MD 20904
Callahan, Patrick, 9110 Belvoir Woods Pkway, No 221, Fort Belvoir, VA 22060
Callahan, Richard, A.P.O. Box 239, Pebble Beach, CA 93953
Caminer, Gerald, 1723 Powell Dr., Ventura, CA 93004
Cammarota, Armand,32 Valencia Ln., Clifton Park, NY 12065
Camp, Peter, 272 1st A ve., New York, NY 10009
Campbell, Gretchen, 701 Corner Ln., McLean, VA 22101

Campbell, James E., 7002 River Oake Dr., McLean, VA 22101
Campbell, Dr. Kenneth, 3701 S. George Mason Dr., No 103N, Falls Church, VA 22041
Campbell, Wesley G.,Hoover Institute, Stanford University, Palo Alto, CA
Campos, Anthony, 9125 Dickens Ave., Surfside, FL 33154
Canoy, Mariano, 50 Rizal St., No 805, San Francisco, CA 94107
Cantergiani, Col Joseph, USAF685 Blackhawk Dr., NE, Albuquerque, NM 87122
Canton, Col John, USMC16 Massanuttten Dr., Fort Royal, VA 22630
Caracristi, Ms Ann, 1222 28th St., NW, Washington, DC 20007
Carino, LtCol James P., USAF1142 Stony Ln., Gladwyne, PA 19035
Carley, LtCol Ronald, AUSRt 2, Lemars, IA 51031
Carley, Wayne H., 311 Rollins St., Falls Church, VA 22046
Carlson, Col Stan, USA6219 Baker Ave., NE, Minneapolis, MN 55432
Carmody, LtCol James, USA8514 Lancashire Dr., Springfield, VA 22151
Carmoy, Herve, Banque Industraile Mobiliere, Paris, France
Carnes, Cdr Calland, USN11078 Saffold Way, Reston, VA 22090
Carosia, Cdr Joseph J., USN1608 Fort Duquesne Dr., Cherry Hill, NJ 08003
Carroll, Charles L., 11710 Parliment St., No 510, San Antonio, TX 78213
Carroll, Edward, 106 Bradock Rd., Williamsburg, VA 23185
Carson, Edward M., First Interstate Bancorp, Los Angeles, CA
Carter, James H., 712 Samuel Chase Ln., W. Melbourne, FL 32904
Carter, William R., 5600 Ridgefield Rd., Bethesda, MD 20816
Cartwright, Cecil J., P.O. Box 227, Yazoo City, MS 39194
Cary, George L., 6900 Breezewood Terrace, Rockville, MD 20852
Casanova, Jean-Claude, Economic Institute for Policy Studies, Paris, France
Casey, Col Edmund, AUS7702 Twinleaf Trail, Orange, CA 92669
Casey, Robert M., 1245 Cresthaven Dr., Silver Spring, MD 20903
Cash, CWO John, USN10514 Greenford Dr., San Diego, CA 92126
Caspersen, LtCol Ralph, AUS5109 S. Washburn Ave., Minneapolis, MN 55410
Castorani, Samuel, 10026 Sageglow, Houston, Tx 77089
Caswell, John F., 2801 New Mexico Ave, NW, No 605, Washington, DC 20007
Cater, Col Maurice, USMC240 Calle De Sereno, Leucadia, CA 92024
Caton, Col Edward, USAF300 Bayview Dr, NE, St. Petersburg, FL 33704
Cavadine, John O., 10708 Norman Ave., Fairfax, VA 22030
Cavalier, SgtM William, USA2826 Huntngton Park Dr., Waterford, MI 48329
Cavanaugh, Joseph, M3310 Fish Canyon Rd., Duarte, CA 91010
Cecchini, Col Louis, USA16200 Laurel Ridge Dr., Laurel, MD 20707
Cesare, Donald J., 2729 Alteza Ln., Colorado Springs, CO 80917
Chaffin, C. Wayne, 6714 Northport, Dallas, TX 75230
Chaffin, Richard, 1051 9th Ave., Huntington, WV, 25701
Chalker, William R., Jr.5 South Trail, Arden, DE 19810
Chamberlain, Gary J., 755 Shaker Dr., Medina, OH 44254
Chanbers, Gregory, 19 Bailey Rd., Millburn, NJ 07041
Chambers, John A., 421 West 5th Ave., Columbus, OH 43201
Champlin, Malcom M., 485 Ellita Ave., Oakland, CA 94610
Chapin, Capt A. Winfield, USNRP.O. Box 789, Palm Beach, FL 33480
Chapman, LtCol Gerald S., USAF13822 Via Alto Ct., Saratoga, CA 95070
Chapman, LtCdr William, USN888 Canyon View Loop, Hamilton, MT 59840
Charriere, Robert F., 332 Waldo Rd., Arlington, MA 02174
Chase, Col Harold B., USAF3112 N. Rosser St., Alexandria, VA 22311
Cherry, Maj Donald, USAF2166 Northam Rd., Columbus, OH 43221
Chesnut, George L., 2306 N. Vernon St., Arlington, VA 22207
Chigos, Dr. David, 651 Silvergate Ave., San Diego, CA 92106
Chillemi, Richard L., 15436 Snowhill Ln., Centreville, VA 22020
Chin, Robert, 10509 Tyler Terace, Potomac, MD 20854
Chino, Yoshitoki, Daiwa Securities Ltd., Tokyo, Japan
Chizewsky Nicholas A., 125 Highway 80, Bisbee, AZ 85603
Chizum, David G., 476 Whitetail Dr., Franktown, CO 80116
Choate, Art, 117 Pine Valley, Williamsburg, VA 23188
Christiansen, Ms. Kathleen, 1022 Simas Ave., Pinole, CA 94564
Christie, Col William, USAF6409 Seven Oaks Dr., Falls Church, VA 22042
Christman, John H., 2055 Oxford Ave., Cardiff, CA 92007
Christopher, Col Stone, USAF5100 John D. Ryan Blvd., No 315., San Antonio, TX 78245
Chron, Dr. Gustav, 7110 N. McAlpin Ave., Chicago, IL 60646
Chu, Kirby P., P.O. Box 26418, San Francisco, CA 94126

Cianci, Salvatore, 1704 Glenkarney Pl., Silver Spring, MD
Cieri, Paul P., CMR 416, Box 251, APO, AE 09613
Cinnamon, LeRoy, 1208 Spicewood Dr., Schertz, TX 78154
Cioci, Mario, 8038 Glendale Rd., Chevy Chase, MD 20815
Claar, Richard, 86 Hancock Pl., NE, Leesburg, VA 22075
Clapper, LtGen James, USAF5366 Ashleigh Rd., Fairfax, VA 22030
Clare, Kenneth, 1600 North Oak St., No 320, Arlington, VA 22209
Clark, MajGen Arthur, USAF3540 Rugby Rd., Durham, NC 27707
Clark, Donald D., 17 W. 514 Victory Parkway, Addison, IL 60101
Clark, Galen L., 30 Holly Way, Parachute, CO 81635
Clark, J. Ransom, PoliSci Dept., Muskingum College, New Concord OH 43762
Clark, John M., 40 Santa Macia Dr., Novato, CA 94947
Clark, Ned, 8701 Contee, Rd., Laurel, MD 20708
Clarke, Charles R., P.O. Box 22121, Santa Clara, CA 95055
Clarke, LtCol Robert F., USAF5846 S. Wilshire Dr., Tucson, AZ 85711
Clary, Carter, P.O. Box 80074, Albuquerque, NM 87198
Cline, Dr. Raymond, 3027 N. Pollard St., Arlington, VA 22207
Clinton, Babes van Dillen, 131 Sycamore Ave., San Mateo, CA 94402
Clontz, Col Ralph C. USA, 2229 Queens Rd., East, Charlotte, NC 28207
Clothier, William J., 215 S. 16th St., Philadelphia, PA 19102
Clough, Herbert D. Jr., 14315 Riverside Dr., No 106, Sherman Oaks, CA 91423
Clutter, LtCol Roderick, USAF121 N. 7th St., Boonville, IN 47601
Coats, LtCol J. C., USAF1409 Camino Cerrito, SE, ALbuquerque, NM 87123
Cochran, Farrett, 1619 Greenbrier Ct., Reston, VA 22090
Coco, John J., 695 Johnson St., North Andover MA 01845
Coffee, Edward, 226 N. Oakland St., Arlington, VA 22203
Coffey, Raymond, 28 Harbor View Ct, NE, Decatur, AL 35601
Coffin, Charles E., 260 S. 300 W, Lebanon, IN 46052
Colby, Maj George, USAF1422 Cypress, St. Cloud, FL 32769
Colby, William E., 3028 Dent Place, NW, Washington, DC 20007
Cole, John D.420, South Alexandria, Los Angeles, CA 90020
Cole, Michael R., 12020 Sunrise Valley Dr., No. 100, Reston, VA 22091
Coleman, Dr. Robert, P.O. Box 1101, Lake Elsinore, CA 92531
Coleman, Francis I.G., 1807 Kalorama Square, SE, Washington, DC 20008
Coleman, Col John, USA191 Folsom Dr., Dayton, OH 45405
Colgan, Frederick, R.1543 Longfellow Ct., McLean, VA 22101
Collazo, Jose, P.O. Box 12142, Loiza Station, Santurce, PR 00914
Collie, David W., 242 Portland, Houston, TX 77006
Collier, Col Daniel, USAR1199 Park Ave., No. 7F, New York, NY 10028
Collin, Barry C., 1325 Howard Ave., No. 301, Burlingame, CA 94010
Collingwood, Dr. Ronald, 10615 G Tierrasanta Blvd., No 344, San Diego, CA 92124
Collins, Edward M., 816 Eagle Ln., Apollo Beach, FL 33572
Collins, Col Frank, USAF7362 Rebecca Dr., Hollin Hills, VA 22307
Collins, J. Foster, 6804 Sorrell St., Mclean, VA 22101
Collins, LtCol James, USAR3420 Eliot Rd., Erie, PA 16508
Collomb, Bertrand, Lafarge Coppee, Paris, France
Collins, Ms. Mary Rose, 5688 Bayberry Dr., Cincinatti, OH 45242
Combemalle, Jean-Loup, RR1, Box 309, Fainsville, VA 22065
Comras, Peter, 2431 Del Air Blvd., Apt. D, Delray Beach, FL 33445
Conaty, Joseph, 11519 Bucknell Dr., Silver Spring, MD 20902
Condon, Joseph, P.O. Box 10231, Naples, FL 33941
Conner, William E., 46911 Bushwood Ct., Sterling, VA 20914
Connolly, Col George, USA681 Village Rd., North Palm Beach, FL 33408
Connolly, LtCol Philip, USAF7115 11th Ave., West, Badenton, FL 34209
Connor, John, 91 Richardson Rd., Coventry, RI 02816
Connors, John J., 6912 Clemson Dr., Alexandria, VA 22307
Conway, Donald, 13003 Melville Ln., Fairfax, VA 22033
Cook, Arie, 20275 Quesada Ave., Port Charlotte, FL 33952
Cook, RAdm Ralph, USN153 Nawilliwili St., Honolulu, HI 96825
Cook, R. W., 762 Lunallio Home Rd., Honolulu, HI 96825
Cooke, Richard K., RR4, Box 129, Keyser, WV 26726
Colley, Ms Laura, 424 Heron Pt., Chestertown, MD 21620
Coombe, G.W., 555 California St., San Francisco, CA 94104
Cooper, C.E., 11623 46th Ave., NE, Marysville, WA 98217

Cooper, Capt David, USN3805 Winterset Dr., Annandale, VA 22003
Cooper, Mrs. Lucille V., 6635 Montarbor Dr., Colorado Spings, CO 80918
Cooper, Paul, 4417 Lowell St., NW, Washington, DC 20016
Copher, Paul B., 9032 E. 33rd Pl., Tuscon, AZ 85710
Corn, Milton W., 300 N. State St., No 5417, Chicago, IL 60610
Corry, Cecil, 625 N. Lincoln St., Arlington, VA 22201
Corsa, Richard,, 2819 Moselle Ct., Walnut Creek, CA 94598
Corson, William, Col, USMC9550 River Rd., Potomac, MD 20554
Costanzo, Christopher, RR1, Box 74, Randolph, VT 05060
Coster, Dr.Abraham, 3541 West Braddock Rd., Alexandria, VA 22302
Cosialle, Bertrand, BNP, 5 Place Massena, Nice 06000 France
Coti, Col William, USMC8247 Clifton Farm Ct., Alexandria, VA 22306
Courtney, John, 12012 Valleywood Dr., Wheaton, MD 20902
Covault, Ms Grace, 3309 Canningate Rd., No 102, Fairfax, VA 22031
Cowan, Bruce, 17 Washinigton St., Rutland, VT 05701
Cowgill, Col Ralph, USAF3610 Crede Dr., Charleston, WV 25302
Cowles, Floyd R., 3945 S.W. Marigold St., Portland, OR 97219
Crabb, LtCol Merle, USMC8110 Kings Point Dr., Springfield, VA 22153
Craig, CWO-4 Joseph, USMCRP.O. Box 30005, Chicago, IL 60630
Craig, Robert J., P.O. Box 74, St. Michaels, MD 21663
Craigmile, Dr. James, 810 Forest Hill Ct., Colmbia, MO 65203
Cramer, Martin G., 5205 Benton Ave., Bethesda, MD 20814
Cramer, Col William, USAF817 San Marcos Ln., Bedford, TX 76021
Crampton, Kevin, 22 Rancho Novato Dr., Pomona, CA 91766
Crandall, Dr. Maureen, 5100 38th St., NW, Washington, DC 20016
Crandall, LtCol Walter M., USA4802 Tara Woods Dr., East, Jacksonville, FL 32210
Creighton, John, 1116 Fernwood Dr., Millbrae, CA 94030
Cremins, Patrick J., 3253 Chrisland Dr., Annapolis, MD 21403
Crilly, Cdr Eugene, USNR276 J St., Coronado, CA 92118
Crippen, Roy E., 801 Peterson Dr., Silver City, NM 88061
Critchfield, Col James, USA1552 Harbor Rd., Williamsburg, VA 23185
Critchfield, Lois, 1552 Harbor Rd., Williamsburg, VA 23185
Critides, A. Byron, 439-16 Camille Circle, San Jose, CA 95134
Crivelli, Capt Joseph, USAR18 Hastings Ln., Hicksville, NY 11801
Cronin, Paul E., 2512 K St., NW, No 12, Washington, DC 20037
Cronin, Peter, 36 Concord Dr., Madison, CT 06443
Crosby, Kenneth M., 3000 K St., NW, Suite 620, Washington, DC 20007
Cross, Richard L., RR 14, Box 2549, Kennewick, WA 99337
Crouter, Cdr Robert W., USN18 Foundry St., Box 573, Amherst, NH 03031
Crow, Col Robert S., USAR2205 Ryan Dr., Alvin, TX 77511
Crowley, Henry, 1003 Devere Dr., Silver Spring, MD 20903
Crowley, Robert, 2818 Cathedral Ave., NW, Washington, DC 20008
Crumpler, Hugh, 17205 Montero Dr., Silver Spring, MD 20903
Culp, Dr. Mildred, 3313 39th Ave., W, Seattle, WA 981888
Cummings, Richard, Strassburgerstr. 10, D-800809, Munich, Germany
Cummings, Richard M, P.O. Box 349, Bridgehampton, NY 11932
Cunningham, Robert, P.O. Box 588, Pawleys Island, SC 29585
Curley, Cdr E. Patrick, USN7501 Maritime Ln., Springfield, VA 22153
Currie, Clare-Adair, 7580 Dunwood Way, San Diego, CA 92114
Curry, Thomas H., 2613 Steeplechase Dr., Reston, VA 22091
Curtis, Gerald L., Columbia University, New York, NY 10027
Curts, Robert I., 5755 W. Ada Ln., Larkspur, CO 80118
Cwiek, Mitchell S., 1926 Bernardo Ave., Escondido, CA 92025

– D –

Dabrowski, Edmund, 148-A Wallworth Park, Cherry Hill, NJ 08002
Dalby, Cranford, 300 N. Washington St., No 400, Alexandria, VA 22314
Dale, Mrs. J. Thomas, 7603 North Ocean Blvd., No 3B, Myrtle Beach, SC 29577
Dalenberg, Philip, P.O. Box 7722, Fort Gordon, GA 30905
Daly, Ralph T., 99 Cloverdale Heights, Charles Town, WV 25414
Daniel, Dr. Gerard L, 25 Canada St., Swanton, VT 05488
Daniluck, Serge, 716 N. Belgrade Ct., Silver Spring, MD 20902
Darcy, Thomas, 12821 Sunset Terrace, Clive, IA 50325
Darer, Stanley, 22 Wilton Rd., Beaconfield, Bucks, IP9 2DE, England

Dann, Charles, 1 Fairway Dr., Manhasset, NY 11030
Davidov, Dr. Michael, 9112 Mill Pond Valley Dr., McLean, VA 22102
Davidson, Philip, 83 Devon Rd., Albertson, NY 11507
Davis, Alton D., 5606 Mirror Light Place., Columbia, MD 21045
Davis, Curtis C., 10 Overhill Rd., Baltimore, MD 21210
Davis, Donald, 4241 Riverside Dr., Evans, GA 30809
Davis, LtGen John, USA 2346 South Mende St., Arlington, VA 22202
Davis, Mrs. Norma, 4241 Riverside Dr., Evans, GA 30809
Davis, LtCol Sidney, USAF 231 Greenwood Dr., Petersburg, VA 23805
Dawson, Mrs. Mary, 1131 Compass Ln., No 306, Foster City, CA 94404
Dawson, Raymond, 6357 Dawson Blvd., Mentor OR 44060
Day, David W., P.O. Box 1296, Mukilteo, WA 98275
Day, Mrs. Mary Louise, 4928 Sentinel Dr., No. 304, Bethesda, MD 20816
De Angelo, Mrs. Alice, 2500 Virginia Ave., NW, No 306-S, Washington, DC 20037
De Candio, LtCol Michael, USA2505 Childs Ln., Alexandria, VA 22308
de Vore, Ralph, 3828 Baltimore, Shreveport, LA 71106
De Wald, LtCdr Bruce, USN5131 SE Naef Rd., Milwaukie, OR 97267
Deahl, Albert, P.O. Box 277792, San Diego, CA 92128
Deahl, Warren, 6125 Tamerlane Dr., South Bend, IN 46614
Dean, Mary Evelyn, 1436 Woodacre Dr., McLean, VA 22101
Dean, Warren, 9908 Fernwood Rd., Bethesda, MD 20817
DeBruier, Wilburn, 10308 Florian Rd., Louisville, KY 40223
Deck, Mrs. Helen P., 1640 Atares Dr., No 8, Punta Gorda, FL 33950
Dee, Col Chester H., AUS 510 S. Hi Lusi Ave., Mt. Prospect, IL 60056
Deffenbaugh, Berman, 331 Ave Maria Dr., San Antonio, TX 78216
DeGenare, William, 12808 Woodview Ct., Burnsville, MN 55337
DeKuyper, Frederick, 4422 Underwood Rd., Baltimore, MD 21218
Del Favero, Dario, 210 Southland Station Dr., No256, Warner Robins, GA 31088
Delaney, Col John, USA 5621 Granada Blvd., Miami, FL 33146
Delanty, Timothy, 8351 Forrester Blvd., Springfield, VA 22152
DeLashmit, William, 2462 River Rd., Plymouth, NU 03264
Dell, George, 11909 Hickory Creek Dr.,·Fndericksburg, VA 22407
Delia Santa, Walter, 16327 Lindsay Rd., Yelm, WA 98597
De Long, Earl, 1602 N. Greenbrier St., Aiiington, VA 22205
DeLong, Richard, 2250 East Imperial Highway, No 323, El Segundo, CA 90245
del Olmo, Frank, Los Angeles Times, Times Minor Square, Los Angeles, CA 90053
Demich, Capt Fred, USN 3106 Mereworth Ct., Oakton, VA 22124
Demello, Ronald, P.O. Box 627, Hampton Falls, NU 03844
Denisevich, LtCol Peter, USA24 Heather Ct., Nashua, NU 03062
Dennett, Garland L., 1156 East Blaine Ave., Salt Lake City, UT 84105
DeNora, John, 4019 Goldfinch St., No 155, San Diego, CA 92103
Derrick, Robert, 55 Atlantic Rd., Cloucester, MA 01930
Deveresuz, Robert, 7423 Brad St., Falls Church, VA 22042
Devore, Dixon, P.O. Box 1010, Greenville, NH 03048
Dewaid, Frank, 6960 NW 6th Ct., Margate, FL 33063
de Genova, Joseph, 5307 Hill Burne Way, Chevy Chase, MD 20815
Di Trolio, Jerry, 1002 N. 65th St., Philadelphia, PA 19151
Dick, Herman, P.O. Box 22464, Honolulu, Hi 96833
Dickey, Mrskiloma, 29605 Chaparral Dr., Temecula, CA 92592
Dickow, Daniel, P.O. Box 1470, Duxbury, MA 02332
Dickson, Philip, 7800 Hidden Meadow Terrace, Potomac, MD 20854
Dietsche, Herbert, 917 Teakwood Dr., Richardson, TX 75080
Diliberti, Col Angelo, USAP.O. Box 295, South Elgin, IL 60177
Dillingham, RAdm Paul, USNRR2, Box 66, Roch Hall, MD 21661
Dillon, Floyd, 11423 Costa Del Sol NE, Albuquerque, NM 87111
Dillon, Col Francis, USA 9204 Maria Ave., Great Falls, VA 22066
Dinn, Edith, P.O. Box 591330, San Francisco, CA 94118
DiNoto, Joseph, 4621 Bronx Blvd, New York City, NY 10470
DiNieho, Anthony, 2250 Union St., San Francisco, CA 94123
Diosdado Cesar, 1774 Vale St., Chula Vista, CA 91912
Disney, Raymond, 212 North Glen Ave., Annapolis, MD 21401
Diver, Ms. Ruth, 4339 W. Braddock Rd., No 20, Alexandria, VA 22311
Dixon, LtCol William, USA 600 Crowder Ct., Fort Walton Beach, FL 32547
Dodge, Dr. Norman, 8000 Northumberland Rd., Springfield CVA 22153

Dodson, James, 2005 Calvin Cliff Ln., Cincinatti, OH 45206
Doherty, George, 553 Fairhaven St., Anaheim, CA 92801
Dolan, MSgt Francis, USAF 2914 Caprice Dr., Corpus Christi, TX 78418
Dolan, Capt J., USMC P.O. Box 374, Garrett Park, MD 20896
Doleman, LtGen Edgar, USA 1341 Pueo St, Honolulu, RI 96816
Domingos, Mrs. Agnes, 188 Florida Ave., Macon, GA 31204
Donahue, Frank J., 13 Plumrose Ln., Schaumburg, IL 60194
Donahue, LtCdr Thomas, USN 3704 Sprucedale Dr., Annandale, VA 22003
Donahue, William, 4300 18th St West, No 207C, Bradenton, FL 34205
Donlea, Patrick, 119 Waverly Rd., Barrington, IL 60010
Donohue, Jerome, 8030 McKenstry Dr., Laurel, MD 20723
Donovan, Arthur, 312 Owaissa Rd., SE, Vienna, VA 22180
Dooley, Arthur, 3O3l North Nottingham St., Arlington, VA 22207
Dorffi, Maj William, USAF 497 N. Arbona Circle, Sonora, CA 95370
Dorman, E. (Viktor A. Zelenko), 350 5th Ave., New York, NY 10018
Dorr, Colgate, 26290 Valley View Dr., Carmel, CA 93923
Dorsey, John, P.O. Box 101, Quinton, VA 23141
Dougherty, Col Andrew, USAF10 Mile Post Ln., Pittsford, NY 14534
Dougherty, Robert, 2619 S. Kihei Rd., No 408-A, Maui, HI 96753
Douglas, Terrance, 1833 Quartet Circle, Vienna, VA 22182
Douglas, Thomas (A.L Korochev), P.O. Box 381, Organ, NM 88052
Dountas, Peter, P.O. Box 36647, Albuquerque, NM 87176
Douris, Charles, 236 Lexington Rd., Schwenksville, PA 19473
Dowd, Capt Robert, USN 3 Grouse Ln., Brevard, NC 29712
Downing, Thomas E, 8 Pingree Farm Rd., Georgetown, MA 01833
Doyle, David, 65 Hanapepe Loop, Honolulu, III 96825
Doyle, Edward, 19715 Ames St., Fairfax, VA 22032
Doyle, Mrs. Elizabeth, 5807 Wilshire Dr., Bethesda, NM 20816
Drake, Robert, 19470 Saddlebrook Ct., Fort Meyers, FL 33903
Dravis, Michael, 1807 Merrimac Dr., Adelphi, NM 20783
Drawdy, Vance, P.O. Box 10167, Greenville, SC 29603
Dreher, Robert, 4141 N. Henderson Rd., No 907, Arlington, VA 22203
Dreyfuss, Robert, 6904 Park Terrace Dr., Alexandria, VA 22307
Dribben, Col William, USA 108 East 38th St., New York, NY 10016
Drisin, David, 41 Rue des Thermopyles, 75014, Paris, France
Driver, Carl, P.O. Box 8157 Rolling Hills, Greenville, TX 75404
Driver, Garston W., 2540 Clairemont Dr., No 305, San Diego, CA 92117
Drum, Col James, USA 311 Essex Meadows, Essex, CT 06426
Dryan, Philip, 116 Calle Nivel, Los Gatos, CA 95030
DuBrul, Stephen, 610 Fifth Ave., Suite 605, New York, NY 10020
Dudik, Dr. Rollie, 2308 Floral Park Rd., Clinton, MD 20735
Dudley, Col Paul, USAF 4606 Gaslight Circle, Las Vegas, NV 89119
Duffy, Paul, 3850 Sweet Grass Ln., Charlotte, NC 28226
Dukes, Robert, 10087 Windstream Dr., No 2, Columbia, MD 21044
Duncan, Lewis, 1744 Hacienda Pl., El Cajon, CA 92020
Dunlevy, Mrs. Elizabeth, 4701 Willard Ave., No 417, Chevy Chase, MD 20815
Dunlop, Cdr Edwin, USNR P.O. Box 1012, Burbank, CA 91507
DuPre, Col Paul, USMC 226 E. Garden Green, Port Hueneme, CA 93041
Dupre, Robert, 28 Williams St., Salem, NH 03079
Durham, Leonard, 4612 Twinbook Rd., Fairfax, VA 22032
Durr, Dr. Frank, 7337 Brookview Circle, Tampa, FL 33634
Duval, Thomas, 77 Michael Manor Rd., Berkeley Springs, WV 25411
Dyckman, Wesley, P.O. Box 301, Livermore, CA 94551
Dyer, James H., 218, Capitol, Washington DC

– E –

Eames, Edward J., 4601 Cavillo Ct., SE, Rio Rancho, NM 87124
Earnest, Edwin P., 6686 Midhill Pl., Falls Church, VA 22043
Easley, LtCol Claudius, USA3601 Connecticut Ave., NW, Washington, DC 20008
East, John W., 4822 N. 15th St., Arlington, VA 22205
Eaton, BrigGen Richard, USA1448 Westlake Dr., NW, Gainesville, GA 30501
Eavenson, L. Chandler, 491 Whippoorwill Ln., Sautee-Nacoochee, GA 30571
Eckels, Vernon, 718 Kings Ln., Fort Washington, MD 20744
Edgar, Major Scott, USAF334 Esquina Dr., Henderson, NV 89014

Edwards, Duval, 566 E. Hampton No 238, Tucson, AZ 85712
Edwards, Henry, 6412 Sewanee, Houston, TX 77005
Edwards, Capt John, USN100 E. Ocean View Ave., Norfolk, VA 23503
Egermeier, Ms Phyllis, 900 E. Wilcox Dr., No 124, Sierra Vista, AZ 85635
Eifler, Col Carl, AUS22700 Picador Dr., Salinas, CA 93901
Elder, Arthur G., 2411 Romney Rd., San Diego, CA 92109
Elkins, Allen, 105 Gullane Dr. Williamsburg, VA 23188
Ellenwood, Robert, 5133 Grandon Dr., Hilliard, OH 43026
Elliker, John, 1054 Darrell Dr., NE, New Philadelphia. OH 44663
Elliott, Carter, 640 Black Bear Run, Christiansburg, VA 24068
Elliott, Charles P., 312 La Peninsular Blvd., Naples, FL 33962
Elliott, Joe Wilson, P.O. Box 74699, Los Angeles, CA 90004
Elliott, John, 1655 Larchmont Ave., Lakewood, OH 44107
Ellis, John F., 1801 East 12th St., Cleveland, OH 44114
Ellis, Capt William, USN4101 Downing St., Annandale, VA 22003
Ellithrope, Major Gilbert, AUS358 Santa Margarita Dr., San Rafael, CA 94901
Ellwanger, Edward, 5915 Alan Dr., Clinton, MD 20735
Elser, Cinda, P.O. Box 43, North Lima, OH 44452
Elston, Paul, White City 201, London W12 7TS, England
Emley, Warren, 936 St. Andrews Blvd., Naples, FL 33962
Encher, Cazimier V., 6745 S. Tripp Ave., Chicago, IL 60629
Endel, Max, 7323 Staffordshire No 3, Houston, TX 77030
Enkelmann, Robert, 10133 Concord School Rd., St. Louis, MO 63128
Enney, MajGen James, USAF1914 Rose Mallow Ln., Orange Park, FL 32073
Enochs, John, 17316 Ash St., Fountain Valley, CA 92708
Epperson, J. B., 2440 E. 45th St., Tulsa, OK 74105
Epstein, LtCol Lawrence, USAR115 Hatteras Rd., Barnegat, NJ 08005
Epstein, Dr. Mark, 9522 E. Stanhope Rd., Kensington, MD 20895
Erikson,, LtCol James, USARP.O. Box 10097, Lynchburg, VA 24506
Erkko, Aatos, Helsingin Sanomat, Helsinki, Finland
Erman, Dr. Seneca, 7341 E. Sabino Visitia Dr., Tucson, AZ 85715
Eskes, James, 1453 Montelegre Dr., San Jose, CA 95120
Esser, Mrs. Erna, 1620 Wrightson Dr., McLean, VA 22101
Estey, Col Hayden, USAR5341 Westpath Way, Bethesda,MD 20816
Etheridge, Obie, 138 Seaview Ln., Corpus Christi, TX 78411
Evans, James, 3209 Riviera Pl., NE, Albuquerque, NM 87111
Evans, Jean, 2105 Reynolds St., Falls Church, VA 22043
Evans, John, RR2, Box 1755, Arlington, VT 05250
Evans, Joseph, 605 Winged Foot Ct., New Bern, NC 28562
Eye, Ralph, P.O. Box 291, Bucksport, ME 0441

– **F** –

Fahey, Paul, P.1807 Calas Way, Virginia Beach, VA 23454
Fairchild, Brian, 500 Wall St., No 510, Seattle, WA 98121
Falbaum, Bertram, 4921 N. Fort Verde Trail, Tucson, AZ 85715
Farmer, Jack, PSC 76, Box 1671, APO, AE 09720
Farnham, David, 2169 Pond View Ct., Reston, VA 22091
Farnham, Col John, F. USAF3817 Wisconsin Ave., Tampa, FL 33616
Farrand, Robert K., 11 Quantum Pl., Gaithersburg, MD 20877
Farrell, Thomas, 2713 W. Gum St., Rogers, AR 72756
Fascia, BrigGen John, USA115 Ann St., Clarendon Hills, IL 60514
Faulkner, David, 2311 Frizzellburg Rd., Westminister, MD 21158
Faurer, LtGen Lincoln, USAF1438 Brookhaven Dr., McLean, VA 22101
Featherstone, James, 319 South Pitt St., Alexandria, VA 22314
Fedor, William, 9607 Westport Ln., Burke, VA 22015
Fedornak, Michael, Old RR1, Box 71E, Steuben, ME 04680
Fee, Russell, 66 Douglas St SMW, Homosassa, FL 32646
Feeney, Cdr Harold, USN3442 Arkansas St., Corpus Christi, TX 78411
Feeney, William, PoliSci Dept., S. Illinois University, Edwardsville, IL 62026
Feer, Frederic, 22910 Portage Circle, Topanga, CA 90290
Fell, Col John, USA5550 Feltin Rd., San Jose, CA 95182
Fenyvesi, Charles, 1150 15th St., NW, Washington, DC 20017
Feltman, David, 705 O'Neill House Office Bldg, Washinigton, DC 20515
Ferguson, George, 2515 West 14th St., Yuma, AZ 85364

Ferguson, LtCol John, USA9980 Caminito Chirimolla, San Diego, CA 92131
Ferguson, Kenneth, 7021 Westbury Rd., McLean, VA 22101
Fernandez, Joseph, 9542 Whitecedar Ct., Vienna, VA 22180
Ferrell, Mrs. Mary, 4406 Holland Ave., Dallas, TX 75219
Ferrese, LtCol Ralph, USA2201 S. Grace St., No 105, Lombard, IL 60148
Ferrer, Carlos, Bank of Europe, Barcelona, Spain
Ferrier, CWO-3 James, USMC4029 S. 70th St., Milwaukee, WI 53220
Fetterolf, Wallace, 6800 Fleetwood Rd., No 918, McLean, VA 22101
Fetzer, Clarence, 14901 N. Swan Rd., Tucson, AZ 85737
Ffolkes, Rodgers, P.O. Box 584, Claremont, CA 91711
Field, Mrs. Mary, 4701 W. Braddock Rd., Alexandria, VA 22311
Fields, Bryan, 3527 Jamestown Rd., Davidsonville, MD 21035
Fields, LtCol Thomas, USAF135 Club Terrace, Lebanon, PA 17042
Fimbel, Richard, 1311 Redwood Ln., California, MD 20619
Finder, Joseph, 401 Commonwealth Ave., Boston, MA 02215
Fink, W. Gordon, 1510 Knollwood Rd., Annapolis, MD 21401
Finke, Robert F., 5056 Tanaga Ct., Stone Mountain, GA 30087
Finlay, Richard, 400 Balsam Dr., Severna Park, MD 21146
Finley, Irving, 4369 Talmadge Trace, Lithonia, GA 300058
Firment, Conrad, 204 Tapawingo Rd., SE, Vienna, VA 22180-
Fischer, Addison, 20 14th Ave., South, Naples, FL 33940
Fischer, Col. Howard, USAF803 Spyglass Ln., Las Vegas, NV 89107
Fischer, Dr. Henry A., P.O. Box 780068, Sebastian, FL 32978
Fischer, Robert, Hall House, Nichols College, Dudley Hill, MA 01570
Fishel, Edwin, 3819 Albermale St., Arlington, VA 22207
Fisher, George, 502 Grandview Dr., Sun Prarie, WI 53590
Fisher, Mrs. Renee, 5003 Spring Lake Dr., Tampa, FL 33629
Fisher, W. Douglas, 6721 Michaels Dr., Bethesda, MD 20817
Fisk, Nan, 50 Palmetto Bay Rd., Hilton Head, SC 29928
Fitchett, James, P.O. Box 1271, Harrisonburg, VA 22801
Fitzgerald, John, 2 Magnolia Ave., St. Augustine, FL 32804
Flanders, Sherman, 1306 Lencoe Dr., Stockton, CA 95210
Flannery, James, 1812 River Rd., Elizabeth City, NC 27909
Fleming, LtCol Dennis, USAF108 W. Azalea Dr., Long Beach, MS 39560
Flowers, Earl, 9704 Mantauk Ave., Bethesda, MD 20817
Flynn, Henry, 31 Rowayton Woods Dr., Norwalk, CT 06854
Flynn, Michael, 374 Kyle Rd., Herald Harbour, MD 21032
Flynn, MajGen Thomas, USA7813 Brookstone Ct., Ellicott City, MD 21043
Fogarty, James E., 1036 Park Ave., No 3D, New York, NY 10028
Folensbee, Scott, 3930 Kathryn Jean Ct., Fairfax, VA 22033
Foley, Charles, 81 Spring Ln., Fairfax, CA 94930
Foley, Capt Robert, USNR4625 North 26th St., Arlington, VA 22207
Force, Capt Herbert, USCGR7448 Agradar Dr., Rancho Murietta, CA 95683
Ford, Harold P., 415 Russell Ave., No 609, Gaithersburg, MD 20877
Ford, Lawrence, 2737 Casa del Norte Ct., NE, Albuquerque, NM 87112
Forde, Rev. Norman, 226 High Timber Ct., Gaithersburg, MD 20879
Forrette, Gerald, 6142 Arctic Way, Edina, MN 54436
Fort, Bernard (Horst Gruber), P.O. Box 1690, Truckee, CA 95734
Fosmire, Thomas G., 3329 W. Lakeshore Dr., Florence, SC 29501
Fossett, Col John, USA1261 Creel Rd., NE, Palm Bay, FL 32905
Foster, Gary E., 2151 Cabots Point Ln., Reston, VA 22091
Foster, Mayhew, 1006 W. Greenough Dr., Missoula, MT 59802
Fountain, Col Ernest, USA742 W. Emaus Ave., Allentown, PA 18103
Foust, CWO-4 Frank, USN2815 S. Atlantic Blvd., No 606, Cocoa Beach, FL 32931
Fox, Thomas, 2439 Villa Nova Dr., Vienna, VA 22180
Frankenfield, Capt Robert, USN1255 Madison St., Alexandria, VA 22314
Franklin, William, 1836 Green Hill Rd., Virginia Beach, VA 23454
Franz, John B., P.O. Box 10568, Pompano Beach, FL 33061
Frederick, Christian, 2832 Berryland Dr., Oakton,VA 22124
Frederickson, Robert, 3810 Manor Dr., Greensboro, NC 27403
Freed, Mrs. Abigail Berlin, 2700 Virginia Ave., NW, Washington, DC 20037
Freund, Matthew, 1203 N. Quebec St., Kennewick, WA 99336
Freund, Col Philip, USAN53, W14458 Aberdeen Dr., Menomonee Falls, WI 53051
Friar, James, 16 The Crescent, Short Hills, NJ 07078

Frice, Gene, P.O. Box 3940, San Luis Obisbo, CA 93403
Frick, LtCol William, USAFP.O. Box 463/1004, Tucumcari, NM 88401
Frierson, Dr. David, P.O. Box 31, Mt. Pleasant, SC 29464
Frisch, Donald, 3300 Gessner, No 200, Houston, TX 77063
Fritz, Russell, P.O. Box 151282, Los Angeles, CA 90015
Frizzell, Arthur, 15331 Sherwood Forest Dr., Tampa, FL 33647
Froendt, Carl, 4375 Collins Rd., Spring Hill, FL 34606
Fromm, William, 1104 Castle Harbour Way, No 2B, Glen Burnie, MD 212061
Frost, Edmund, 4490 Sweet Bay Ave., Melbourne, FL 32935
Fry, LtCol Clifford, USA802 Maverick Trail, SE, Albuquerque, NM 87123
Funabashi, Yoichi, Ashai Shimbun, Washington, DC
Furnas, Capt Wendell, USN746 19th St., Santa Monica, CA 90402
Furst, LtCol Howard, USAFP.O. Box 400, El Toro, CA 92630
Fuss, David, 8714 Preston Pl., Chevy Chase, MD 20815

– G –

Gable, Lamar, 2600 Golden Gate Parkway, Naples, FL 33942
Gabriel, James, 268 S. South St., Wilmington, OH 45177
Gaddy, David, The Riverside, Box 46, Tappahannock, VA 22560
Gagner, Wayne, 9104 Charred Oak Dr., Bethesda, MD
Gaines, Stanley, 3040 Cedarwood Ln., Falls Church, VA 22042
Gallagher, Patrick, 7271 Swan Point Way, Columbia, MD 21045
Gallagher, Thomas, 11400 Washington Pl., No..W 1102, Reston, VA 22090
Garbler, Paul, 6222 West Miramar Dr., Tucson, AZ 85715
Gardemal, Cdr Robert, USN3123 S. Ninth St., Chickasha, OK 73018
Gardner, David, 8477 Menicoor Blvd., Largo, FL 34647
Gardner, Theodore, 4606 Jones Creek Rd., No 270, Baton Rouge, LA 70817
Garner, Arthur, MHPCC/DOD Facility, 590 Lipoa Parkway 3100, Kihei, HI 06753
Garrison, David, 3731 Olympia Dr., Houston, TX 77019
Garrison, Mrs. Mildred, 100 South Osceola Dr., Indian Harbour Beach, FL 32937
Gartland, Edward, 7 Cypress Rd., Milford, NH 03055
Garvey, Geoffrey, 1287 Merion Ct., Murrells Inlet, SC 29576
Gaston, Col Arthur, USAF 370 Sandringham Rd., Rochester, NY 14610
Gaumond, Ms. Marian, 12052 North Shore Dr., No. 221B. Reston, VA 22090
Gautier, Len, P.O. Box 3166, Oakton, VA 22124
Gavaghen, William, 1165 Silver Beech Rd., Herndon, VA 22070
Gavello, Alfred, 36 San Carlos Ct., Walnut Creek, CA 94598
Gay, Earle, 50 Park Ave., New York, NY 10016
Gay, Richard, P.O. Box 1027, Blue Hills, ME 04614
Geary, Dr. Fred, 434 Rolling Hill Dr., Sebastian, FL 32958
Geary, Mrs. Ruth, 3130 Duke St., Alexandria, VA 22314
Geer, Sgt Galen, USMCR 1310 Reed Ln., Canon City, CO 81212
Geiger, RAdm Robert, USN 3273 Charles MacDonald Dr., Sarasota, FL 34240
Geise, Dr. Marion, 1600 S. Joyce St., No C812, Arlington, VA 22202
Gelwick, Dr. Robert, 1708 Berwick Ln., Middletown, OH 45042
Geohegan, Paul, 4111 Platt Dr., Kenner, LA 70065
George, Clair, 5026 Allan Rd., Bethesda, MD 20816
Gerard, Thomas, Berth 38, West Pier, Rappas Marina, Sausalito, CA 94965
Gerber, Burton, 2311 Connecticut Ave., NW, No 305, Washington, DC 20008
Gerber, William, 16 Princes Ave., Chelmsford, MA 01863
Getsinger, Norman, P.O. Box 575, Flint Hill, VA 22627
Ghormley, LtCol William, USAF 4125 Granada Dr., Georgetown, TX 78628
Giambri, Philip, 131 SW 194th St., Normandy Park, WA 98166
Gibbens, LtCol Edward, USAF 4675 S.18th St., East, Mountain Rome, fD 83647
Gibson, Albert, 9110 Deer Park Rd., Great Falls, VA 22066
Gibson, Sgt Jonathan, USA P.O. Box 15514, West Palm Beach, FL 33416
Gibson, Roger, 912 Ortega Ave., Coral Gables, FL 33134
Gibson, William, 21 Brandon Pl., Cleveland, ON 44116
Gillard, Ruth, 3747 Terra Grande Dr., No. 1A, Walnut Creek, CA 94595
Gillette, LtCdr Halbert, USN 1355 Leslie Dr., Merritt Island, FL 32952
Gilliam, Mrs. Clare, 5908 Cedar Parkway, Chevy Chase, MD 20815
Gilligan, Dr. Robert, 18 Kirkwood Circle, Brigantine, NJ 08203
Gillingham, LtCdr W., USNR 5433 Landau Dr., No. 22, Dayton, OR 45429
Gillis, James, 1518 Notre Dame Dr., Davis, CA 95616

Giovinazzo, Anthony, 840 Weymouth Rd., Medina, OH 44256
Girard, Harlan, P.O. Box 58700, Philadelphia,PA 19102
Gittinger, John, 1022 Thistle Wood Rd., Norman, OK 73072
Givans, Robert L., 2275 W. Nottingham St., Springfield, MO 65810
Given, David R., 235 11th Avenue, Huntington, WV 25701
Givens, John C., 1330 Ponder Point Dr., Sandpoint ID 83864
Gleisberg, Harold E., P.O. Box 536, Roswell, NM 88202
Glover, LCDR Norman J., USCGR271 Central Park, West New York, NY 10024
Glunt, E. Merle, RR 1, Box 303, Mount Union, PA 17066
Glunt, CDR Elliott H., USN10411 Brunswick Ave., Silver Spring, MD 20902
Goeller, Carl G., 4605 Lanterman Rd., Youngstown, OH 44515
Goepper, Forrest S., 1595 N. Atlantic Ave., No.301, Cocoa Beach, FL 32931
Goerder, Col Robert L., USAF 902 South Garner St., State College, PA 16801
Goff, CPT Ronald L., 251 Pauline Ave., Akron, OH 44312
Gold, Barry A., 90 State St., Albany, NY 12207
Goldberg, Col Nathan S., USAF 603 N. Doheny Drive, #2A, Beverly Hills, CA 90210
Golden, Maj Robert J., USA751 5 La Madera Ct., NE Albuquerque, NM 87109
Goldman, Edward H., 46 Noyes St., Portland, ME 04103
Goldman,.Elmer M., 52 Gregory Rd., Framingham, MA 01701
Goldsher, Marvin, 5733 N. Sheridan Rd #220, Chicago, IL 60660
Goloway, Edward, D. RR. 3, Box 5850, Berryville, VA 22611
Gonakis, Mike S., 1044 E. Dartinoor Ave., Seven Hills, OH 44131
Gooden, Royal T., Box 1090, Fort Myer, VA 22211
Goodfield, Dr. Barry Austin, 1060 Clay St., San Francisco, CA 94108
Goodjoin, Al, P.O. Box 632, New Rochelle, NY 10801
Goodman, Billy L., 1703 McKay Ct., Jefferson City, MO 65109
Goodwin, Joseph C,. 415 Roebling Rd., South Belleair, FL 34616
Gordon, Charles J., 1924 Blair Blvd., Wooster, OH 44691
Gordon, BrigGen Dudley J., USA320 Palm Court, Indialantic, FL 32903
Gordon, Gordon, 6145 Jochums Drive, Tucson, AZ 85718
Gordon, Steven, 77 Terapin St., Mastic, NY 11950
Gorman, Ms. Judith E., 19 Ripley St., Somerset, MA 02725
Gorsline, Capt Samuel G., USN225 Deddie Terrace, Fallbrook, CA 92028
Goss, Porter J., US House of Rep. 509 Cannon Building, Washington, DC 20515
Gottschalk, Capt Jack, USAR12 Crossbrook Road, Livingston, NJ 07039
Goulden, Joseph C., 1534 29th St., N.W. Washington, DC 20007
Gourlay, Lawrence, 4660 Ocean Blvd. No.1-2, Sarasota, FL 33581
Gourley, William, 3120 Myrtle Ave 6094 San Diego, CA 92104
Govia,. Philip Anthony, P.O. Box 941, Millville, NJ 08332
Gowin, Maj Robert W., AUS8517 Lakinhurst Ln., Springfield, VA 22152
Grabo, Ms. Cynthia M., 2001 Columbia Pike No.606 Arlington, VA 22204
Grady, J. William, 7510 Glenbrook Rd., Bethesda, MD 20814
Graff, Ms. Eleanora, 6145 Beachway Dr., Falls Church, VA 22041
Graham, Gordon, 21 Beacon St., No.8-H, Boston, MA 02108
Graham, Thomas B., 716 Forest Park Rd., Great Falls, VA 22066
Grasle, Milton, 111 Donald St. East Saint Louis, IL 62206
Graves, Hunter Lee, 2995 Old Lynchburg Rd. N. Garden, VA 22959
Gray, LtCol George W., AUS5550 36th NE, Seattle, WA 98105
Gray, Peter J., 20420 Lake Rd., Rocky River, OH 44116
Graybeal, Sidney N., 10101 Langhorne Ct., Bethesda, MD 20817
Greaney, John K., 6112 Western Ave., Chevy Chase, MD 20815
Greaves, Fielding, P.O. Box 150368, San Rafael, CA 94915
Green, Dr. Gilbert, P.O. Box 98, Gaithersburg, MD 20884
Green, Mrs. Jacqueline R., Rt 2 Box 347, Lovettsville, VA 22080
Green, James F., 6522 Heather Brook Ct., McLean, VA 22101
Greenblatt, Col Owen, USAF4125 Century Ct., Alexandria, VA 22312
Greene, Harris, 3671 N. Harrison St., Arlington, VA 22207
Greene, Ms. Nancy D., P.O. Box 7339, Incline Village, NV 89450
Greenfield, Alfred I., 18 Bradstreet Rd. Hampton, NH 03842
Greenman, Roger, 1173A Second Ave, No. 313 New York, NY 10021
Greenwald, Col Robert, USAR21509 S. Figueroa St., Carson, CA 90745
Greico, Rev. Charles F., P.O. Box 635, Chester, NJ 07930
Grier, E. Phillips Sr., 13201 Conrad Court Woodbridge, VA 22191
Gries, David D., 4855 Reservoir Rd., NW Washington, DC 20007

Griffith, B. Herold M.D.S.C, 320 Greenwood St., Evanston, IL 60201
Griffith, Carl F., P.O. Box 845, Middlebury, CT 06762
Griffith, Mrs. Jeanne B., 320 Greenwood St., Evanston, IL 60201
Griffith, Richard A., 511 N. Highland St., Arlington, VA 22201
Griffith, Dr. Richard R., RR. 1, Box 373-70, Randolph, VT 05060
Griffith, William, P.O. Box 7294, State Capitol, Albany, NY 12224
Grigg, Harry K., 61 Longview Dr., Green Brook, NJ 08812
Grigrovich-Barsky, Gleb B., RR I Box 432, Kilmarnock, VA 22482
Grill, LtCol Jack, USA2280 South 19th St., Mount Vernon, WA 98273
Grillo, Cdr Pat L., USN 1330 Victorian Crescent, Virginia Beach, VA 23454
Grimm, Howard, 38-40 Regatta Pl., Douglaston, NY 11363
Gross, Walter H., P.O.Box 1804, Sedona, AZ 86339
Gross, Maj William J., USAF1760 Valleybrook Pl.,. Dayton, OH 45459
Grostephen, Ms. Marjorie L, 6145 Beachway Dr., Falls Church, VA 22041
Grubbs, Judson B., 1037 Rodeo Rd., Pebble Beach, CA 93953
Guay, BrigGen Georges R., USAFP.O. Box 16, APO, AE 09777
Guenther, LtCol John J., USMC265 Sea Woods Dr. North St., Augustine, FL 32084
Guernsey, Douglas D., 305 Hamden Kells, Peachtree City, GA 30269
Guffin, LtCol Robert A., USAF 5148 Splitrail Ct., Colorado Springs, CO 80917
Guider, James J., 385 Abbott Ave., P.O. Box 630, Ridgefield, NJ 07657
Gunn, Edward M., M.D. 300 Wood Haven Dr., No.1507, Hilton Head Island, SC 29928
Gustafson, Harry M., 237 East Prospect, Mt. Prospect, IL 60056
Guth, Robert M., 3800 Powell Ln., Falls Church, VA 22041

– H –

Hacherian, Jack, 2726 Sinton Pl., Pepper Pike, OH 44124
Hackl, Robert, 4145 Sunnyslope Ave., Sherman Oaks, CA 91423
Hackman, Col Jeffrey, USAF P.O. Box 35, Round Hill, VA 22141
Haendle, Col Karl, USA 4543 Carriage Run Circle, Murrels Inlet, SC 29576
Hagaman, BGen Harry, USMC222 E. Fallen Rock Rd., Grand Junction, CO 81503
Hagerling, Col Sidney, USMCRP.O. Box 452, Ft. Collins, CO 80522
Hagle, Mrs. Nina, 2608 Ridge Road Dr., Alexandria, VA 22302
Hahn, Alfred, 14 Quay Ct., Centerport, NY 11721
Hahn, LtCol B. Albert, AUS427 Greenwich St., Bergenfield, NJ 07621
Haig, Mrs. Elizabeth, 222 Reeds Landing, Springfield, MA 01109
Haig, Ransom, 17443 Plaza Destacado, San Diego, CA 92128
Hall, David, 804 N. High St., Duncannon, PA 17020
Hall, Keith D., 1020 School Station Dr., Folsom, CA 95630
Hall, Dr. Richard N, 6353 Meadowrue La., Erie, PA 16505
Halpern, Samuel, 2202 Popkins Ln., Alexandria, VA 22307
Halpin, Daniel D., 9 Eastman Ave., Bedford, NH 03110
Hamilton, William, 8810 Lynnhurst Dr., Fairfax, VA 22031
Hamit, Francis, 11669 Valerio, No 247, North Hollywood, CA 91605
Hammond, Col Walter, USAF 7994 Breezy Point Rd., West, Melrose, FL 32666
Hammond, LtCol William, AUS8622 Oak Ledge Dr., San Antonio, TX 78217
Hampson, Thomas R., 680 Hillcrest Blvd., Hoffman Estates, IL 60195
Hanable, Cdr William, USNR P.O. Box 1464, Westport, WA 98595
Hancock, Gus H., 11463 Waterview Cluster, Reston, VA 22090
Handlin, James, 185 Hemmh Ave., Alamo, CA 94507
Hanna, Philip, Vernon Junior College, 4400 College Dr., Vernon, TX 76384
Hanneman, Leroy, 14421 Southeast 60th St., Bellevue, WA 98006
Hanrahan, James, 11111 Gainsborough Rd., Potomac, MD 20854
Hansen, LtCol Lester, USA.F 12767 Hunters Ridge Dr., Bonita Springs, FL 33923
Happersett, LtCol Newlin, USA 850 E. Roberts Rd., Phoenix, AZ 85022
Harder, Ms. Dorothy, 2800 Woodley Rd., NW, Washington, DC 20008
Harding, Mrs. Nancy, 1803 Westwind Way, Mclean, VA 22102
Hardy, Major George, USA6027 Pine Crest Dr., Los Angeles, CA 90042
Harney, John, 8603 Powhatan St., New Carrollton, MD 20784
Harnish, James, 2865 Mourning Dove Way, Titusville, FL 32780
Harper, John, 7910 Fort Hunt Rd., Alexandria, VA 22308
Harpham, LtCdr Richard, USNRP.O. Box 5713, Santa Barbara, CA 93105
Harris, Charles, 4402 S. Garnett Rd., No 113, Tulsa, OK 74145
Harris, Col Jimmy, USA 1429 Walden Oaks Pi., Plant City, FL 33566
Harris, Raymond, 5320 Nichols Dr. East, Lakeland, FL 33813

Harrison, Stuart, RR3, Box 648 Belfast, ME 04915
Harroll, Benjamin, 425 F St., San Diego, CA 92101
Hart, Col Donald, USA P.O. Box 127, Cornwall, CT 06796
Hart, John L., 2767 Unicorn Ln., NW, Washington, DC 20015
Hart, Joseph, 1441 Waggaman Circle, Mclean, VA 22101
Hart, Peter, 181 Lester St., New Britain, CT 06053
Harvey, Arthur, P.O. Box 974, Derry, NH 03038
Harvey, Mrs. Clara, 1611 Northwood Dr., Indianapolis, IN 46240
Harvey, Deborah, 8203 Jeb Stuart Rd., Potomac, MD 20854
Harvey, RAdm Donald, USN 8203 Jeb Stuart Rd., Potomac, MD 20854
Harvey, Patrick, P.O. Box 5186, Santa Fe., NM 87502
Harvey, Richard, 11 Admiral Rd., Severna Park, MD 21146
Hatch, Capt William, Mill Road Farm, RR2, Box 107, Leesburg 22075
Hauck, Paul, 796 102nd Ave., N. Naples, FL 3399963
Hawkins, Charles H., 121 Medicine Springs Rd., Conner, MT 59827
Hawkins, Frank, 204 Ocean Dr., Tavernier, FL 33070
Hawkins, Col John, USARP.O. Box 5969, Texarkana, TX 75505
Hayden, Col Charles, AUS 401 Via Casitas, No. 9, Greenbrae, CA 94904
Hayden, Ms. Kathleen, 4904 Pelican Blvd., Cape Coral, FL 33914
Hayes, James, 5569 Glen Abby Ct., Delray Beach, FL 33484
Hayes, Jimmy, 5 East Circle Dr., Cocoa Beach, FL 32931
Hayes, Louis, Dept. of PoliSci, University of Montana, Missoula, MT 59812
Hays, Donald, 501 East 79th St., New York, NY 10021
Hays, James, 1427 S.W. 53rd Terrace, Cape Coral, Fl, 33914
Hays, Adm Ronald, USN 869 Kamoi Pl., Honolulu, HI 96825
Hayward, Capt Thomas, USMC6767 Reflection St., Redding, CA 96001
Heacock, George, 5696 Montilla Dr., Fort Myers, FL 33919
Healey, David, 12203 Hollow Tree Ln., Fairfax, VA 22030
Healey, Donald, 2100 Lee Highway, No. 433, Arlington, VA 22201
Healy, Michael, 6658 Meadowlawn, Houston, TX 77023
Hearn, Dan L., 2534 S. Granada, Rancho San Diego, CA 91977
Heber, Robert, 2860 Evergreen Way, Cooper City, FL 33026
Heddy, Marc, 150 Appleton St., No. 4C, Boston, MA 02166
Hedges, Daniel K., 700 Lousiana, Suite 3500, Houston, TX 77002
Heibel, Robert, 5800 Millfair Rd., Fairview, PA 16415
Heiede, Ernest, 555 Freeman Rd., No 53, Central Point, OR 97502
Heinz, LtGen Edward, USAF 515 Davis St., SW, Leesburg, VA 22075
Heires, John, 245 Kilmarnock Dr., Millersville, MD 21108
Helms, Richard, 4649 Garfield St., NW, Washington, DC 20007
Hemphill, Col William, AUS 1200 S. Courthouse Rd., Arlington, VA 22204
Henderson, Lindsey, P.O. Box 1014, Saluda, NC 28773
Hendrick, Lyle G., P.O. Box 24013, Columbia, SC 29224
Henger, Charles, 50 Business Parkway, Richardson, TX 75081
Hennelly, Edmund, 84 Sequams Lane East, West Islip, NY 11795
Hennings, Mrs. W.M., RR2, Box 164, Bryans Rd., MD 20616
Henry, James M., Back Bay Annex, P.O. Box 1187, Boston, MA 02117
Henschel, William, 120 North Harmony St., Medina, OR 44256
Herr, Mrs. Lifley, P.O. Box 433840, San Ysidro, CA 92143
Herr, Cdr William, USNR P.O. Box 433840, San Ysidro, CA 92143
Herring, LtCol Lorenzo, USAF370 Hill N'Dale, Lexington, KY 40503
Herron, William, 204 Liberty St., Murfreesboro, NC 27855
Hersh, Burton, P.O. Box 433, Bradford, NU 03221
Heuer, Richards, 47 Alta Mesa Circle, Monterey, CA 93940
Hicks, W.B., 161 4th Ave., No A, Chula Vista, CA 92010
Hildago, Balmes, 240 Treasure Lake Rd., DuBois, PA 15801
Higbee-Glace, Mrs. Anne, P.O. Box 85, Bolton, MA 01740
Highbarger, Robert, 7509 Hackamore Dr., Potomac, MD 20854
Hull, Dr. Wayne, P.O. Box 2315, Traverse City, Ml 49685
Hilliard, John, 13005 Chalfont Ave., Fort Washington, MD 20744
Hirschhorn, LtCdr W., USNR 4 Yale Rd., Norristown, PA 19401
Hirst, R.NLA., Mathildenstr.4, D-65189 Wiesbaden, Germany
Hirzy, Franz, 318 Old Hunt Rd., Fox River Grove, IL 60021
Hiscott, George E., 1745 Spruce Ave., Highland Park, IL 60035
Histed, Cliff, 575 W. Madison St., No 2412, Chicago, IL 60661

Hitchcock, Edward C., 7013 Old Cabin Lane, Rockville, MD 20852
Hoar, Mrs. Elanore, 50 Oak St., New Canaan, CT 06840
Hobbs, Ms. Madge, 260 Saint Daniel Ln., Florissant, MO 63031
Hockeimer, Henry, 2801 New Mexico Ave., NW, Washington, DC 20007
Hodge, Walter P., 5953 Oakland Park Dr., Burke, VA 22015
Hoes, Ms Lauarie C., 3413 Wood Creek Dr., Suidand, MD 20746
Hoffman, Ray, 375 South End Ave., No 8B, New York, NY 10280
Hoffmeier, Mrs. Frances, 2447 Lockhill-Selma, No 301, San Antonio, TX 78230
Hoffsis, James, 7513 Dellwood Rd., NE, Albuquerque, NM 87110
Hoggan, Robert, 1626 Montmorency Dr., Vienna, VA 22192
Hoke, Jonathan, P.O. Box 534, Goshen, IN 46526
Holcombe, Col Harold, USAR 23 Grapetree Bay, Christiansted, VI 00820
Holman, Wayne, 800 4th St., SW, No S-525, Washington, DC 20024
Holmes, Kent, 1 John Lynch Rd., Compton, MD 20627
Holmes, Robert, Cannon St., Inc., 88 Kearny St., No 825, San Francisco, CA 94108
Holmes, Robert, P.O. Box 180, Somers Point, NJ 08244
Holstein, Dudley, 1406 Cedar Park Rd., Annapolis, MD 21401
Holt, James, 16115 Kennedy St., Woodbridge, VA 22191
Hoobler, Dr. James, 11410 Strand Dr., No 410, Rockville, MD 200852
Hopkins, Ms Christine, 8380 Greensboro Dr., No 5-623, McLean, VA 22102
Hopler, Samuel, 2020 Jacaranda Dr., Fort Pierce, FL 34949
Hoppy, Ms. Louise, 1320 North Bryant Ave., Tucson, AZ 85712
Horan, Mrs. Yolanda, 1791 Massachusetts Ave., NW, No 405, Washington, DC 20036
Horgan, Mrs. Eileen N., 18905 Olney Mill Rd., Olney, MD 20832
Horkan, George A., Cleremont Farm, RRI, Box 34, Upperville, VA 22176
Horn, Capt William, USN 301 G St, SW, No 822, Washington, DC 20024
Hornaday, Col William, AUS 26770 Stardust Dr., Bonita Springs, FL 33923
Horne, Cdr Edward, USN 1005 Olive Ave., South Island, Coronado, CA 92118
Horton, John R., P.O. Box 234, Hollywood, MD 20636
Hoskins, Capt Floyd E., USN 109 Ridley Dr., Carrollton, GA 30117
Hottel, David, 110 Leisure St., Stafford, VA 22554
Houchins, Dr. Lee, 1323 Windy Hill Rd., McLean, VA 2221202
Houkal, Henry C., 500 Roosevelt Blvd., No 427, Falls Church, VA 222044
Houtehad, Gary, 11438 E. Huffman Rd., No 5, Parma Heights, OR 44130
Houston-Jones, Cheyd, 4814 Glencoe Ave., No 7, Marina Del Ray, CA 90292
Howard, Andrew, 4400 Massachusetts Ave., NW, Washington, DC 20016
Howe, William, 4940 Lowell St., NW, Washington, DC 20016
Howell, Ms Lucille, 4038 S.E. 73rd Ave., Portland, OR 97206
Howrigen, Lois D., 3920 Mainlands Blvd.,S. Pinellas Park, FL 34666
Hubbard, Ralph, 415 West Lyon Farm Dr., Greenwich, CT 06830
Hubbart, Gerald, 2825 Espanola NE, Albuquerque, NM 871 1 0
Hudson, LtCol Denis, USAF 381 Bush St., No 200, San Francisco, CA 94104
Hudson, Herbert, 4005 Rickover Rd., Silver Spring, MD 20902
Hudson, Jerry, 6938 Norchester Ct., Charlotte, NC 28227
Huefner, Donald, 905 Country Club Dr., NE, Vienna, VA 22180
Hugel, Max, 18 Horn Rd., Windham, NH 03087
Huggins, James, 22 Fairview St., Belfast, ME 04915
Hulnick, Arthur, 216 Summit Ave., No E 102, Brookline, MA 02146
Hunt, David, 3503 Fulton St., NW, Washington, DC 20007
Hunt. E. Howard, 1401 B St., NW, Washington, DC 20005
Hunter, Col David, USA 185 Bar R Dr., Athens, GA 30605
Huntington, John, P.O. Box 1006, Tiburon, CA 94920
Huntington, Capt Stuart, P.O. Box 2906, Reston, VA 22090
Huray, Col Frank, 11130 Ft. George Rd., E, Jacksonville, FL 32226
Hudburt, LtCol Arthur, AUS 190 High St., No 314, Medford, MA 02116
Hurley, Kenneth, 5020 45th St., NW, Washington, DC 20016
Huse, Thomas, 3512 Whitehaven Dr., Walnut Creek, CA 94598
Hussey, William, 5563 B. Via Portola, Laguna Hills, CA 92653
Hutchinson, II. Frederick, 3404 White Oak Ct., Fairfax, VA 22030
Hyde, Joseph, 559 Colecroft Ct., Alexandria, VA 22314
Hyink, LtCol James, USA 1962 Gomez Dr., Los Lunas, NM 87031
Hyndman, James, 4811 Brookwood Dr., Mableton, GA 30059

– I –

Iannaccone, Thomas, S.6914 14th Ave., Brooklyn, NY 11228
Ill, Col Paul, AUS970 Mayflower Ave., Melbourne, FL 32940
Immel, William J.,106 Sunset Dr., Otley, IA 50214
Inda, James, 420 S. 22nd St., La Crosse, WI 54601
Inge, Col Leon, USAF4100 Century Ct., Alexandria, VA 22312
Ingraham, Mrs. Anne Mary, 827 S. Royal St., Alexandria, VA 22314
Inman, Adm Bobby R., USN3200 Riva Ridge, Austin, TX 78746
Innis, Donald R., 676 Murex Dr., Naples, FL 33940
Isserman, Manfred A., County Home Rd., Thompson, CT 06277

– J –

Jackson, Clarence A., P.O. Box 75007, St. Paul, MN 55175
Jackson, Daniel G., 3408 Chiswick Ct., No 3H, Silver Spring, MD 20906
Jackson, Donald, 8305 Private Ln., Annadale, VA 22003
Jackson, Col Joseph, USA1412 Chesapeake Ave., Hampton, VA 23661
Jacobs, Charles T., 103 Brown St., Box 7, Washington Grove, MD 20880
Jacobs, Eli S., 641 Lexington Ave., 31st Floor, New York, NY 10022
Jacobsen, Eric P., 10402 Lakeshore Blvd., Bratenahl, OH 44108
James, Robert G., 80 Ludlow Dr., Chappaqua, NY 10514
Jamison, Katherine, 1600 S. Eads St., No 113m South, Arlington, VA 22202
Jamison, Ms. Sara Jane, 12191 Clipper Dr., Lake Ridge, VA 22192
Japikse, Ms. Catherine, 80 Lyme Rd., Hanover, NH 03755
Jasin, Peter W., 4900 N. Ocean Blvd., No 1113, Fort Lauderdale, FL 33308
Jasper, Kenneth, 7351 Eldorado Ct., McLean, VA 22102
Jastrow, Robert E., 2508 West Straford Dr., Chandler, AZ 85224
Jemilo, John, 3581 N. Avers Ave., Chicago, IL 60618
Jenkins, Carl E., BHPS PSC No 80, Box 10461, APO, AP 96367
Jenkins, Dale A., Tower Hill Rd., Tuxedo Park, NY 10987
Jenkins, RAdm John, USN5809 Helmsdale Ln., Alexandria, VA 22310
Jenks, Airell, 4 Sunset Farm, Woodstock, VT 05091
Jenks, Donovan R., 5007 Auckland Ave., North Hollywood, CA 91601
Jenne, Dr. Herbert, 1481 Patriot Dr., Melbourne, FL 32940
Jentsch, Heber, 6331 Hollywood Blvd., Los Angeles, CA 90028
Jerawski, Edward, 32556 Mound Rd., Warren, MI 48092
Jilli, Edmund, 8700 N. La Cholla No 2134, Tucson, AZ 85741
Jirles, LtCol Edward, USAF2773 Cady Way, Winter Park, FL 32792
Joannides, George E., 8817 Tuckerman Ln., Potomac, MD 20854
Johannessen, John, Box 315, 52 Fairway Dr., Grantham, NH 03753
Johanson, Cdr Donald, USN8260 Hornbuckle Dr., Springfield, VA 22153
Johnson, MSgt Charles, USAF317 Jan Lynn, Kenton, TN 38233
Johnson, Douglas W., 16421 S.E. 42nd Pl., Issaquah, WA 98027
Johnson, Herbert J., 527 Seminiole Dr., Erie, PA 16505
Johnson, John B., 221 Flower Ave., West, Watertown, NY 13601
Johnson, Kenneth T., 3509 North Valley St., Arlington, VA 22207
Johnson, Mrs. Lucy A., 3014 Brinkley Rd., No 108, Temple Hills, MD 20748
Johnson, Norman, 6017 Saturn Ln., Mira Loma, CA 91752
Johnson, Ronald, 7300 Reservation Dr., Springfield, VA 22153
Johnson, Terry D., 25200 Baronet Dr., Salinas, CA 93908
Johnson, Thomas, P.O. Box 1297, Littleton, CO 80160
Johnson, William O., P.O. Box 145, Leander, TX 78641
Johnson, William P., 1911 Camino de la Costa No 501, Redondo Beach, CA 90277
Johnson, William R., 317 Foxtail Ct., Boulder, CO 80303
Johnson, William W., RR 9, Box 244, Mountain Home, AR 72653
Johnstone, William W., P.O. Box 18380, Shreveport, LA 71138
Jones, Major Bruce, USMC98-1870K Kaahumanu St., Pearl City, HI 96782
Jones, George E., 225 Sycamore Ave., Shrewsbury, NJ 07702
Jones, Joseph, 12123 Sage Glen Ct., Maryland Heights, MO 63043
Jones, Col Marvin, 175 Stewart Dr., Merritt Island, FL 32952
Jones, Major Paul, USAF8712 Clydesdale Rd., Springfield, VA 22151
Jones, Col Richard, USA350 Myrtlewood Rd., Melbourne, FL 32040
Jordan, Joseph L., 2615 Waugh Dr., No 301, Houston, TX 77006
Joscelyn, Kent, 11 Southwick Ct., Ann Arbor, MI 48105
Jose, Virgil, 14415 Frankton Ave., Hacienda Heights, CA 91745

Jost, Dr. Charles, 118 Doubloon Dr., North Ft. Myers, FL 33917
Jost, Dr. Patrick, 3020 Fredsen Pl., Falls Church, VA 22042
Joy, Robert, 795 Montecello Rd., San Rafael, CA 94903
Joyce, James G., 12399 Falkirk Dr., Fairfax, VA 22033
Joyce, Col Jean K., USA4522 Swann Ave., Tampa, FL 33609
Joyce, Richard, 4626 Alton Pl., NW, Washington, DC 20016
Joyeuse, Dr. Rene, P.O.Box 329, Dannemora, NY 12929
Jozwiak, Vincent, 7759 Chars Ln., Springfield, VA 22153
Juarez, Capt Robert, USN3217 Wynford Dr., Fairfax, VA 22031
Judy, Chesley, 11820 Wynford Dr., Fairfax, VA 22031
Julitz, BrigGen Frank, USA5832 N. Virginia Ave., Chicago, IL 60659
Julitz, John A., 10011 Seymore, Schiller Park, IL 60176
Julliard, Jacques, Le Nouvel Observateur, Paris, France
Jungel, Paul, 744 E. Hayward Ave., Phoenix, AZ 85020
Jurchenko, Col Andrew, 603 Preserve Pl., Peachtree City, GA 30269
Justman Jacob, Poul Louis, Kon. Ned. Hoogovens & Staalfabrieken N.V. Netherlands

– K –

Kahdeman, Tyler, P.O. Box 7465, Las Cruces, NM 88006
Kaiser, Robert G., 1150 15th St.,NW, Washington, DC 20017
Kalitka, Col Peter, USAP.O. Box 305, Waterford, VA 22190
Kallini, LtCol Thaddeus, USAF5100 John D. Ryan Blvd., No 717, San Antonio, TX 78245
Kanellos, Constantine, 6416 Berkshire Dr., Alexandria, VA 22310
Kappes, George M., 709 Cascade Dr., Golden, CO 80403
Karlow, S. Peter, 43 Fair Oaks Ln., Atherton, CA 94027
Karr, R. Michael, P.O. Box 1762, Bothell, WA 98041
Kassebaum, Dr. Peter, 1545 Rio Nido Ct., Petaluma, CA 94954
Katheder, Thomas, P.O. Box 22671, Lake Buena Vista, FL 32830
Katsirubas, William P., 7126 Merrimac Dr., McLean, VA 22101
Kaufman, Col Raymond, USAP.O. Box 1009, Litchfield, CT 06759
Kaufman, Walter J., 11 Ruxview Ct., No 302, Ruxton, MD 21204
Kavanaugh, Maj Kevin, USAR206 N. Trenton St., No 3, Arlington, VA 22203
Kaylor, Ms. Pattie, 4977 Battery Ln., No 307, North, Bethesda, MD 20814
Kearns, Capt Michael, USAF826 Orange Ave., No 128, Coronado, CA 92118
Keat, Augustus, 8547 S. Zypher, Littleton, CO 80123
Keats, Col James, USAR2000 S. Eads St., No 607, Arlington, VA 22202
Keefe, Stephen R., 5600 Small Oak Ct., Woodbridge, VA 22192
Keeler, Ray M., 860 Rudder Way, Annapolis, MD 21401
Keenan, Gerard P., 1005 Celia St., West Islip, NY 11795
Keikuatov, Oleg, 1311 Ross St., SW, Vienna, VA 22180
Keiser, LtCol Melville, USAR6904 Hutchison St., Falls Church, VA 22043
Kellaher, Frank J., 7518 Dover Ln., Lanham, MD 20706
Kellar, Michael, 45-401 Mokulele Dr., No 32, Kanehoe, HI 96744
Keller, Dennis M., 2226 Calle Opalo, San Clemente, CA 92673
Keller, E. John, 2906 Southlake Blvd., Southlake, TX 76092
Keller, George R., 305 Lee Dr., Baltimore, MD 21228
Kelly, Capt William, USNR465 Canton Rd., Kingsport, TN 37663
Kelso, LtCol Joseph, USAF3645 S. Poplar St., Denver, CO 80237
Kempa, Erich, 3115 NW 93rd St., Seattle, WA 98117
Kennedy, James P., 506 Granite St., Ashland, OR 97520
Kenney, James, 1100 NW Loop 410, Suite 200, San Antonio, TX 78213
Kent, Alexander, 14816 East Dunton Dr., Whittier, CA 90604
Kent, William, 320 Burning Tree Rd., Pinehurst, NC 28374
Kenyon, Dr. Paul, 1314 S. King St., No 664, Honolulu, HI 96814
Kephart, Cdr Robert, USNERLACH, RR1, Box 335, Faber, VA 22938
Kerbe, Wilmer, 3237 Brushwood Ct., Clearwater, FL 34621
Kern, Erson, 4576 Crimsonwood Dr., Redding, CA 96001
Kerns, Arthur J., 6852 Grande Ln., Falls Church, VA 22043
Kessler, Peter, 2199 Holland Ave., No 5G, Bronx, NY 10462
Kesterson, Mrs. Goldie Mae, 2001 Columbia Pike, No 202, Arlington, VA 22204
Kida, Anthony, 3102 North 47th St., Phoenix, AZ 85018
Kiechlin, Edmond F. Jr., 10022 Wheatfield Ct., Fairfax, VA 22032
Kierce, Robert R., 47784 Fathom Pl., Sterling, VA 20165
Kies, Dr. Rudolf, P.O.Box 295, San Fernando, CA 91341

Kim, Arthur, 7117 Idylwood Rd., Falls Church, VA 22043
Kimble, Wilford L., 24 Edmiston Ln., Comfort, TX 78013
King, Col Dale M., USA2743 Spicer Ln., Decatur, GA 30033
King, Daniel C., 26425 Millinix Mill Rd., Mt. Airy, MD 21771
King, Daniel P., 5125 N. Cumberland Blvd., Whitefish Bay, WI 53217
King, George W., 9839 Mendota Dr., Peoria, AZ 85345
King, Ms. Mary, 5601 Seminary Rd., No 1617N, Falls Church, VA 22041
King, William P., 2850 S. Ocean Blvd. No 502, Palm Beach, FL 33480
Kirby, Oliver, RR5, Club Lake, Box 229E, Greenville, TX 75401
Kirchman, Charles V., 14801 Notley Rd., Silver Spring, MD 20905
Kirk, Grayson L., Columbia University, New York, NY 10027
Kirkpatrick, Rita, P.O. Box 429, Middleburg, VA 22117
Kirschner, Calvin, P.O. Box 777, Garden City, MI 48136
Kizirian, Col John, USA98-1032 Alania St., Aiea, HI 96701
Klager, Roy B. Jr., 3001 Hedgetree Ct., Wichita, KS 67226
Kleber, Col Victor, USMC907 Forrest Ln., Beaufort, SC 29902
Kleebauer, Charles, 1833 Baldwin Dr., McLean, VA 22102
Klein, Edward V., P.O. Box 597, Dillsboro, NC 28725
Klein, Col Frank O., USAF30180 Santiago Rd., Tememcula, CA 92592
Klein, Rev Theodore, USAF69 Groton Long Point Rd., Groton, CT 06340
Kleyla, Mrs. Helen H., P.O. Box 161, Nags Head, NC 27959
Kleyla, Robert L., 730 24th St., NW, No 400, Washington, DC 20037
Kmentt, Todd A., 10681 Oak Lake Way, Boca Raton, FL 33498
Knickman, Carl V., Torweg Haus, P.O. Box 677, Madison, VA 22727
Knoll, Col Rudolph, AUS9412 Northridge Dr., NE, Albuquerque, NM 87111
Kobernicki, Lesek, 59 Elmleigh Rd., Hampshire, POO 2AB, England
Kobetz, Dr. Richard W., Arcadia, RR 2, Box 3645, Berryville, VA 22611
Koczak, Crd Edward, USN2500 Virginia Ave., NW, Washington, DC 20037
Koczak, Stephen A., 2932 Macomb St., NW, Washington, DC 20008
Kodmur, Milton J., 2734 Bordeaux Ave., Las Jolla, CA 92037
Koehler, John, 1 Strawberry Hill Ave., No 4H, Stamford, CT 06902
Kohlhaas, George, 1580 Tarpon St., Merritt Island, FL 32952
Koier, Mrs. Virginia R., 36 DeVries Circle, Lewes, DE 19958
Kokot, Ms. Mary Anna, 970 Virginia St., No 310, Dunedin, FL 34698
Koletar, Joseph, 53 Berkeley Pl., Glen Rock, NJ 07452
Koller, Col Rudolph, USAF1404 Stanley Dollar Dr., No 4A, Walnut Creek, CA 94595
Kolombatovic, Vadja, 1171 Dolley Madison Blvd., McLean, VA 22101
Kolon, LtCol Walter V., AUSP.O. Box 21063, Port Authority, New York, NY 10129
Kopera, John A., 1016 S. Wayne St., No 307, Arlington, VA 22204
Koplowitz, Wilfred, 410 E. 57th St., New York, NY 10022
Kopp, Dr. Guido, P.O. Box 1040, D-55100, Mainz, Germany
Koppel, Ted, 1717 DeSales St., Washington, DC 20017
Kosal, Ozmer, 245 Collington Dr., Ronkonkoma, NY 11449
Kostolich, Marcus, 12815 Teasberry Rd., Wheaton, MD 20906
Kotapish, William R., 1702 Bradmore Ct., McLean, VA 22101
Kourembis, Ms Mary, 926-Q Avenida Majorca, Laguna Hills, CA 92653
Kovacevich, Mrs. Ruth, 4800 N. 68th St., No 142, Scottsdale, AZ 85251
Kovar, Richard, 1913 Wintergreen Ct., Reston, VA 22091
Kray, Edward, 309 Tampa Ave., Indiatlantic, FL 332903
Krick, Samuel W., RR2, Box 2070, Duncannon, PA 17021
Kreibel, Norman F., 601 Montgomery Ave., No 201, Bryn Mawr, PA 19010
Krisel, Capt Lionel, USN100840 Savona Rd., Los Angeles, CA 90077
Krisman, Col Michael, USADrury Lane, Cragston, Highland Falls, NY 10928
Kroh, Herman, 2876 Forest Lodge Rd., Pebble Beach, CA 93953
Kronemeyer, Cdr Robert, USNR 7717 Ludington Pl., La Jolla, CA 92037
Krueger, Richard, 700 Muirfield Circle, Ft. Washington, MD 20744
Krueger, LtCol Robert A., 2212 Lakecrest Dr., Greer, SC 29651
Kryza, Honorable E. Gregory, 2035 Franklin Cluster Ct., Falls Church, VA 22043
Kubiszewski, LtCol S., USA5315 66th Ave., Court W, Tacoma, WA 89464
Kuethe, LtCol Ralph, USA6450 Queen Anne Terrace, Falls Church, VA 22044
Kuhn, Mrs. Nancy Z., 4204 Flower Valley Dr., Rockville, MD 20853
Kulberg, Raoul, 3916 McKinley St., NW, Washington, DC 20015
Kunen, Jeremy, 4475 White Egret Ln., Sarasota, FL 34238
Kuntzman, Major John C., USA11204 Trippon Ct., North Potomac, MD 20878

Kurtz, Howard, 1150 15th St., NW, Washington, DC 20017
Kustra, Richard J., 7331 Eldorado St., McLean, VA 22102
Kuzmuk, Walter, 854 Boatswin Way, Annapolis, MD 21401
Kvetkas, William, 595 Coover Rd., Annapolis, MD

– L –

Labar, Sherwood M., 8775 20th St., No 814W, Vero Beach, FL 32960
LaClair, Cameron, 4201 Cathedral Ave., NW, No 315E, Washington, DC 20016
LaFaver, Richard N., 1 North Hornbeam Pl., The Woodlands, TX 77380
Lafferty, Fred B., P.O. Box 9300, Minneapolis, MN 55440
Laggan, Francis P., 2217 Great Falls St., Falls Church, VA 22046
LaGuex, Conrad, 2317 N. Pocomoke St., Arlington, VA 22205
Lahnstein, Manfred, Bertelsman AG, Gutersloh, Germany
Lambert, Robert, 1919 Killarney Way, Bellevue, WA 98004
Lamkin, James, P.O. Box 210, Starkville, MS 39760
Lamon, Ralph, 6363 Christie Ave., No 1517, Emeryville, CA 94608
Lampshire, Cdr Harvey, USN2145 N. Quebec St., Arlington, VA 22207
Lancer, Col Thomas, USA9048 Belvoir Woods Parkway, Fort Belvoir, VA 22060
Landau, Yechil, 60 Division Ave., No 2C, Brooklyn, NY 11211
Landreth, Edward, 544 E. 86th St., New York, NY 10028
Landreth, Ted, 1211 S. Genesee Ave., Los Angeles, CA90019
Lane, Albert, 138 Germany Rd., Verona, NY 13478
Lane, Buford, 3611 Antiem St., San Diego, CA 92111
Lange, Col H.W., USA9000 Belvoir Woods Pkway, No 302, Fort Belvoir, VA 22060
Langevin, Henry R., 4 Longview Dr., Bow, NH 03304
Langfield, Millard, 3330 N. Leisure World Blvd., No 926, Silver Spring, MD 20906
Langholz, Marcus, P.O. Box 94, Rapidan, VA 22733
Langlie, Gary, 4103 Wexford Dr., Kensington, MD 20895
Languit, Col Gerard, USAF6415 Cleghorn Rd., NW, Albuquerque, NM 87120
Lankford, Blaine, 4480 Bella Mia Ct., Howell, MI 48843
Lanterman, Col John, USA8502 Whittier Blvd., Bethesda, MD 20817
Lanterman, Mark T., 132-A Plymouth Ave., Oreland, PA 19075
Lantos, Thomas, 2217 Rayburn House Office Bldg., Washington, DC 20515
Lapham, Lewis, 65710 E. Desert Trail Dr., Tucson, AZ 85737
Lapinier, Major Arnold, AUS5893 Grove Rd., Trumansburg, NY 14886
Larkin, MajGen Richard, USA1517 Night Shade Ct., Vienna, VA 22180
Laroche, Richard, 150 Sportsmans Dr., West Lakes, SA 5021, Australia
Larsen, Harold A., 1314 Kurtz Rd., McLean, VA 22102
Larson, Ms. Florence, 5903 Mt. Eagle Dr., No 601, Alexandria, VA 22303
Larum, Norman, 3225 Eldora Ln., Missoula, MT 59803
Larzelier, Henry, 16903 Kilwinning, Houston, TX 77084
Lascaris, Constant, P.O. Box 3172, Clearwater, FL 34630
Laster, Clarence C., 10915 Burr Oak, San Antonio, TX 78230
Latzen, Capt. Murray, 57-45 74th St., Unit 309, Elmhurst, NY 11373
Laub, Charles, 949 S. Hope St., Suite 3030, Los Angeles, CA 90015
Laufman, David, 9303 Sibelius Dr., Vienna, VA 22182
Law, Richard, 9713 Ceralene Dr., Fairfax, VA 22032
Law, Major Robert S., AUS472 Argyle Rd., Brooklyn, Ny 11218
Lawton, Edward F., 4865 Carriagepark Rd., Fairfax, VA 22032
Layton, LtCol Benjamin, USA10700 Brunswick Ave., Kensington, MD 20895
Lazar, Charna, 501 NW 7th St., Boca Raton, FL 33432
Leader, John L., 5052 Westpath Terrace, Bethesda, MD 20816
Leaf, Edward121 N., Chestnut St., Lindsborg, KS 67456
Learnard, Edwin, 1010 16th Ave., No 6, San Diego, CA 92101
Leary, William, Dept. of History, University of Georgia, Athens, GA 30602
Leavitt, John H., P.O. Box 1182, Wellfleet, MA 02667
Leavitt, Robert W., 7129 Rolling Forest Ave., Springfield, VA 22152
Ledoux, Sylvester P., 1106 Main St., No 5, Buffalo, NY 14209
Lee, Mrs. Barbara, P.O. Box 137, Harwichport, MA 02646
Lee, Bruce115 E., 67th St., New York, NY 10028
Lee, John F., 2010 Meadow Springs Dr., Vienna, VA 22182
Lee, Terence M., 1480 Garfield Ave., San Marino, CA 91108
Lee, Col Thomas, USAF9605 Atwood Rd., Vienna, VA 22182
Lefebre, Albert, 36 Sea Spray Dr., Biddeford, ME 04005

Lefkowitz, Alan, 2488 Mt. Royal Rd., Pittsburgh, PA 15217
LeGallo, Andre, 2 Bridgeberry Ct., The Woodlands, TX 77381
Lehman, Frederick J., 3706 E. 3rd St., No 1, Dayton, OH 45403
Leibacher, Ernst, 1931 Park Skyline Rd., Santa Ana, CA 92705
Leifer, Capt N. David, USARP.O. Box 960748, Miami, FL 33296
Leighton, Ms. Marian, 2081 Wethersfield Ct., Reston, VA 22091
Lelesz, Spec George, USAP.O. Box 670881, Brink, NY 10467
Lengel, Capt John, 8451 Stafford Dr., Strongsville, OH 44136
Lennox, Cdr Alexander, USN324 Devonshire Ln., Orange Park, FL 332073
Lentol, Edward S., 107-43 113th St., Richmond Hill, NY 11419
Leonard, Col Eugene, USARP.O. Box 501, Lexington, VA 24450
Leusner, James, 5471 Lake Howell Rd., No 106, Winter Park, FL 32792
Leven, Barry K., 5665 Phelps Luck Dr., Columbia, MD 21045
Leveridge, William, 9409 Shouse Dr., Vienna, VA 22181
Levin, Mrs. Elizabeth, 10420 Royal Rd., Hillandale, MD 20903
Levin, M.J., 10420 Royal Rd., Hillandale, MD 20903
Levy, Frank, 6504 Smoot Dr., McLean, VA 22101
Lewis, Ernest A., 3720 SE 1st Place, Cape Coral, FL 33904
Lewis, Orme, 100 West Washington St., Phoenix, AZ 85003
Lewis, Stanton ,2447 NCNB Center, Houston, TX 77002
Lewton, Lewis, 28131 Coolidge Dr., Euclid, OH 44132
Librandi, Frank J., 3723 W. Grovers Ave., Glendale, AZ 85308
Lieberman, Dr. Alan, 18425 Long Lake Dr., Boca Raton, FL 33434
Lincoln, PNCS Charles, USN300 E. Evergreen Ave., Philadelphia, PA 19118
Lindenauer, S/A Julian, 12975 SW 186th Terrace, Miami, FL 33177
Lindsley Winston J., 4913 Tydfil Ct., Fairfax, VA 22030
Linn, Mrs. Betty, 3130 Duke St., Alexandria, VA 22314
Linton, Mrs. Jean, 5216 Farrington Rd., Bethesda, MD 20816
Lipton, Maurice, 611 John Marshall Dr., NE, Vienna, VA 22180
Liskey, Russell, 1230 Kings Tree Dr., Michelville, MD 20721
Liszka, Dr. Victor, 12171 Fort Caroline Rd., Jacksonville, FL 32225
Literento, Anthony, 1304 57th St.West, Bradenton, FL 34209
Littig, Cdr Gerald, USNR2511 Lomond Dr., Kalamazoo, MI 49008
Little, Arthur F., 9718 St. Andrews Dr., Fairfax, VA 22030
Little, Warren, P.O. Box 8127. Missoula, MT 59807
Lium, Elli, 3806 49th St., NW, Washington, DC 20016
Livingston, James, 804 Greenwood Rd., Wilmington, DE 19807
Livingston, Robert G., 3415 Raymond St., Chevy Chase, MD 70815
Lock, Owen, 2 Gary Ct., Holmdel, NJ 07733
Loeb, James, 2 Sutton Place South, No 15D, New York, NY 10022
Loehr, Major Rodney, USAR8106 Highwood Dr., No Y 321, Bloomington, MN 55438
Loesche, Paul, 301 Plantation Dr., Bent Creek Plantation, Lexington, SC 29072
Loeser, Paul, 3310 N. Leisure World Blvd., No 1025, Silver Spring, MD 20906
Loesere, Ms. Antoinette, USA5422 Long Boat Ct., Fairfax, VA 22032
Loftin, William, 12509 Millstream Dr., Bowie, MD 20715
Logan, Major Glenn, USARP.O. Box 6268, Colorado Springs, CO 80934
Lograsso, Peter P., 12220 Blanchester Dr., Lyndhurst, OH 44124
Long, Richard, 1615 Evers Dr., McLean, VA 22101
Longanecker, MajGen W., USAF5653 Rayburn Ave., Alexandria, VA 22311
Loomis, Capt Robert, USN1418 Independence Ave., Melbourne BVeach, FL 32940
Looney, John R., 9122 St. Andrews Pl., College Park, MD 20740
Loosararian, Armen, 10703 Edgewood Ave., Silver Spring, MD 20901
Lopez, John, 2315 MacDonough Rd., Wilmington, DE 19805
Lore, Nicholas, 5429 Honors Dr., San Diego, CA 92122
Loucopolos, Tom, 29 Brookside Pl., Livingston, NJ 07039
Louie, Henry, 11420 Bedfordshire Ave., Potomac, MD 20854
Love, LtCol Gale AUS11596 Lower Circle Dr., Grass Valley, CA 95949
Lovorovich, Chris, 3669 Ireland Dr., Indianapolis, IN 46236
Lowe, LtCol Darrell, USMC1432 Buckner Rd., Valrico, FL 33594
Lower, Michael, 6214 Amberwood Dr., Alta Loma, CA 91707
Lucas, Floyd, 2011 12th St., NW, Hickory, NC 28601
Lucas, Harry Jr., P.O. Box 56467, Houston, TX 77256
Ludewig, Walter, 120 Mashodack Rd., Nassau, NY 12123
Lugar, Richard, 7841 Old Dominion Dr., McLean, VA 22102

Lumovich, LtCol Victor, USAF7401 Churchill Rd., McLean, VA 22101
Luntzel, Major James, USAF18962 Symeron Rd., Apple Valley, CA 922307
Lupsha, Peter, 617 Dartmouth NE, Albuquerque, NM 87106
Lusby, David, 1937 S. Abrego Dr., Green Valley, AZ 85614
Luthy, Raymond, 2825 Royal Ann Ln., Concord, CA 94518
Lyles, Bobby Neal, 2496 Orchid Bay Dr., No 204, Naples, FL 33942
Lyman, Mrs. Dorothy, 3300 Ocean Shore Ave., No 502, Virginia Beach, VA 23451
Lynch, David, 14512 Chesterfield Rd., Rockville, MD 20853
Lynch, Ray, 100 Maple Ln., Annapolis, MD 21403
Lyons, Kenneth, 9372 Avery Rd., Broadview Heights, OH 44147

– M –

Macartney, John, 2119 O St., NW, Washington, DC 20037
MacCormack, Robin, P.O. Box 15573, Boston, MA 02215
Maciel, Joseph, 1992 Jack Rabbit Ln., New Bern, NC 28562
MacKenzie, John, 2150 Gulf Shore Blvd, N, Naples, FL 33940
Mackie, Major Thomas, AUS77 W. Washington St., Rm 1518, Chicago, IL 60602
McKinnon, Colin, 1724 N. Quebec St., Arlington, VA 22207
MacMillian, Ronald, 19 Laurelwood Ct., San Rafael, CA 944901
MacMullen, Col Douglas, USAP.O. Box 5201, Sherman Oaks, CA 91413
Macones, Mrs. Dorothy, 20151 Laurel Hill Way, Churchill, Germantown, MD 20874
MacPhee, Keith, 406 14th Ave., NE, St. Petersburg, FL 33701
MacVane, Matthew, 99SW 14th Ave., Boca Raton, FL 334432
Madigan, Col John, USA7647 Tiverton Dr., Springfield, VA 22152
Madigan, Mrs. Mary, 1410 Alban Ave., Tallahassee, FL 32301
Maechling, Charles, 3403 Lowell St., NW, Washington, DC 2016
Magill, Francis, 3564 Reynolds Rd., Douglasville, GA 30135
Magnusson, Warren, 1608 East Ave., McLean, VA 22101
Mahlman, Robert, 20 Sunset Dr., Orono, ME 04473
Mahoney, Harry, 1110 Shady Ln., Wheaton, IL 60187
Mahoney, Timothy, 24 Yarmouth Rd., Chatham Township, NJ 07928
Main, Frederick, 4723 Garfield Ln., La Mesa, CA 92041
Mainardi, Mrs. Marilyn, 1402 ½ Central Ave., No 305, Evanston, IL 60201
Maire, Joseph, 47783 Fathom Pl., Sterling, VA 20165
Major, David, 1516 Stoneleigh Ct., Huntingtown, MD 20639
Maki, Arnold, 2005 Lancecrest Dr., Garland, TX 75044
Malec, Andrew, 2107 Jefferson Ave., St.Paul, MN 55105
Mallon, Capt Harry, USNR1113 Overbrook Dr., Ormond Beach, FL 32074
Mallory, George, 5148 Shorewood Dr., Dunkirk, NY 14048
Malmquest, Carl, 2425 Constitution Blvd., Sarasota, FL 34231
Maltenfort, Martin, 10952 A Roebelini Palm Ct., Boynton Beach, FL 33437
Manchester, Col B.B., USMCRR1, Box 1176, Hayes, VA 23072
Mandigo, Guy C., P.O. Box 6013, MacDill AFB, FL 33608
Mansi, LtCdr Leon, USN319 Harrisburg Dr., Encinitas, CA 92024
Manthorpe, William, 12707 River Rd., Potomac, MD 20854
Manwearing, LtCdr James, USNR3 Kenilworth Dr., West, Stamford, CT 06902
Marelius, Donald C., 7364 Player Dr., San Diego, CA 92119
Marini, Frank, 42 Church St., Hudson, MA 01749
Marini, Laura, 3340 W. 57th St., No 5E, New York, NY 10019
Mark, David, 4800 Trail Crest Circle, Austin, TX 78735
Markarian, MajGen Ronald, USA8547 N. Calavaras, Fresno, CA 93711
Markovic, Cedomir, 3111 N 20th St., No C-211, Arlington, VA 22201
Marks, Henry, 5029 Bonadventure Ct., Cincinatti, OH 45238
Markulis, Thomas, 202 4th Ave., SE, Glen Burnie, MD 21061
Marling, George, 2626 Meridith Dr., Vienna, VA 22180
Marocchi, RAdm John, USNP.O. Box 229, Sperryville, VA 22740
Marscelli, Frank, 429 Willow Dr., Greensburg, PA 15601
Marsh, Charles, 1254 NE 39th Rd., Ocala, FL 34470
Marshall, Brian, 5304 Albermarle St., Bethesda, MD 20816
Marshall, John, Box 436, Overlook Dr., Drum Point, Lusby, MD 20657
Marshall, Walter, 31 Durham St., Nashua, NH 03063
Martel, Sinclair, 6702 Bowie Dr., Springfield, VA 22150
Martin, Capt Barney, USNP.O. Box 2589, Rancho Santa Fe, CA 92067
Martin, Dr. Carlos, 73290 NW 3rd St., Miami, FL 33126

Martin, Charles, 9626 Blackbrook Rd., Mentor, OH 44060
Martin, Col Edgar, AUS922 26th Pl., South, Arlington, VA 22202
Martin, Ms. Marjorie, 230 Broadway Village Dr., Columbia, MO 65201
Martin, Peter, Chateau de Monplan, Valprionde, 46800 Montcuq, France
Martin, Robert, 2014 Wolftrap Oaks Ct., Vienna, VA 22182
Martin, LtCol William, AUS63031 Moonstone Ln., Bend, OR 97701
Martines, Lawrence J., P.O. Box 11673, Pueblo, CO 81001
Marvin, James, 109 Glenview Ave., Wyncote, PA 19095
Mason, Christopher ,P.O. Box 25765, Arlington, VA 22313
Mason, Frederick, 2440 Virginia Ave., NW, N D 501, Washington, DC 20037
Mason, Harold, 435 West St., NW, Vienna, VA 22180
Mastrovito, James, 7120 Aztec Rd., NE., Albuquerque, NM 87110
Matanky, Arnie, 1920 N. Clark St., No 6B, Chicago, IL 60614
Matheny, Mr. Ruth, 3760 Comet Dr., Lake Havasu City, AZ 86403
Mathews, Jack, P.O. Box 40507, Santa Barbara, CA 93140
Mathisen, Arthur, 3724 Calliandra Dr., Sarasota, FL 34232
Mattas, Dr. Barbara, 2021 Mock Orange Ct., Reston, VA 22091
Matthewson, Quinn, 1513 Hillsmont Dr., El Cajon, CA 92020
Mattison, Mrs. Alma, 9212 Cedar Way, Bethesda, MD 20814
Mattison, Dr. James, 234 San Miguel Ave., Salinas, CA 93901
Maxwell, Donald, PSC 2, Box 6618, APO, AE 09012
May, Christopher, 4516 38th St., NW, Washington, DC 20016
May, Major Donald, USAF4017 107th St., West, Leona Valley, CA 93551
May, Col Lynwood, USAFR10228 Leslie St., Silver Spring, MD 20902
Mayer, Luke, 1007 N. Pitt St., Alexandria, VA 22314
Mayhew, Mrs. Mary, RR 7, Box 124 BB, Santa Fe, NM 87505
Mayhew, Robert, RR 7, Box 124 BB, Santa Fe, NM 87505
Mazzocco, William, 5403 Newington Rd., Bethesda, MD 20816
McAllan, Col James, USA3804 Whispering Ln., Falls Church, VA 22041
McAllister, Major Robert, USAF3800 N. Fairfax Sr., No 211, Arlington, VA 22203
McAniff, Edward, 3315 San Pasqual St., Pasadena, CA 91107
McBride, Maurice, 15067 Meadow Oak, Salinas, CA 93907
McBride, CMSgt Richard, USAF660 East First Place, Mesa, AZ 85203
McCabe, Ward, 935 Eden Ave., San Jose, CA 95117
McCaddon, Jeff, 1099 Gainard St., Crescent City, CA 95331
McCaffrey, Daniel, 17 Melant Dr., Orchard Park, NY 14127
McCann, John, P.O. Box 4882, Poughkeepsie, NY 12602
McCarthy, Charles, 11 Bayberry Ln., Beverly, MA 01915
McCarthy, Ms. Dorothy, 15111 Glade Dr., No 3F, Silver Spring, MD 20906
McCarthy, Mrs. Melba, 6501 Allview Dr., Columbia, MD 21046
McCarthy, Richard, 530 East 23rd St., No 11 B, New York, NY 10010
McCarthy, Roger, 2054 Sutton Way, Henderson, NV 89014
McCarthy, William, 59 Topaz Way, San Francisco, CA 94131
McCausland, Mrs. Mary, 8014 Greeley Blvd., Springfield, VA 22152
McClellan, George, 5000 Olde Mill Dr., Marietta, GA 30066
McClintick, LtCol Robert, USAF2723 Vanderbilt Ln., No 18, Redondo Beach, CA 90278
McConkey, Harry, 3553 Lum Ave., Kingman, AZ 86401
McConnell, Donald, 4211 Howard, No 3, Los Alamitos, CA 90720
McConnell, Col John, USAF11313 Cromwell Ct., Woodbridge, VA 22192
McConnell, Col Robert, USAF823 S. Columbus St., Alexandria, VA 22314
McConnon, B.Ray, 6464 Woodridge Rd., Alexandria, VA 22312
McCord, Howard, 16035 Placer Hills Rd., No B, Meadow Vista, CA 22312
McCord, James, P.O. Box 780131, San Antonio, TX 78278
McCormick, Ms. Maureen, 107 S. West St., No 257, Alexandria, VA 22314
McCoy, Tidal, 330 Chesapeake Dr., Great Falls, VA 22066
McCrary, Col Thomas, USA975 Great Street Circle, Gainesville, GA 30501
McDonald, Gilman, 207 South Pitt St., Alexandria, VA 22314
McDonald, Capt Richard, USN16017 Malcom Dr., Laurel, MD 20707
McDowell, RAdm Don, USN7206 Pinehurst Pkway, Chevy Chase, MD 20815
McElroy, Walter, 1672 Jupiter Rd., Venice, FL 34293
McFarlin, Mark D., 21134 Woodland Green Dr., Katy, TX 77449
McGarry, LtCol William, AUS1421 Lehia St., Honolulu, HI 96818
McGettigan, Edward, 2105 King Garden Way, Falls Church, VA 22043
McGinley, BrigGen Donald, USAF5229 Melody Ln., Willoughby, OH 44094

McGinnis, Neal, 631 De Sales St., San Gabriel, CA 91775
McGinnis, William, 700 S. Gondola Dr., Venice, FL 34293
McGlade, Joseph, 7141 Pelican Island Dr., Tampa, FL 33634
McGrath, Edward, 10201 Cedar Pond Dr., Vienna, VA 22180
McGraw Thomas, 9034 Ashmede Dr., Fairfax, VA 22032
McGreenery, William, 21 Bradford Rd., Box 587, East Dennis, MA 02461
McGregor, LtCol Alexander, USA9705 Ladbrook Way, Fairfax, VA 22032
McGuiness, Thomas, 41 Homestead Ave., Garden City, NY 11530
McGuire, James, 4912 North 26th St., Arlington, VA 22207
McGuire, John F., 2412 59th Pl., Cheverly, MD 20785
McHale, Dr. Vincent, 3070 Coleridge Rd., Cleveland Heights, OH 44118
McIntosh, Mrs. Elizabeth, 42485 Cochi an Mill Rd., Leesburg, VA 22075
McKeon, Thomas, 11012 Earlsgate Ln., Rockville, MD 20852
McKnight, Capt Phillip, USN309 Yoakum Parkway, No 1515, Alexandria, VA 22304
McLeod, Karl B., P.O. Box 218, Boling, TX 77420
McMahon, Edward, 31 Commodore Ln., East Falmouth, MA 12536
McMahon, James, 10301 NW 16th Ct., Plantation, FL 33322
McMahon, John, 2355 Friars Ln., Los Altos, CA 94024
McManus, Doyle, Los Angeles Times, Times Mirror Square, Los Angeles, CA 90053
McManus, Joseph, 100 Chinquapin Circle, Columbia, SC 29212
McMichael, LtCol George, USAF8333 Seminole Blvd., No 253, Seminole, FL 34642
McMichael, John, 10346 S. Horizon View, Morrison, CO 80465
McMillan, Patrick, P.O. Box 9612, Las Vegas, NV 89193
McNabb, Col David, 903 Setter Ct., Seffner, FL 33584
McNamara, Francis, 8040 Cindy Ln., Bethesda, MD 220817
McRae, John, 258 Fox Meadow Rd., Scarsdale, NY 10583
McTigue, William, 1510 Haviland Pl., Frederick, MD 221701
Measley, Wilbur, 72 Dawn Dr., Mount Holly, NJ 08060
Meanen, John, RR1, Box 269, Keene, NH 03431
Medigovich, William, 2227 Laguna Vista Dr., Novato, CA 94945
Medina, Thomas, 4937 Fairhaven Way, Roswell, GA 30075
Meese, Norman, 110 N. Hampton Ct., Sanford, FL 32773
Meghdadi, Freeman, 1630 Calle Vaquero No 403, Glendale, CA 91206
Mehl, Ralph E., 21 Lipscomb Ct., Sterling, VA 20165
Mehosky, Col Edward, USAP.O. Box 757, Solomons, MD 20688
Meisenheimer, Daniel, 404 Longmeadow Rd., Orange, CT 06477
Meisinger, H. Peter, 8618 Wolftrap Rd., Vienna, VA 22180
Mellen, James, N 5004 Madison, Spokane, WA 99205
Melli, Rev. Richard, 20253 Twin Oaks Rd., Spring Hill, FL 34610
Melton, H. Keith, P.O. Box 5755, Bossier City, LA 71171
Mendez, Orlando, P.O. Box 34574, Las Vegas, NV 89133
Mendoza, Ms. Ethel, 915 Hathaway Rd., No 306, New Bedford, MA 02740
Mercer, Dudley, 2734 N. Yucatan St., Arlington, VA 22213
Mercill, Alan, 802 S. Oakland St., Arlington, VA 22204
Merkel, Peter, 5001 King Richard Dr., Annandale, VA 22003
Merritt, Mark, 7211 Normandy Ln., Falls Church, VA 22042
Mertz, John, 458 Norma Ct., Punta Gorda, FL 33950
Merz, Ms. Mary Frances, 2800 Woodley Rd., NW, No 130, Washington, DC 20008
Merz, Robert, 1182 N. Reed Ave., Reedley, CA 93654
Mescall, Patrick N., 150-22 21st Ave., Whitestone, NY 11357
Meserve, Edward, 532 Broxburn Ave., Tampa, FL 33617
Mesick, Ms. Charlotte, 5922 N. Placita del Conde, Tucson, AZ 85718
Meyer, Frad, 3600 Jeanetta Rd., No 901, Houston, TX 77063
Meyer, John H., 1900 Allanwood Pl., Silver Spring, MD 20906
Meyers, Charles, 1400 McHaney St., Eldorado, IL 62930
Micara, Capt Francis, USN2545 S. Atlantic Ave., No 1808, Daytona Beach Shores, FL 32118
Middleton, Dr. James, 1230 Leslie Lane., Des Plaines, IL 60018
Mihelic, Randall, 2011 San Jose Ave., Las Vegas, NV 889104
Mikulecky, Col Richard, USAFR127 West 18th St., Lombard, IL 60148
Miler, Newton, 18 Loblolly Trail., Hampstead, NC 28443
Milich, Wallace, 28 Roxbury Rd., Port Washington, NY 11050
Miller, James, 2810-K Carriage Dr., Winston Salem, NC 27106
Miller, Mrs. John S., 850 Hamilton St., Alcoa, TN 37701
Miller, Mitchell, 1166 Point View St., Los Angeles, CA 90035

Miller, Stan, P.O. Box 3481, Evergreen, CO 80439
Millian, Kenneth, 3527 Winfield Ln., NW, Washington, DC 20007
Milligan, LtCol Edward, USARP.O. Box 25765, Alexandria, VA 22313
Millis, John, 1652 Oak Spring Way, Reston, VA 22090
Mills, Col Francis, USA3729 Acosta Rd., Fairfax, VA 22031
Millson, Col Chris, USAF516 Fox Hunt Circle, Highlands Ranch, CO 80126
Milton, Donald, Overlook at Skunks Misery, Locust Valley, NY 11560
Minihan, Col Daniel USA2222 Fuller Rd., No 1015 A, Ann Arbor, MI 48105
Minnick, Wendell, 427 South 31st St., Terre Haute, IN 47803
Minogue, James, RR1, Box 126A, Bentonville, VA 22610
Mintz, Col Ronald, USAF4917 Ravenswood Dr., No 1214, San Antonio, TX 78227
Miscavige, David, 6331 Hollywood Blvd., Los Angeles, CA 90028
Miskovsky, Milan C., 5500 Chevy Chase Pkw., NW, Washington, DC 20015
Mistler, J.D., 2775 Mansway Dr., Herndon, VA 22071
Mitchell, Bruce, 400 Montgomery St., No 1002, San Francisco, CA 94104
Mitchell, Elizabeth, 6113 Hillcrest Rd., Cary, IL 60013
Mitchell, Capt John, USN35 Mayfair Dr., Westwood, MA 02090
Mitchell, Dr. William, 6202 Winston Dr., Bethesda, MD 20817
Moberly, Hayden, 7106 McKamy Blvd., Dallas, TX 75248
Moeller, James, 18 Edgebrook-Peck Rd., Kirkville, NY 13082
Mogen, Philip, 1705 Pedregoso Pl, SE, Albuquerque, NM 87123
Mogus, Jack N., 9532 Whitecedar Ct., Vienna, VA 22181
Monahan, James, 4321 East Mercer Way, Mercer Island, WA 98040
Monahan, Stephen, 228 S. Main St., Burlington, CT 06013
Mondani, Eugene, 3024 West Springlake Circle, Colorado Springs, CO 80906
Mongno, LtCol Thomas, USAF5515 Camino Vista, Yorba Linda, CA 92686
Montague, Capt Lloyd, USN8623 Chantily Ave., San Diego, CA 92123
Montecino, Allen J., 6060 Burnside Landing Dr., Burke, VA 22015
Montgomery, Philip, 9 Edgewater Dr., Old Greenwich, CT 06870
Montgomery, Stephen, 421 West Main St., Fredericksburg, TX 78624
Moody, Mrs. Juanita M., P.O. Box 416, Murrells Inlet, SC 29555576
Moody, Ms. Margaret, 3440 S. Jefferson St., No 1227, Falls Church, VA 220241
Moon, Thomas, 2604 E. Washington, Orange, CA 92669
Mooney, E. Brooke, 1417 E. Abingdon Dr., No 3, Alexandria, VA 22314
Moore, Col Lloyd T., USAF1023 Chestnut Hill Dr., Erie, PA 16509
Moore, MajGen William, USA8424 Weller Ave., McLean, VA 22102
Moos, Stanley, 814 W. Chula Vista Rd., Tucson, AZ 85704
Moravek, B.J., 520 Senate Hart Bldg., Washington, DC 20501
Morehouse, Ms. Maureen, 1413 Belleview Blvd., No B1, Alexandria, VA 22307
Morgan, Francis, 196 Lancelot Way, Lawrenceville, GA 30245
Morgan, Ray, 6815 Flint St., Shawnee Mission, KS 66203
Morgan, Russell, 4144 Center Gate Blvd., Sarasota, FL 34233
Morgan, LtCdr William, USN1169 Laurel Loop NE, Albuquerque, NM 87122
Morgenroth, Herbert, 2428 Sherbroke Ct., NE, Atlanta, GA 30345
Morinelli, Joseph, 901 Fairfax Rd., Drexel Hill, PA 19026
Moritz, Milton, 7723 Avondale Terrace, Harrisburg, PA 17112
Moriyama, Col Charles, USAR95-100 Mahuli Pl., Miliani, HI 96789
Morrell, David, 642 Camino Lejo, Santa Fe, NM 87501
Morris, Anthony, 2412 N. Madison St., Arlington, VA 22205
Morris, C. Carson, 5392 Brunswick Ln., Broad Run, VA 22014
Morris, Capt C. Ward, USN5915 Reservoir Heights Ave., Alexandria, VA 22311
Morris, Donald, P.O. Box 271667, Houston, TX 77277
Morris, Jack, P.O. Box 1327, Loomis, CA 95650
Morrison, MajGen John, USAF3471 Constellation Dr., Davidsonville, MD 21035
Morrison, Roland, 45-123 Mahalani Circle, Kaneohe, HI 96744
Morrison, Capt Vance, USN3120 McGeorge Terrace, Alexandria, VA 22309
Moses, Dr. Elbert, 2001 Rocky Dells Dr., Prescott, AZ 86303
Moskowitz, Jerome, 3215 Chrisland Dr., Annapolis, MD 221403
Mossotti, Louis, 989 Orchard Lakes, Creve Cour, MO 63146
Mott, RAdm William, USN9 Dogwood Ln. N., Charlottesville, VA 22903
Mosseau, Wilfred, 5240 Cronan Rd., Sheboygan, MI 49721
Mower, Jack, 4436 48th St., NW, Washington, DC 20016
Moy, Robert S., 2934 North 22nd Pl., Phoenix, AZ 85016
Mueller, James, 9028 Greylock, Alexandria, VA 22308

Muhoray, Cornel, 279920 Osborn Rd., Bay Village, OH 44140
Mula, S. James IV, P.O. Box 61001, Denver, CO 80206
Mulcahy, Donald, 4631 Denpat Ct., Annandale, VA 22003
Mullady, Mrs. Elizaeth, 3300 Juniper Way, Falls Church, VA 22044
Mullan, William, 80706 E. Lavender Dr., Gold Canyon, AZ 85219
Mulledy, William H., 3 Willow Oak Rd., Hilton Head Island, SC 29928
Muntz, Ms. M. Lucille, 550 N St., SW, No S-301, Washington, DC 20024
Muratti, LtCol Jose, USA316 Rossi-Baldrich, Hato Rey, PR 00918
Murchison, R. Bruce, 242 Rimpau Blvd, South, Los Angeles, CA 90004
Murphy, David E., 40 Ocean Dr., Punta Gorda, FL 33950
Murphy, George, 7702 Maryknoll Ave., Bethesda, MD 20817
Murray, Graham, 4423 SE 14th Pl., Cape Coral, FL 33904
Murray, Dr. Kent, 608 Forest Blvd., Hastings, NE 68901
Murray, Dr. Paul, P.O. Box 1117, Centerville, MA 02632
Murray, Dr. Thomas H., 2915 No. 27th St., Arlington, VA 22207
Murtha, Bruce, 17 Kelly Ln., Granby, CT 06035
Murtha, Col Edmund, AUS410 Linwood Ave., Bel Air, MD 21014
Musladin, LtCol William, USAF838 Commons Dr., Sacramento, CA 95825
Mutzig, Andy, 4321 Springbranch Dr., Fort Worth, TX 76116
Myers, Major Charles, USA1520 Stage Coach Ln., SE, Albuquerque, NM 87123
    – N –
Nadler, S.I., 4820 Linnean Ave., NW, Washington, DC 20008
Naftali, Tim, Yale University, New Haven, CT 06520
Naftzinger, Col Joseph, USA104 Surf View Dr., No 1401, Palm Coast, FL 32137
Nagle, Capt Frederick, USARR3, Box 4, Old Post Rd., Bedford, NY 10506
Nall, Julian, 4631 N. 27th St., Arlington, VA 22207
Nashold, Dr. James, 1819 Glendale Ave., Durham, NC 27701
Natsios, Nicholas, 77 Liincoln Parkway, Lowell, MA 01851
Nebel, Robert, P.O. Box 94, Clarksburg, NJ 08510
Neff, Paul, 2111 Jefferson Davis Hiway, No 1105 South, Arlington, VA 22201
Nelsen, Dr. Harvey, 2410 Vandervort Rd., Lutz, Fl 33549
Nelson, Robert, 537 E. 36th St., Erie, PA 16504
Ness, Gordon, 824 Winslow, No 253, Redwood City, CA 94063
Neumann, Warren, P.O. Box 584, Englewood, NJ 07631
New, James, 27 Farm Haven Ct., Rockville, MD 20852
Newcomb, Norton, 215 N. Woodlawn Ave., Decatur, IL 62522
Newdeck, Frank, 4004 Francine Dr., Hatboro, PA 19040
Newell, Richard, 6212 N 35th St., Arlington, VA 22213
Newsham, Mrs. Richard, 7401 Rebecca Dr., Alexandria, VA 22307
Newton, Ms. Betty Jane, 3618 Villa Verde Rd., No 125, Dallas, TX 75234
Newton, Donald, RR2, Box 343, St. Alabans, VT 05478
Nichols, MajGen Stephen, USAP.O. Box 146, West Buxton, ME 04093
Nicholson, Col Robert, USAF11370 Ethan Ct., Issue, MD 20645
Nielsen, Capt Don, USNRR1, Box 464, Huntly, VA 22640
Nielsen, John, 1005 S. Columbus St., Arlington, VA 22204
Nihart, Col F.B., USMC6208 Kellogg Dr., McLean, VA 22101
Noble, Armond, 2509 Donner Way, Sacramento, CA 95818
Nobles, Major Ellsworth, USMC1321 Eastside Highway, Corvallis, MT 59828
Nolan, James E., P.O. Box 765, Mt. Jackson, VA 22842
Nolan, John A. III, 9629 Waldrop Dr., SE, Huntsville, AL 35803
Nolan, W. Robert, 18 Woodbury Way, Fairport, NY 14450
Norland, Seimer, 3310 N. Leisure World Blvd., No 926, Silver Spring, MD 20906
Northam, Col William, F.USA229 West lake Faith Dr., Maitland, FL 32751
Norton, George, 177 Riverbrook Ave., Lincroft, NJ 07738
Norton, Maurice, 6453 N. College Ave., Oklahoma City, OK 73132
Norton, William, 16-B Mallard St., Lakehurst, NJ 08733
Norwood, Billy T., 7209 16th St., NW, Washington, DC 20012
Nottingham, Milton, 4849 Upton St., NW, Washington, DC 20016
Noukas, John, P.O. Box 1963, Houston, TX 77251
Nousen, Douglas, P.O. Box 30383, Richland, WA 99352
Novak, Robert, 7249 Reservoir Rd., Springfield, VA 22150
Nugent, Col Robert, USAF1838 W. Camino Urbaano, Green Valley, AZ 85614
Nuthall, Jane Hoerrner, 5 Eagle Circle, Brervard, NC 28712

– O –

O'Brien, Francis X., 934 S. Artery, No 206, Quincy, MA 02169
O'Brien, Thomas, 121 Edge Hill, Sherwood Forest, MD 21405
O'Connell, Edward, 2016 Westwood Terrace, Vienna, VA 22180
O'Connell, Kevin, 516 San Vincente Blvd., No 105, Santa Monica, CA 90402
O'Connor, David, 150 St. Botolph St., No 36, Boston, MA 02166
O'Connor, Francis X., 9055 Moving Water Lane, Columbia, MD 21046
O'Connor, Jeremiah, 69 Taylor St., Qunicy, MA 02170
O'Connor, John, 23 Waterville St., North Grafton, MA 01536
O'Connor, Kathleen, 2539 27th Ave., San Francisco, CA 94116
O'Connor, Robert, 4 Dartmouth Dr., Framingham, MA 01701
O'Donnell, James, 61C St. Andrews Blvd., Clifton, NJ 07012
O'Donnell, Msgr William, 2665 Woodley Rd., NW, Washington, DC 20008
O'Donovan, Major Brendan, USAF5615 Wyoming Blvd., NE, Albuquerque, NM 87109
O'Keefe, E. Stephan, 2770 Westchester Dr. S., Clearwater, FL 34621
O'Mallley, Edward, 706 Peggy Stewart Ct., Davidsonville, MD 21035
O'Neil, Robert, 248 Pine Branch Circle, Columbus, GA 31909
O'Neill John J., 2624 N. 2nd Rd., Arlington, VA 22201
O'Rourke, Major Daniel, USAFRBox 878, Fort Walton Beach, FL 32549
O'Shea, Cornelius, 9628 Hillock Ct., Burke, VA 22015
Obucina, Joseph, 680 South Lake Sybelia Dr., Maitland, FL 332751
Offenbacher, Rosmarie, 560 S. Brevard Ave., No 631, Cocoa Beach, FL 32931
Oftedahl, Douglas, P.O. Box 13, Westminister Station, VT 05159
Oldchurch, LtCol Gerald, AUSP.O. Box 8722, Tucson, AZ 85738
Oleson, Peter, 12109 Beaver Creek Rd., Clifton, VA 22024
Olveira, Sinval, 2917 Devil's Tower, El Paso, TX 79904
Olson, Robert, Barter's Island, Trevett, ME 04571
Olson, Frederick, 3979 Burning Bush Ct., Fairfax, VA 22033
Olson, James, 311 Crescent Dr., Sheridan, WY 82801
Oney, Earnest, 28 Peyton St., Winchester, MA 22601
Oostmeyer, Paul A., 305 207th Ave., NE, Redmond, WA 98053
Opdahl, LtCol O., USAF9131 Olive Ln., Sun Lake, AZ 85224
Opper, Clifford, 1515 22nd St., S. Arlington, VA 22202
Ord, Marian, 2540 Massachusetts Ave., NW Washington, DC 20008
Orr, Irene, 339 N. Wood St., Mahopac, NY 10541
Ortiz, Horacio, 4170 Monaco Dr., Corpus Christi, TX 78411
Ostensoe, Omer, 7123 Thrasher Rd., McLean, VA 22101
Otepka, Otto, 4229 SE 19th Pl., No 2B, Cape Coral, FL 33904
Otomo, John H., 1528 Mill St., Selma, CA 93662
Otstot, Charles, 5124 North 33rd St., Arlington, VA 22207
Owen, William, 20-203 Plantation Dr., Vero Beach, FL 32966
Owens, John P., 519 South 10th St., Elkhart, IN 46516

– P –

Pacalo, Capt.Patrick, USAR4787 West 130th St.No 204, Cleveland, OH 44135
Page, William, 1718 Woodridge Dr., Abilene, TX 79605
Page, William R., P.O. Box 556, Rio Grande City, TX 78582
Painter, Robert, 10304 Pierce Dr., Silver Spring, MD 20901
Paladino, LtCol Vito, USAP.O. Box 268, Newfield, NJ 08344
Palevich, John E., 6200 Swords Way, Bethesda, MD 20817
Palmer, Richard O., 652 Main St., Harwich Port, MA 02646
Palumbo, Carl J., 7142 Swift Run Trails, Fairfax Station, VA 22039
Palumbo, Louis F., 7980 N. Biscayne Point Cir., Miami Beach, FL 33141
Pamplin, Mrs. Jack C., 300 Westminster-Canterbury Dr.,Winchester, VA 22603
Panek, John R., 6137 Monlaco Road ,Long Beach, CA 90808
Pangburn, Gerold W., RR 7 Box 249, Staunton,VA 24401
Papich, Sam J., 4908 General Hodges NE, Albuquerque, NM 871 11
Pappas, Tommy, 26-09 24th Avenue, Astoria, NY 11102
Parcher, Capt Stuart M., USN 1115 Fallsmead Way, Rockville, MD 20854
Parker, Col Franklin Jr., USA4613 Braeburn Dr., Fairfax, VA 22032
Parker, Col Howard C., USA 1545 Valley Forge Lane, Melbourne, FL 32940
Parker, Phillip A., 5231 Riverwood Road, Norfolk, VA 23502
Parks, Lt Col Benjamin, USAF525 King's Town Dr., Naples, FL 33940
Parlor, Maj.Michael B., USMCP.O. Box 568, Tustin,CA 92681

Parmeter, LtCol Glenn L., AUS1815 Daniel Dr. , Missoula, MT 59802
Parris, Col Joe W., USAF14 Chaumont Square NW, Atlanta, GA, 30327
Parrish, James D.Jr., 523 Bayview Dr., Seabrook,TX 77586
Parsons, Donald L., 12230 Shadetree Lane, Laurel, MD 20708
Passarella, CMSgt Donald, USAF3718 Meadowbreeze Dr., Tampa, FL 33619
Pattakos, Col Arion N., USA 4216 Knowles Ave. , Kensington, MD 20895
Patten, James S., P.O. Box 1321, Torrington, CT 06790
Patterson, LtCol Betty, USAF930 S. Aurora Ave.,Tacoma, WA 98465
Patterson, LtCol Michael P.O.Box 392, Forestville,CA 95436
Patton, MajGen George S., USA 650 Asbury Street, South Hamilton, MA 01982
Patton, James V., 20239 Catlett Place, Ashburn, VA 22101
Patton, MajGen John S., USAF1429 Labumum St., McLean, VA 22011
Patton, Thomas J., 3514 Wentworth Dr., Falls Church, VA 22044
Patty, Robert, 7180 Pah Rah Dr., Sparks, NV 89436
Paul, Mr.Allen T., 1231 Surrey Run, East Aurora, NY 14052
Paul, Jon D., 42 Truman Dr., Novato, CA 94947
Paulich, John, 4401 Gulf Shore Blvd., No.1708 , Naples, FL 33940
Pavlakis, Major Gregory, USAFR6590 West 92st St., No.205, Overland Park, KS 66212
Pavlin, Ivan C., 1011 Bay Drive North, Bradenton Beach, FL 34217
Pawlowski, Dr.Edward J.P., 422 North Center St., Vienna, Va 22180
Peabody, Malburne J., 3222 Patrick Henry Dr., Falls Church, VA 22044
Preacher, MajGen D, USMCR1001 Genter St., No. 3-1, La Jolla, CA 92037
Peacock, Mrs.Mary Eyre, P.O. Box 1047, Cheriton, VA 23316
Peake, Hayden B., 502 S.St. Asaph St., Alexandria, VA 22314
Pease, LtCol Charles M., USAF1575 Mercury St., Merritt Island, FL 32953
Peck, Major Samuel W., USA 5220 Fiore Ter. No.M-314, San Diego, CA 92122
Peck, Stephen T., 8500 Westover Ct., Springfield, VA 22152
Peisen, Gary L., 106 Otey Dr., Meridianville, AL 35759
Pelletier, LtCol Robert, USA 9056 Bellwart Way, Columbia, MD 21045
Pendragon, Mr. Merlin J., 10084 Bromont Ave., Sun Valley, CA 91352
Penne, James J., 2708 Via Pacheco, Palos Verdes Estates, CA 90274
Pepper, Edward L., 8 Robinson Park, Winchester, MA 01890
Perdue, Thomas E., 2486 47th Ave., San Francisco, CA 94116
Perkins, Cdr Samuel, USNR964 East Shore Dr. , Culver, IN 46511
Perlman, Lee A., 224 Arbor Lane, San Mateo, CA 94403
Perry, Mrs.Bernice R., 1002 61st St., So., Gulfport, FL 33707
Perry, Donald W., 3705 Alameda Way, Bonita, CA 92002
Perry, Gerald L. Jr., 217 D Fifth Ave.,North, Edmonds, WA 98020
Perry, Samuel, 734 N. LaSalle St.,No 1158, Chicago, IL 60610
Perry, Col Stephen M., USA99 Battery Place No. 21-G, New York, NY 10280
Peters, Franklin, 8 Tulip Rd., Holland, PA 18966
Peters, Gary, 2725 Connecticut Ave, NW. No 108, Washington, DC 20008
Peters, Mark D., 17 Purple Martin Dr., Hackettstown, NJ 07840
Petersen, George A., P.O. Box 605, Springfield, VA 22150
Petersen, Neal, 5429 N.19th St., Arlington, VA 22205
Peterson, LtCol Alden, USAF 7200 Easy St., Camp Springs, MD 20748
Peterson, David L., 8155 East 31st Court, Tulsa, OK 74145
Peterson, Maj H.C.Jr, USMC39 Halawa Dr., Honolulu, HI 96818
Peterson, Lee, 972 Pasque Dr., Longmont, CO 80501
Petras, A.J., 129 Benefit St. , Providence, RI 02903
Petti, Robert D., RR 42, Box 286-A, Wiscasset, ME 04578
Pfeiffer, Capt Carl A., USAR1265 Castelton Ave., Staten Island, NY 10310
Pforzheimer, Walter L., 2500 Virginia Ave.,NW, Washington, DC 20037
Philcox, Norman W., P.O. Box 471, Amherst, NH 03031
Phillippe, Ms. Suzanne E., 9706 Ranger Road, Fairfax, VA 22030
Phillips, Jim, P.O. Box 168, Williamstown, NJ 08094
Phillips, Mrs. David Atlee, 10942 Whiterim Dr., Potomac, MD 20854
Pialet, Joseph, 26151 Lakeshore Blvd Euclid, OH 44132
Pickoff, Col Julius, USAF4469 W. Sentinel Rock Terrace., Larkspur, CO 80118
Pidgeon, Ms Marion R., 1057 Forest Lakes Dr.,No 203, Naples, FL 33942
Pierucki, Capt Ervin J., USN6118 Edith N.E.,No 134, Albuquerque, NM 87107
Pincus, Walter, 1150 15th St., NW, Washington, DC 20071
Platt, Dr.Edward E., 325 N. Ben Franklin Rd. , Indiana, PA 15701
Platt, John C. 9618 Beach Mill Rd., Great Falls, VA 22066

Platt, Dr.Rorin M., 1512 Oakland Hills Way, Raleigh, NC 27604
Pletcher, LtCol John S., USAF P.O. Box 1075, Anna Maria, FL 34216
Ploetz, Col Raymond C., USAR 2700 Brookdale Dr., Minneapolis, MN 55444
Plowman, Col Harry B., USA 26345 Montgomery Dr., Bonita Springs, FL 33923
Polgar, Thomas, 2430 Lauder Dr., Maitland, FL 32751
Poll, Stanley, 430 E. 56th St.,No 9-E, New York, NY 10022
Pollock, James.C., 1200 Zack Lane, Charlottesville, VA 22901
Poole, Mrs.Rose M., 8221 7th Street,North, St. Petersburg, FL 33702
Popovich, Ms Eva M., 1600 South Eads St.,No 1218-South, Arlington, VA 22202
Porcaro, LtCol Michael, USAFR P.O. Box 402, Whitestone, NY 11352
Porter, Gary C., 29524 Southfield Rd., Southfield, Ml 48076
Porter, Harry W.III, 5120 Woodmire Lane, Alexandria, VA 22311
Porter, LtCol John D., USA2214 Via Monserate Rd., Fallbrook, CA 92028
Poshepny, Tony, 775 La Plays, No 2, San Francisco, CA 94121
Postove, Herman, 3001 Veazey Ter. N.W. ,No 1130, Washington, DC 20008
Poteat, S.Eugene, 1318 Titania Lane, McLean, VA 22102
Potoocki, Anita A., 3606 North Vernon St., Arlington, VA 22207
Potor, Mrs.Gill A. PhD 2535 Big Woods Trail, Fairborn, OH 45324
Potterton, Richard Lee, P.O. Box 1718, Winchester, VA 22604
Potts, James M., 5235 Massachusetts Ave., Bethesda, MD 20816
Potts, Raymond B., 1556 Eton Way, Crofton, MD 21114
Potts, Prof.Rinehart S., 1223 Glen Terrace, Glassboro, NJ 08028
Povolovski, Albert K., 104 Blaisdell St., Haverhill, MA 01832
Powell, Mrs.Ruth M., 12240 S.W. 39th Terrace.,S., Miami, FL 33175
Powers, Thomas, P.O. Box 35, So. Royalton, VT 05068
Prados, John, 7218 Spruce Ave.,Takoma Park, MD 20912
Prager, Stanley E., 2300 Lowell St., Aurora, IL 60506
Pratt, Alex, 45 Main St., Kennebunk, ME 04043
Prendergast, LtCol C., USA2410 Sarasota Dr., Friends Wood, TX 77546
Price, Douglas R., 5122 Cannon Bluff Dr., Woodbridge, VA 22192
Price, Frank L., 1141 Van Nuys St., San Diego, CA 92109
Price, Larry E., 222 S. Edgewood Dr., Statesboro, GA 30458
Price, BrGen William H., USA7713 Falstaff Rd., McLean, VA 22102
Pringle, Glen Eugene, 7828 Garner Dr., Manassas, VA 22110
Prins, Dougal W.S., 124 Archie Smith Rd., Hattiesburg, MS 39402
Printz, Ms M.Jean, 1123 Dryden Lane, Charlottesville, VA 22901
Prior, Mrs.Nancy Fife, 10570 Main St., No B-219, Fairfax, VA 22030
Prisley, Captain John P., P.O.Box 1219, Leesburg, VA 22075
Pritchard, Charles G., 10612 Margate Rd., Silver Spring, MD 20901
Pritikin, BrigGen R., ILANG1200 Talcott Building,, Rockford, IL 61 1 01
Prokopowicz, Col John H., USA13207 Memory Lane, Fairfax, VA 22033
Pruefer, Capt Clifford, USNR 3407 Barkley Dr. , Fairfax, VA 22031
Prugh, Mrs.Frances B., 11705 Eden Rd. , Silver Spring, MD 20904
Prugh, Thomas A., 11705 Eden Rd., Silver Spring, MD 20904
Puchnick, Ms. Barbara J., 823 Railroad St., Forest City, PA 18421
Purdom, Todd229 W., 43rd St., New York, NY 10036
Purvis, Floyd E. CPP, P.O. Box 795309, Dallas, TX 75379
Putman, Forrest S., 8808 Chambers Pl.NE, Albuquerque, NM 87111

– Q –

Quesada, Gonzalo, 1285 Lynwood Dr., Novato, CA 94947
Quesenberry, John M., 9806 Brightler Dr., Vienna, VA 22181
Quigg, Stuart M., 2011 Hopewood Dr. Westmorland Sq., Falls Church, VA 22043
Quilici, Leo J., 5110 Harlan Dr,, El Paso, TX 79924
Quinlan-Towey, Ms Miriam A, 1016 So. Wayne St.,No 309, Arlington, VA 22204
Quinn, John F., 7607 Scotch Haven Dr., Vienna, VA 22181
Quirk, John Patrick, 44 Boston Post Rd., Guilford, CT 06437
Quis, Col Francis R., AUS230 Highland Rd., Southern Pines, NC 28387

– R –

Rachel, BrigGen Allen K., USAF 10285 Viacha Dr., San Diego, CA 92124
Rademaker, Theodore, 21 River Bend Rd., Great Falls, VA 22066
Rader, Ms.Stephanie C., 1108 Key Drive, Alexandria, VA 22302
Raff, LtCdr Lori, USN2122 Whisperwood Glen, Reston, VA 22091
Railey, Raymond E., 2522 Gold Rush Dr.,#2, Colorado Springs, CO 80906

Raimer, LtCol Mark, USA4806 Pacer Lane, Colorado Springs, CO 80917
Rall, Col Lloyd L., USA301 Cloverway, Alexandria, VA 22314
Ramfors, Bo, Skandinaviska Enskilda Banken, Stockholm, Sweden
Rambo, Col Charles R., USA 5078 37th St., N., Arlington, VA 22207
Ramsey, Lt Col Cletis E., USAF6911 Compton Valley Ct., Centreville, VA 22020
Ramsey, Lt Col David A., USMC1619 Palm Springs Dr., Vienna, VA 22182
Ransom, Prof Harry H., 511 Belle Meade Blvd., Nashville, TN 37205
Rapalus, Henry W., 201 Mt. Vernon Place, Rockville, MD 20852
Rauch, George W., 1415 9th Avenue E., Bradenton, FL 34208
Rausch, John T., Mitre Corp PSC No 2, Box 8868, APO, AE 09012
Rawls, Hubert F., 323 Flagstone Dr., Myrtle Beach, SC 29577
Raymond, Dr.Gale J., 13164 Memorial Dr., No.185, Houston, TX 77079
Ream, Harold D., 4366 Albacore Circle, Port Charlotte, FL 33948
Reardon, Raymond M., 3928 Clare's Ct., Fairfax, VA 22033
Reaume, LtCdr Paul A., USNR734 Green Briar Lane, Lake Forest, IL 60045
Reckford, Thomas J., 4717 Asbury Pl., NW, Washington, DC 20016
Rectanus, VAdm Earl, USNCoquina 5C, 6100 Estero Blvd, Ft. Myers Beach, FL 33931
Rector. Harry C., 12522 Lt. Nichols Rd., Fairfax, VA 22033
Redican, Col. Edward C., USAF5208 Olley Lane, Burke, VA 22015
Reed, Daniel E., 6774 E. Paseo Penoso, Tucson, AZ 85715
Reed, James Michael, P.O. Box 3215, Long Beach, CA 90803
Reed, BrigG Joseph H., USAR 606 Cherokee St., Medford, OK 73759
Regenstein, Lewis G., 4290 Raintree Lane, Atlanta, GA 30327
Regnier, Mrs.Maxine N., 4023 Mischire, Houston, TX 77025
Rehm, George M., 143 Skyline Dr., Würzburg, D97074, Germany
Reich, Carl W., 255 N.El Cielo, Ste 302, Palm Springs, CA 92262
Reich, Gerald J., 420 Howard St., Lodi, CA 95242
Reiser, John R., P.O. Box 990280, Redding, CA 96099
Relyea, Ms Helen W., 4853 Bayard Boulevard, Bethesda, MD 20816
Remes, LtCol Waino, AUS138 Timberlane Trail, Salisbury, NC 28144
Remick, Allen Thomas, 573 Rock Springs Dr., Atlanta, GA 30324
Reno, Joseph David, 791 Tremont St. W-113, Boston, MA 02118
Reske, Charles F. X., 47 Homestead Court, Traverse City, MI 49686
Restum, A. A., 105 Poplar Dr., Falls Church, VA 22046
Revis, Ms. Sara M., 1809 37th St., N.W., Washington, DC 20007
Reynolds, Ms. D., Joyce 2000 S. Eads St.,No 812, Arlington, VA 22202
Reynolds, M. Sedano, 748 Merrick Ave., East Meadow, NY 11554
Rhoads, Col Robert C. AUS1220 Oakhaven Dr., Roswell, GA 30075
Riach, Col Douglas A., 2609 Trousdale Dr., Burlingame, CA 9401 0
Ricardo, Angel, 6430 SW 20 Terrace, West Miami, FL 33155
Rice, Millard F., 14032 Beech Tree Court, Hudson, FL 34667
Rich, Richard S., 2670 Mineral Point Rd., Friday Harbor, WA 98250
Rich, Robert E., 10106 E. Bexhill Dr., Kensington, MD 20895
Richard, Joseph E., 17315 Donora Rd., Silver Spring, MD 20905
Richards, Gerald B., 15307 Alan Dr., Laurel, MD 20707
Richards, Jeff, 7180 Arcadia Lane, Yuma, AZ 85364
Richardson, Donald L., 352 Caprino Way, No 25, San Carlos, CA 94070
Richardson, William N., 3901 Indian School Rd NE, No C-206, Albuquerque, NM 87110
Richie, George E., 3380 Club Heights Dr., Colorado Springs, CO 80906
Rieder, Eugene W., 12320 Melody Turn, Bowie, MD 20715
Rigney, James C., 3850 Galt Ocean Dr., No 1 708, Ft. Lauderdale, FL 33308
Rigsbee, Ms. F. Catherine, Tryon Estates 615 Peniel Rd., Columbus, NC 28772
Riley, Ms Margaret F., 254 School St. , Worcester, MA 01505
Ring, Dennis, 318 New Meadows Rd., RR 1, Box 318, West Bath, ME 05430
Ripley, Capt Paul H. Sr., USA4506 Amherst Rd., College Park, MD 20740
Robbins, Christopher M., 4419 N. 4th Rd., No 2 , Arlington, VA 22203
Roberts, Dr. Calinn, 555 California St., San Francisco, CA 94104
Roberts, George, 47868 Kamehameha Highway, Kaneohe, Oahu, Hi 96744
Roberts, Jerry E., 4576 Hawley Blvd. No I, San Diego, CA 92116
Robinson, Ms. Jeanne S., 1054 Anna Knapp Blvd., 434G Mt. Pleasant, SC 29464
Robinson, Dr. James T., 2307 Crestlawn Ave., Cheverly, MD 20785
Robohm, Ms. Peggy Adler, 32 Founders Village, Clinton, CT 06413
Rockhill, Charles D. Jr., 3382 W. Camino De Amigos, Tucson, AZ 85746
Rockstroh, Col S., USAF 113 Peckham St. S.E. , Port Charlotte, FL 33952

Rodell, Fred, 12223 Maple Rock, Houston, TX 77077
Rodgers, George C., 408 West Liberty St., Medina, OH 44256
Rodgers, George F., 3544 Queen Ann Dr., Fairfax, VA 22030
Rodney, Marvin C., 5775 Devon Lane, Burke, VA 22015
Roehl, Charles A., 1563 MeNeer St., McLean, VA 22101
Roepe, Herbert B. Jr., 2109 N. Illinois Street Arlington, VA 22205
Rogers, Col Herbert J., USAF 433 East Hildebrand Ave., San Antonio, TX 78212
Roscoe, Dr. John H., 20 Holden Ct., Portola Valley, CA 94028
Rosenbaum, David M., 4620 Dittmar Rd. , Arlington, VA 22207
Rosenbaum, Col E., USAFR 10801 Decatur Rd., Philadelphia, PA 19154
Rosenbaum, Marcus A., 47 Observatory Cir., NW, Washington, DC 20008
Rosendahl, Ellen R., 11446 Links Dr., Reston, VA 22090
Ross, G. Perry, 221 Smith Neck Rd., South Dartmouth, MA 02748
Ross, Rosalinda C., 90 Home Acres Ave., Milford, CT 06460
Rossing, Col. Dennis E., USAF 27006 Granite Path , San Antonio, TX 78258
Rost, Rachel F., 13515 Furman Rd., Houston, TX 77047
Roukis, George S., Davison Hall, 4200C, Hofstra University, Hempstead, NY 11550
Roush, Col John, USAR 27 Terrace Ave., Kentfield. CA 94904
Row, Maurice F. Sr., 3830 Pickett Court, Annandale, VA 22003
Rowan, Donald J., 8501 Aquaduct Rd., Potomac, MD 20854
Roy, LtCol Lawrence B., USAAcademy Hill Road RR 1, Box 497, Newcastle, ME 04553
Roy, Cdr William G., USN222 Harbour Dr., Naples, FL 33940
Rudka, Col Joseph ,SMR, IRR 941 Jones St., San Francisco, CA 94109
Ruffini, Lt Col Joseph, USA8892 Estebury Circle, Colorado Springs, CO 80920
Runyon, J. Robert, 254222 Estrada Circle, Punta Gorda, FL 33955
Rupp, Capt Heinrich F., USA17702 E. Arapahoe Rd., Aurora, CO 80016
Russ, Mr. Virgil T. ICS, P.O. Box 6255, Gulf Shores, AL 36547
Russo, Gus G., 221 Blakeney Rd., Baltimore, MD 21228
Russoniello, Joseph P., 100 St. Francis Blvd., San Francisco, CA 94127
Rustmann, Frederick W. Jr., 529 South Flagler Dr., West Palm Beach, FL 33401
Ruth, Charles P., 3004 Cactus Dr., Edmond, OK 73013
Ruth, LtCol Robert J., USA 2015 Gunnell Fauns Dr., Vienna, VA 22180
Ryan, David, 4026 North 27th Rd., Arlington, VA 22207
Ryan, Francis E., 1540 Red Rock Court, Vienna. VA 22180
Ryan, George W., P.O. Box 644, Al-Khobar 31952, Saudi Arabia
Ryan, LtCol John J., USAF 1623 Frontier Dr., Melbourne, FL 32940
Ryan, Michael Richard, 3208 Louise, Dodge City, KS 67801
Ryan, LtCol Philip J., USMC 4868 North Hulbert, No. 101, Fresno, CA 93705
Rydell, William P., 9610 Laurel Oak Place., Fairfax Station, VA 22039

– S –

Sachs, LtCol Martha, USA 5045 North 5th St., Arlington, VA 22203
Saenz, Adolph B., P.O. Box 12884, Albuquerque, NM 87195
Safreed, Robert B., 6290 Bataan St., Cypress, CA 90630
Sagan, LtCol Stanley D., USAF 3218 Bluefield Dr., San Antonio, TX 78230
Salazar, Timothy, 11248 Silver Buckle Way, San Diego, CA 92127
Sampson, Mr. Richard A., 1408 Westwood Pl., Escondido, CA 92026
San Fellipo, George J., 1593 Colonial Ter., No. 305, Arlington, VA 22209
Sanders, Nicholas , 3902 Gannon Road, Silver Spring, MD 20902
Sanford, Wayne F., 901 Madison Lane, Falls Church, VA 22046
Santa, Ms. Jeanine M., 11000 Wilshire Blvd., No. 1700 Los Angeles, CA 90024
Sartiano, Joseph F., 140 Cerritos Ave., San Francisco, CA 94127
Saul, Joseph H., 9634 Green Moon Path, Columbia, MD 21046
Sauls, Dr. F. Clark, 201 Chesterfield Rd., Hattiesburg, MS 39402
Sauner, Col Richard G., USAF 1600 South Eads St.. No 612, South Arlington, VA 22202
Sawallesh, LtCol Robert, USA 2541 Brimhollow Dr., Vairico, FL 33594
Sax, Capt Samuel W., USNR237 East Delaware Place, Chicago, IL 60611
Scatterday, George H., 5911 Osceola Rd., Bethesda, MD 20816
Schaad, Col Carl W., 7116 Warbler Ln., McLean, VA 22101
Schaaf, Charles W., 434 Seminole Dr., Erie, PA 16505
Scahefer, Mr. Gene R., P.O. Box 87, Bradenton Beach, FL 34217
Schaf, Col Frank L. Jr., USA6159 Tompkins Dr., McLean, VA 22101
Schall, John T., 5182 San Aquario Dr., San Diego, CA 92109
Schatzley, Col Byron, USAF1442 Devoe Dr., No. 1289, Beavercreek, OH 45434

Scheidt, Edward M., 1048 Dead Run Dr., McLean, VA 22101
Scheiner, Lt. David, USMCR 9341 Abbott Ave., Surfside, FL 33154
Schimmel, Donald W., RR 4, Box 175, Hedgesville, WV 25427
Schleicher, Richard G., 6103 Wynnwood Rd., Bethesda, MD 20816
Schlesinger, James P., 1800 K Street, NW, No. 520, Washington, DC 20006
Schmaltz, Robert E., 11 Bixby Lane, Westford, MA 01886
Schmidt, Richard, 7903 Jansen Ct. , Springfield, VA 22152
Schmitz, Clarence W., 800 Bridgeport Way, Annapolis, MD 21401
Schmitz, Robert J., 1701 Mountain Laurel Dr., Kerrville, TX 78028
Schmucker, Richard G., RR 2 Box 15-A Brock, NE 68320
Schneider, Alan N., P.O. Box 158, Coral Gables, FL 33134
Scheider, David, 220 M St., NW, Washington, DC 20036
Schoen, Charles J., P.O. Box 33, Crystal Bay, MN 55323
Schoenwetter, Edward J., 1355 Lake Shore Dr., Mt. Dora, FL 32757
Schoeps, Lawrence J., 560 N Street, SW, Washington, DC 20024
Scholz, Otto F., 4349 Greenberry La. , Annandale, VA 22003
Schuler, Donald V., 11425 Tanbark Dr., Reston, VA 22091
Schuler, Richard H., 356 White Oaks Dr. , Albuquerque, NM 87122
Schultheis, Lawrence W., 763 Gretchen Rd., Chula Vista CA 91910
Schulze-Merchinski, WolfgangGeneral Delivery, Naples, FL 33962
Schulz, Ronald R. Sr., 2709 Coxswain Pl., Annapolis, MD 21401
Schvimmer, Joseph H., 4614 Hawksbury Rd., Baltimore, MD 21208
Schwartz, Leon F., 7108 Purdue Place, McLean, VA 22101
Schwartzbard, Richard, 3704 N. Woodstock St., Arlington, VA 22207
Schwasinger, Eugene L., 5231 Sunnyside Rd., St. Paul, MN 55112
Schwenk, George O., 177 Merriam Hill Rd., Mason, NH 03048
Sclaris, Cdr Louis G., USN APO Miami, FL 34037
Scott, Alan, P.O. Box 223, Exton, PA 19341
Scott, Mrs. Almeda H., 7133 Alger Rd., Falls Church, VA 22042
Scott, Col William F., USAF918 Mackall Ave., McLean, VA 22101
Scully, Ms Mary L., 3001 Veazey Terrace, NW, No. 809 Washington, DC 20008
Seale, Mrs. Almets C., 4031 Gulfshore Blvd., No. 93 Naples, FL 33940
Sedoff, Walter, 1013 Meadow Lane, Alberton, MT 59820
Seegren, LtCol Norman W., 3702 Prado Place, Fairfax, VA 22031
Segal, Carl G., 23185 Hemenway Ave., N.E., Port Charlotte, FL 33980
Selgrat, George S., 11426 N. Balboa Dr., Sun City, AZ 85351
Seron, Richard Z., 490 Banning Beach Rd., Tavares, FL 32778
Sesow, Anthony D., 9909 Bamsbury Ct., Fairfax, VA 22031
Severance, Col Michael, USA Gooch's Beach, P.O. Box 631, Kennebunkport, ME 04046
Shackeley, Theodore G., Research Assoc Internat'l, P.O. Box 716, Glen Echo, MD 20812
Shaffer, LtCol John R., USA 835 Oyster Cove Dr., Grasonville, MD 21638
Shaffer, Robert H., 4406 Martin's Way, No. D, Orlando, FL 32808
Shank, David W., 135 N. Edgewood St., Arlington, VA 22201
Shannon, Mrs. Catherine C., 4101 Cathedral Ave., No 1104, Washington, DC 20016
Shapiro, Radm Summer, USN6138 Ramshorn Dr., McLean, VA 22101
Sharp, Frederick D., III 3 Fairwind Lane, Yarmouth, ME 04096
Sharp, Adm Ulysses S. G., USN 876 San Antonio Place, San Diego, CA 92106
Shaw, Donald O., 2613 Sakian Indian Dr., No. 3, Walnut Creek, CA 94595
Shaw, J. Arnold, 2625 Woodmont Circle, Waco, TX 76710
Shaw, Robert T., 12851 E. Speedway Tuscon, AZ 85748
Sheldon, Dr. Rose Mary, Dept of History, Virginia Military Institute, Lexington, VA 24450
Sheley, Edward L. Jr., 6540 Bay Tree Court, Falls Church, VA 22041
Shelko, William S., 8634 N. Gateway Dr., N. Royalton, OH 44133
Shelton, Thomas A., 1317 Oakhill Ave., Fairborn, OH 45324
Shelton, Vernon L., P.O. Box 310, Holder, FL 34445
Shepardson, John W., P.O. Box 9591, Denver, CO 80209
Sheppard, Dr. I Thomas, 14511 Chesapeake Pl., NE, Bainbridge Island, WA 98110
Sherman, John Merchant, 3229 Tranquility Ln., Herndon, VA 22071
Sherman, Col Nahida C., USAF 124 Brimstone Comer Rd., Hancock, NH 03449
Sherman, Roger R., 12488 Alexander Cornell Dr., Fairfax, VA 22033
Sherman, William O., 217 Woodbury Rd., Box 404, Woodbury, NY 11797
Sherrick, David C., 7705 Marbury Rd., Bethesda, MD 20817
Shier, Jerome B., 2588 Saw Mill Rd., North Bellmore, NY 11710
Shingleton, Col Gordon, AUS Cool Spring Farm, Gerrardstown, WV 25420

Shirley, Alick A., 10111 Eastlake Dr., Fairfax, VA 22032
Shirley, Joe, 140 Woodstream Way, Fayetteville, GA 30214
Shivley, James F., 11181 Magdalena Rd., Los Altos Hills, CA 94024
Shonkweiler, John P., 307 Pitt County Courthouse, Monticello, IL 61856
Shore, Col Moyers S., USA P.O.Box 846, Tucumcari, NM 88401
Showers, RAdm Donald, USN 3829 N. 26th St., Arlington, VA 22207
Shubert, Jeffrey M., 3246 Clay St., San Francisco, CA 94115
Shuffelt, BrGen James W., USA 2703 Franklin Ct., Alexandria, VA 22302
Shuffstall, Col Donald, USA P.O. Box 3255, Peachtree City, GA 30269
Shumway, Col Allen, USAF 60 Treaty Dr., Wayne, PA 19087
Sierros, Steve N., 9312 69th Ave., Oak Lawn, IL 60453
Sikich, Capt Geary W., USA P.O. Box 1998, Highland, IN 46322
Silberberg, Mervin, 3700 Sacramento St., San Francisco, CA 94118
Silua, Otto A., 6708 Point Dr., Minneaplis, MN 55435
Simmons, Robert Ruhl, 268 N. Main St., Stonington, CT 06378
Sims, LtCol David, USA9304 Santayana Dr., Fairfax, VA 22031
Sims, William S., 3106 Wake Robin Dr., Shelburn, VT 05482
Sinclair, LtCol Margaret, USA 98-351 Koauka LP, No 1908, Aiea, Hi 96701
Singlaub, MajGen John K., USA 1101 S. Arlington Ridge Rd., Suite 314, Arlington, VA 22202
Singletary, Arthur, 303 Daniels St. N.W., Leesburg, VA 22075
Singleton, John W., 5052 Cliffhaven Dr., Annandale, VA 22003
Singleton, Walter F., 9595 Sherburne Farm Rd., Marshall, VA 22115
Sirks, Robert T., 1200 Paul Lane, Fredericksburg, VA 22406
Skaggs, John R., P.O. Box 571935, Houston, TX 77257
Skeels, Bradley T., 7924 Valmy Ln., Port Richey, FL 34668
Skoog, Ronald D., 1058 S. Winchester, No 6, San Jose, CA 95128
Skromak, Ms. Janet H., 360-3 DeGeorge Circle, Rochester, NY 14626
Skuby, LtCol Vladimir, USAF 7802 Jansen Dr., Springfield, VA 22152
Slack, Cdr Charles E., USN3801 Adrienne Dr., Alexandria, VA 22309
Slaff, Capt Allan P., USN3101 Green Dolphin Lane, Naples, FL 33940
Slain, Michael B., 25318 Cardington Dr., Beachwood, OH 44122
Slane, Daniel M., 8161 Manitou Dr., Westerville, OH 43081
Sleeper, Francis H., 55 Lambert St. No 7, Portland, ME 04103
Smead, Francis, 666 Stoneledge Rd., State College, PA 12683
Smith, Burdette C., 781 Binnacle Point Dr., Longboat Key, FL 34228
Smith, Clarence E., 2606 Lemontree Lane, Vienna, VA 22181
Smith, LtCol Conway J., USMC 7171 E. Horn Rd., Lake Leelanau, MI 49653
Smith, David R., 1717 Mott-Smith Dr., No 2911, Honolulu, HI 96822
Smith, Dr. Derrin Ray, 3746 E. Easter Cir. S., Littleton, CO 80122
Smith, Maj Ernest A., USAR 1296 Robertridge Dr., St. Charles, MO 63304
Smith, Frank C., 756 Wimbrow Dr., Sebastian, FL 32958
Smith, Mrs. Gloria Loomis, 2902 P St., N.W., Washington, DC 20007
Smith, James C., 9911 Colony Rd., Fairfax, VA 22030
Smith, Col John A., USA2676 Caballo Ct., Las Cruces, NM 88001
Smith, John Anson, P.O. Box 2717, Naples, FL 33939
Smith, John E., 15304 Birchcroft Dr., Brook Park, OH 44142
Smith, Col Landgrave T., USAF 2814 Oakton Manor Ct., Oakton, VA 22124
Smith, Col Mason E., USA 6758 War Eagle Place, Colorado Springs, CO 80919
Smith, Nichols J., 41 Sutter St. Suite 1230, San Francisco, CA 94104
Smith, Col Quinn G., AUS 3306 Daniell St., Omaha, NE 68123
Smith, Robert A., 7721 Baggins Rd., Hanover, MD 21076
Smith, Roderick G., P.O. Box 34846, Bethesda, MD 20827
Smith, Dr. Ronald L., 236 West Sixth St., Ste 206, Reno, NV 89503
Smith, Sheila C, 784 Tuscawilla Hills, Charles Town, WV 25414
Smith, Thomas J., 12711 Hugh Graham Rd., NE, Albuquerque, NM 871 11
Smith, Thomas N., 600 E. Medical Centre Blv. Windward Apt 101, Webster, TX 77598
Snell, William R., 17110 N. Bear Creek Dr., Houston, TX 77084
Snow, Stanley A., P.O. Box 33393, Cleveland, OH 44133
Snyder, Thomas D., 4246 Worcester Dr., Fairfax, VA 22032
Sohns, LtCol Ernest R., AUS6311 Kellogg Dr., McLean, VA 22101
Soloranzo, Alexander M., 5553 West Saguaro Dr., West Jordan, UT 84084
Somers, Mr. F. Eugene, 225 Westwood Rd., Annapolis, MD 21401
Somers, LtCdr John A., USNR 10077-2 Windstream Dr., Columbia, MD 21044
Sonek, Mr. Douglass R., 4308 28th Ave., Astoria, NY 11 103

Sorenson, MajGen Ted, USAF 5734 Harvey Ave., LaGrange, IL 60525
Sorenson, Capt Glenn, USNR 1352 Casa Ct., Santa Clara, CA 95051
Sorenson, Loren O., 10582 Sycamore Ave., Stanton, CA 90680
Sovern, Maurice A., EWA 13873 Park Center Rd., Herndon, VA 22071
Spadero, Anthony R., 4634 North 38th St., Arlington, VA 22207
Spangler, Charles G., 7504 Ridgewell Ct., Beltsville, MD 20705
Spasek, Col. Edward, 7 Sherwood Ct., San Francisco, CA 94127
Speers, Michael F., 11 Intervale Rd., Kennebunk, ME 04043
Spelta, Joseph M., 6835 Cologo Ct., St. Charles, MD 20603
Spencer, Thomas R., 801 Brickell Ave., No.1901, Miami, FL 33131
Spera, Mrs. Agnes C., 5913 Kingswood Rd., Bethesda, MD 20814
Spinelli, Ernest, 106 Tuscana Ct., No. 703 Naples, FL 33999
Spirto, Col Leonard A., USA 8 W. Harmon Dr., Carlisle, PA 17013
Spitzer, Larry Sr., RR 1, Box 134, Broadway, VA 22815
Sployar, Col Ludwig J., USAFR 1505 East River Rd., Minneapolis, MN 55414
Sponaugle, S. Woodrow, 8933/301 Tamar Dr., Columbia, MD 21045
Srodes, James L., 1010 Vermont Ave., NW, No. 721, Washington, DC 20005
Stack, Robert S., P.O. Box 611, San Anselmo, CA 94979
Stadermann, Howard A., 4000 Massachusetts Ave., NW, No. 1508, Washington, DC 20016
Stainback, Charles O., 5022 Lauderdale Ave., Virginia Beach, VA 23455
Stakutis, Vincent J., 160 Grant St., Lexington, MA 02173
Stanley, LtCol Arthur J. Jr., 234 Federal Bldg., Leavenworth, KS 66048
Stanton, George T., P.O. Box 262, Anacortes, WA 98221
Starr, Roger S., 721 Scott St., Stroudsburg, PA 18360
Steakley, BrigGen Ralph, USAF 1655 Frontier Dr., Melbourne, FL 32940
Steele, Mr. George T., 1725 Baldwin Dr., Millersville, MD 21108
Steele, LtCol James L., USMC24782 Alanwood St., El Toro, CA 92630
Steele, Robert D., OSS, Inc., 11005 Langton Arms Ct., Oakton, VA 22124
Steeves, Dr.William, USMC 8918 Kenilworth Dr., Burke, VA 22015
Stefanson, Randolph E., 428 So 8th St., Moorhead, MN 56560
Steinfeld, James H., 558 Lake Victoria Circle, Melbourne, FL 32940
Steitz George W., 531 Inverness Ave., Melbourne, FL 32940
Stephens, LtCol James, USAR 650 South Broadway, Box 503, Georgetown, KY 40324
Stephens, John M., 364 Sheffield Rd., Severna Park, MD 21146
Stephens, LtCdr Robert, USNR P.O. Box 821, Bryans Road, MD 20616
Stephenson, John L., 59670 Pheasant Hill Lane, St. Helens, OR 97051
Stevenson, LtCol Charles, USA1398 School St., Indiana, PA 15701
Stevenson, Col Julian L., M/S 10-16, 1313 Production Rd., Fort Wayne, IN 46808
Steward, LtCol. AUS, 5240 Fiore Terrace, J-306, San Diego, CA 92122
Stewart, James P., 1219 Matamoros, Ste. 504, Laredo, TX 78040
Stich, Rodney F., P.O. Box 5, Alamo, CA 94507
Stiely, Bruce L., 69 Rutherford Circle, Sterling, VA 22170
Stiger, Robert D., One Russell Ct, Sterling, VA 22170
Stiles, Charles L., P.O. Box 467, Cabin John, MD 20818
Stilwell, Ms Doris A., 3210 Wisconsin Ave., NW, No. 811, Washington, DC 20016
Stoelzel, William L., 4120 Gladstonbury Rd., Winston-Salem, NC 27104
Stone, Dolly Corbin, 50 Middle Rd., Palm Beach, FL 33480
Stone, Maj George H., USAF 3129 Tablelands Ct., No. 1H, Prescott, AZ 86301
Stone, Sanford J., 5500 Holmes Run Parkway. No. 1115, Alexandria, VA 22304
Stone, Cmdr Scott, USNR-RP.O.Box 119, Volcano, HI 96785
Storer, Ms. E. Barbara, 9 Spiller Dr., Kennebunk, ME 04043
Stras, Dr. Jerald R., c/o 3211 Thomapple St., Chevy Chase, MD 20815
Stratman, LtCol Robert, H.AUS P.O. Box 6116, Malibu, CA 90264
Straub, Joan Garland, 440 Davis Court, San Francisco, CA 941 11
Strauss, Lt.Col.Herbert, USMC7000 Devereux Circle Dr., Alexandria, VA 22310
Strauss, James P., 4694 B 36th St., Arlington, VA 22206
Straw, Mrs. Thelma J., 155 East 93rd St., No. 8G, New York, NY 10128
Strickler, Col Gilbert, USA P.O. Box 787, McLean, VA 22101
Stroh, LtCol Oscar H., USAR1531 Fishing Creek Valley Rd., Harrisburg, PA 17112
Stromberg, Dr. L. O, P.O. Box A600, Boca Raton, FL 33429
Strong, Mr. James T, 13782 Freeport Rd., San Diego, CA 92129
Strong, Mr. Jesse M. Jr., 6904 Edgerton Lane, Springfield, VA 22150
Strunk, Harold K., 4365 Clovewood Ln., Pleasanton, CA 94588
Stump, Capt Jerry D., USN3734 Thomas Point Rd., Annapolis, MD 21403

Stuntz, Lt.Col. Mayo S., USAR2596 Chain Bridge Rd., Vienna, VA 22181
Sturgis, James M. Jr., 1962 Chartridge Court, Dunwoody, GA 30338
Suckow, William J., 717 Meyer Dr., Naples, FL 33964
Suder, Michael N., 1301 N. Court House Rd., No 604, Arlington, VA 22201
Sughrue, Daniel F., P.O. Box 179, Concord, NH 03302
Sulc,. Lawrence B., 129 E Street S.E., Washington, DC 20003
Sullivan, Arthur H., 4613 Harling Lane, Bethesda, MD 20814
Sullivan, CWO Joseph, USA 105 Oldfield Rd., Fairfield, CT 06430
Sullivan, Martin E., 1908 Althea Lane, Bowie, MD 20716
Sullivan, Rocky O., 348 Elm Ave., Woodbury Hts, NJ 08097
Sullivan, Walton J., 505 S. Hammonds Ferry Rd., Linthicum, MD 21090
Surgener, Damon M. Jr, 5749 Pine Tree Dr., Sanibel Island, FL 33957
Susik, Michael, 9067 Turnbull Rd., Warrenton, VA 20186
Sutton, MACM James, USN 417 Westchester Dr., Altamonte Springs, FL 32701
Swailes, Keven C., 10333 Richmond, No. 700, Houston, TX 77042
Swain, Col Donald W., USAF9420 Mt. Vernon Circle, Alexandria, VA 22309
Swan, Mrs. Nancy C., 9502 Culver St., Kensington, MD 20895
Swan, Thaxter, 15401 Bramblewood Dr., Silver Spring, MD 20906
Swannack, Col Buck, USMC 8206 Magnolia, Glen Humble, TX 77346
Swanson, Douglas R., 10782 S. Federal Hwy., Port Saint Lu, FL 33452
Sweany, Maj Donald, USAR 8 Brice Rd, Pendennis Mount, Annapolis, MD 21401
Swenson, Allan A., RR 1, Box 1987, Kennebunk, ME 04043
Switzer, Col W. Homer, USA 8232 Westchester Dr., Vienna, VA 22182
Swope, Richard L., 632 Hickory Rd., Naples, FL 33963
Sword, Jeffrey D., 109 N. Menominee Dr., Minooka, IL 60447
Swover, Jeffrey S., 7003 N. Holly Ct., Kansas City, MO 64118
Sydorko, Major Michael, USA 1332 Hemlock St., NW, Washington, DC 20012
Szatkowski, Peter S. Jr., 2050 Memorial Dr., Chicopee, MA 01020

– T –

Talbert, Charles R., 316 Cape St. John Rd., Annapolis, MD 21401
Talley, Herman R., 11 Martins Lane, Rockville, MD 20850
Tanner, Daniel A., Jr. 26393 Ingleton Ct E., Easton, MD 21601
Taplin, Winn L., 7641 Sandalwood Way, Sarasota, FL 34231
Tardy, Col Walter E., USA6513 Pinecrest Court, Annandale, VA 22003
Tarrington, Robert W., 11409 S. Tongareva St., Malibu, CA 90265
Tasker, Molly J., 268 Lantenback. Dr., Satellite Beach, FL 32937
Tate, Raymond T., 17929 Pond Road, Ashton, MD 20861
Tauber, Bernard L., 13714 Chestersall Dr., Tampa, FL 33624
Tauber, Mrs. Joanne Veverka, 13714 Chestersall Dr., Tampa, FL 33624
Taylor, Col Charles M., 12400 Hunters Glen Blvd., No. 43, Little Rock, AR 72211
Taylor, Col Cortiandt M., USAF4728 Weston St., Fairfax, VA 22030
Taylor, Mrs. Florence K., 3465 North Edison St., Arlington, VA 22207
Taylor, John E., 4600 Yuma St., NW Washington, DC 20016
Taylor, MajGen Larry S., USMC47 South Prado, Atlanta, GA 30309
Taylor, Ralph S., 820 Barbara Ct., Glen Bumie, MD 21061
Taylor, Robert L., P.O. Box 506, Fairfax, OK 74637
Taylor, Prof. Stanley A., 750 SWKT Brigham Young University, Provo, UT 84604
Teagarden, Ernest M., P.O. Box 7, Madison, SD 57042
Tefft, Dr.Bruce D., 13622 Clarendon Springs Court, Centreville, VA 22020
Teixeira, Roy J., P.O. Box 355, Halifax, MA 02338
Terrebonne, Ms Elizabeth, P.O. Box 394, Santa Fe, TX 77510
Terrell, MajGen F., USAF 1341 San Julian Lane, Lake San Marcos, CA 92069
Terry, Col Woodrow, AUS432 East Spruce St., Cherokee, IA 51012
Tesch, Karl F., 1906 NE 94th Ct., Vancouver, WA 98664
Tester, Joseph J., 888 Logan St., No. 5H, Denver, CO 80203
Thayer, Melvin R., 3726 White Oak Court, Lake Wales, FL 33853
Then, Joseph L., 13216 Valley Drive, Rockville, MD 20850
Thibault, Darryl F., 2360 Palo Danzante, Alpine, CA 91901
Thoman, Austin J., 20 China Cockle Lane, Hilton Head Plantation., SC 29928
Thomas, Col Benjamin E., AUS 11500 Kingsland St., Los Angeles, CA 90066
Thomas, Maj Chester, USA 238 N. Galveston St., Arlington, VA 22203
Thomas, Craig L., 1210 NW 43, Oklahoma City, OK 73118
Thomas, Guy, 7372 Kerry Hill Ct., Columbia, MD 21045

Thomas, MajGen Jack E., USAF 5741 MacArthur Boulevard, NW, Washington, DC 20016
Thomas, Mr. James H. Jr., 7170 W. 80th Pl., Arvada, CO 80003
Thomas, Mr. Malcolm C., 8124 River Country Dr., Springhill, FL 34607
Thomas, Mrs. Mary Lou, 6012 Torreon Dr., NE, Albuquerque, NM 87109
Thompsen, Mrs. A. Rebecca, 361 North Calle Del Diablo, NBU 1218, Green Valley, AZ 85614
Thompson, MGen Edmund, USA3 Bayberry Ave., Kennebunk, ME 04043
Thompson, Ms. Honora F., 2014 Klingle Road, NW, Washington, DC 20010
Thompson, Jeffrey L., P.O. Box 1561, Tacoma, WA 98401
Thompson, Peter J., 7119 E. Shea Blvd., No. 109-118, Scottsdale, AZ 85254
Thomson, Dr. Fred W., 3009 Queen St., Missoula, MT 59801
Thorne, Landon K. III, 7350 SW 100 St., Miami, FL 33156
Throop, Homer H., 1822 Hylton Ave., Woodbridge, VA 22191
Ticknor, Joel D., 11517 Running Cedar Rd., Reston, VA 22091
Tidwell, BGen W., USA9327 Pentland Place, Fairfax, VA 22031
Tierney, Herman F., 924 Circle Tower, Indianapolis, IN 46204
Tierney, Joseph L., 250 Holly Ridge Circle, Arnold, MD 21012
Tilley, Michie F., 16095 Rhyolite Circle, Reno, NV 89511
Toensing, Ms. Victoria, 5807 Hillburne Way, Chevy Chase, MD 20815
Toler, Cdr John H., USNR6087 Dumfries Rd., Warrenton, VA 22186
Tomajan, Don K., IBM, 5933 W. Century Blvd., No.316, Los Angeles, CA 90045
Tomas, Edward J., P.O. Box 4682, Toms River, NJ 08754
Toney, Robert L., 22 Kings Trail, Williamsville, NY 14221
Toohey, Sean F., 188 Clinton Ave., Elmhurst, IL 60126
Tortorella, Maj S., USAR 530 East 234th St., Bronx, NY 10470
Tovar, B.Hugh, 3101 New Mexico Ave., NW, No. 229, Washington, DC 20016
Towers, Frederic C., 8033 Herb Farm Dr., Bethesda, MD 20817
Townsend, Patrick L., 93 Winfield Rd., Holden, MA 01520
Tracy, Col Ollie L., USA10223 Locust, Kansas City, MO 64131
Trapp, Arlen, RR 1, Box 1669, Shohola, PA 18458
Traub, Col Richard L., 6543 Corte Montecito Rancho, La Costa Carlsbad, CA 92009
Travesky, Major John J., USAF 2989 Park Village Way, Melbourne, FL 32935
Trento, Joseph, 210 Happy Creek Rd., Front Royal, VA 22630
Trettin, Carl E., 1339 Monroe Ave., Wyomissing, PA 19610
Triantafellu, MGen R., USAF 157 Nawiliwili St., Honolulu, Hi 96825
Trimbi, Dr. Allan H., P.O. Box 832, Palos Verdes Estates, CA 90274
Trosclair, Allan A., P.O. Box 8999, San Francisco, CA 94128
Troupe, David H., 4911 Long Shadow Drive, Midlothian, VA 23112
Troutman, Col James, USAFR5624 Newington Court, Bethesda, MD 20816
Troy, Thomas F., 6101 Rudyard Dr., Bethesda, MD 20814
Trumbull, Robert G., Jr. P.O. Box 191, Culpeper, VA 22701
Tschudy, Dr. James, 3030 West Foothills Way, Flagstaff, AZ 86001
Tucker, Ms. Audrey M., 4631 S. Oxford, Tulsa, OK 74135
Tucker, Wilfred S., 10100 Hiliview Rd., 4629, Pensacola, FL 32514
Tulich, Cdr Eugene N., USCG17110 Wood Bark Rd., Spring, TX 77379
Tuttle, LtCol Roger Lewis, USA3801 Commodore Point Pl., Midlothian, VA 23112
Twentyman, Chester H., 3643 North Harrison St., Arlington, VA 22207
Twiss, John R. Jr., 901 Tumey Run Rd., McLean, VA 22101
Tyson, Edward C., 34 Lighthouse Point, Aliso Viejo, CA 92656
Tyson, Capt Francis D., USMC1720 Sanderson Ave., Scranton, PA 18509
Tyszka, Matthew F. Jr., 129 West Rd., Collinsville, CT 06022

– U –

Uffelman, Malcolm R., 1808 Horseback Trail, Vienna, VA 22182
Ugarte, Lazaro R., 814 Ponce de Leon Blvd., Suite 406, Coral Gables, FL 33130
Ugino, Major Richard F., 37 Bitteroot Trail, Hilton, NY 14468
Uiberall, LtCol Ernest, USAR7204 Beechwood Rd, Hollin Hills, Alexandria, VA 22307
Ulbrich, Ms. Ruth M., 4701 Willard Ave., No 623, Chevy Chase, MD 20815
Umstattd, Ms. Kristen, USNR 353 Foxridge Dr., SW Leesburg, VA 22075
Unger, Maj Hector F., USAF 13785 NW McLain Way, Portland, OR 97229
Unnerstall, Ronald W., 6704 Walker Branch Dr., Laurel, MD 20707
Unsinger, Peter Charles, 1581 Elka Ave., San Jose, CA 95129
Uransky, Norman A., 3801 S. E. 7th Ave., Cape Coral, FL 33904
Urbach, R. Scott, 12515 Jolette Ave, Granada Hills, CA 91344
Urban, John M., 404 Wild Ginger Court, Forestbrook, Myrtle Beach, SC 29577

Urick, Willis E. Jr., 1866 Caminito Del Cielo, Glendale, CA 91208
Usher, MajGen William, USAF11410 Hollow Timber Court, Reston, VA 22094
– **V** –
Vagnini, Lee L., 26069 Mesa Drive, Carmel, CA 93923
Vaivada, Anthony S., 6872 Melrose Dr., McLean, VA 22101
Valadez, Maj Ramon B., USMC 1633 Babcock Rd.. 4155, San Antonio, TX 78229
Valcourt, Richard R., 177 E 77th St. No. 12C, New York, NY 10021
Valentine, LTC McDonald Jr, P.O. Box 29965, Atlanta, GA 30359
Valley, Harry R., 826 Westpoint Parkway., No. 1250, Westlake, OH 44145
Valois, Mr. Rudolph J., 1 Bayberry Dr., Atkinson, NH 03811
Van Buskirk, Cdr George, USN 4118 Hollowtrail Dr., Tampa, FL 33624
Van Cook, Arthur F., 6112 Pinto Place, Springfield, VA 22150
Van Develde, James R., P.O. Box 207272, New Haven, CT 06520
Van Loon, Ernest J., 5215 North 33rd St., Phoenix, AZ 85018
Van Syckle, L. George, 250 Rt 519, Wantage, NJ 07461
Van Tassell,Col Frederick, USA4302 Gull Cove, New Smyrna Beach, FL 32169
Van Wagenen, John, 10 Storm Haven Court, Stevensville, MD 21666
Vanderbilt, Norman L., 5181 Choc Cliff Dr., Bonita, CA 91902
Vanderree, Arthur E., 14392 Ehlen Way, Tustin, CA 92680
Varano, Bishop Anthony C, 617 Breakwater Terrace, Sebastian, FL 32958
Velar, John A., 2869 Ardsley Rd., Wantagh, NY 11793
Vellios, Gus, 2706 East 65th St., Brooklyn, NY 11234
Venable, Mr.& Mrs. Charles L, 13301 Tierra Montanosa N.E., Albuquerque, NM 87112
Ventres, Col Robert, USAF 6213 Glenview Court, Alexandria, VA 22312
Venzke, Ben N., 1197 Boylston St ., No. 34, Boston, MA 02215
Verhaegen, Alix, 2901 S. Sepulveda Blvd., No. 105, Los Angeles, CA 90064
Verr, Steven R., 4911 West Flanders Rd., McHenry, IL 60050
Vertefeuille, Ms Jeanne R., 6800 Fleetwood Rd., No. 407, McLean, VA 22101
Vetrone, Col Phillip L., USA 1626 Sheridan Rd., North Chicago, IL 60064
Vetter, Ms. Elisabeth L., 5335 42nd St., N.W., Washington, DC 20015
Vetter, Michael F., 28 Salem St., Salem, NH 03079
Vezerts, John, 1102 Bellevista Court, Severna Park, MD 21146
Vieler, Col Eric, USA P.O. Box 8611, Incline Village, NV 89450
Vincent, Edward W., 1701 Hinsdale, Toledo, OH 43614
Violette, Donald, P.O. Box 8412, Allenstown, Cent Queensland 4700 AUSTRALIA,
Voelker, Mrs. Genevieve, 5521 80th St., N. No. 416, St. Petersburg, FL 33709
Vogel, Maj Vance V., USAR P.O. Box 638, Gibsonton, FL 33534
Voigt, Frederick A., 5016 25th St., South Arlington, VA 22206
Voigt, Henry K., 210 Mendell Pl., New Castielle, DE 19720
Volenick, William G., 2525 Jonathan Rd., Ellicott City, MD 21042
Vollono, Ralph, 14109 28th Ave., No. 50, Flushing, NY 11354
von Oito, Mrs.Mary Eloise S., 2818 36th Place, NW, Washington, DC 20007
Von Peterffy, George A., 105 Field Point Circle, Greenwich, CT 06830
Vorona, Dr. Jack, 3337 Manfield Rd., Falls Church, VA 22041
– **W** –
Wade, Robert B., 10198 Wavell Rd., Fairfax, VA 22032
Wade, Robert P., 11307 Owl Lane, Port Richey, FL 34668
Wagley, Elizabeth, 544 E. 86th St., New York, NY 10028
Waldman, Richard J., 40th Postal Box R, CMR 462 Box 682, APO, AE 09089
Walker, Capt Bruce, USNR 1226 E. Willow, Wheaton, IL 60187
Walker, Earl M., 6475 Wishbone Terr., Cabin John, MD 20818
Walker, Capt George, USN 8622 Appleton Court, Annandale, VA 22003
Walker, Richard J. Jr., P.O. Box 888, Marshfield, MA 02050
Walker, Ambassador Richard, 700 Spring Lake Rd., Columbia, SC 29206
Walker, Col William L., USAF635 Cinnamon Court, Satellite Beach, FL 32937
Wallace, Howard H. Jr., 2204 Glasgow Rd., Alexandria, VA 22307
Waller, John H., 708 Beigrove Rd., McLean, VA 22101
Wallerstein, Lee, 3505 Thornapple St., Chevy Chase, MD 20815
Walley, James E., Route I, Taylorsville, MS 39168
Wallsten, Richard P., P.O. Box 320, Alton Bay, NH 03810
Walrath, Barry A., 1490 Hampton Hill Circle, McLean, VA 22101
Walsh, Len, 1529 Laurel Hill Rd., Vienna, VA 22182
Walsh, LtCol Robert F., USAR 4323 Center Oak Woods, San Antonio, TX 78249

Walsh, Thomas M. Jr., 436 Montauk Dr., Westfield, NJ 07090
Walton, Col Frank, USMCR Colony Surf, 2895 Kalakaua Avenue, Honolulu, HI 96815
Wannall, Mrs. Trudic C., 305 Southwest Dr., Silver Spring, MD 20901
Wannall, Mr. W. Raymond, 305 Southwest Dr., Silver Spring, MD 20901
Ward, Francis H., 200 South Birch Rd., No 304, Fort Lauderdale, FL 33316
Ward, Ms. Juliet Blume, 44 Hilicrest Rd., Mill Valley, CA 94941
Wardinski, Col Michael L., USA8602 Cherry Valley Lane, Alexandria, VA 22309
Ware, Col. Joseph M., USAF505 Balfour, San Antonio, TX 78239
Warner, Charles J., 4616 Kitsap Way, Bremerton, WA 98312
Warner, Glen T., 2527 E Irwin Court, Mesa, AZ 85204
Warner, John S., 4081 E. Pontatoe Canyon Dr., Tucson, AZ 85718
Warner, Capt William T., The Parc Vista, No 314, 801 15th St., S. Arlington, VA 22202
Warren, Ward W., 1314 Garden Hall Circle, Reston, VA 22094
Warrick, Moudina C., 5428 W. State Ave., Glendale, AZ 85301
Watkins, Quentin H., P.O. Box 191, Hamilton, IN 46742
Wattles, Robert S., 1700 No Jefferson St., Arlington, VA 22205
Waugh, Michael J., 2814 Jorwoods Dr., Austin, TX 78745
Weaver, Col Donald E., USAF620 Herr's Ridge Rd., Gettysburg, PA 17325
Weaver, Robert W., 1910 36th St., Missoula, MT 59801
Weber, Ralph E., 7420 Grand Parkway, Milwaukee, WI 53213
Webster, Dr. Thomas J., 3 Appomattox Court, Coran, NY 11727
Webster, Hon William H., 9409 Brooke Dr., Bethesda, MD 20817
Wege, LtCol Hans F., AUS 1300 Carmelita Dr, Sierra Vista, AZ 85635
Weidul, Ernest G., Ocean Ave., Kennebunkport, ME 04046
Weil, Hugh H., 4406 Greenwich Pky., NW Washington, DC 20007
Weimar, Vernon H., 13110 Hathaway Dr., Wheaton, MD 20906
Weinbrenner, Col George, USAF 7400 Crestway, San Antonio, TX 78239
Weiner, Mr. Michael, 693 Summit Dr., Webster, NY 14580
Weiner, Tim, 1627 I St., NW, Washington, DC 20006
Weininger, Janet Ray, 17901 SW 84th Ave., Miami, FL 33157
Weinschel, George, P.O. Box 1278, Corsicana, TX 751 1 0
Weinstein, LtGen Sidney, USAEWA 13873 Park Center Rd., Hemdon, VA 22071
Weisman, Jacob, 535 East 86th St., New York, NY 10028
Welborn, James F., P.O. Box 120888, Clermont. FL 34712
Welch, Col Emmett E., USA2118 No. Berwick Dr., Prestwick, Myrtle Beach, SC 29575
Welk, Robert L., 6722 Melrose Dr., McLean, VA 22101
Welkom, LtCol Jerome, USAF 4 Cambridge Ct., Buffalo Grove, IL 60089
Wells, Col Thomas J., USA919 Punabele Place, Honolulu, HI 96821
Wenk, Max, 2300 Army Navy Dr. No 521, Arlington, VA 22202
Wesolik, Kenneth F., 1511 Linden Hurst Ave., McLean, VA 22101
Wessell, Earl R., 35013 Camino Capistrano, Capistrano Beach, CA 92624
West, LtCdr Maxwell C., USN3124 Lippizaner Lane, Walnut Creek, CA 94598
Westerberg, Sandra B., 8N433 Shady Ln., Elgin, IL 60123
Westin, Peter G., 1142 Fairwood Close, NW Acworth, GA 30101
Wetzel, Francis K., 104 W. Marion Drive, Dothan, AL 36301
Weymouth, David E., 126 Madrona Ave., Belvedere, CA 94920
Whatton, Capt James E., USN154 Vistas Drive, Sequim, WA 98382
Wheaton, Roger S., 5595 Marshall House Ct., Burke, VA 22015
Wheeler, Charles B., 117710 Maryknoll Ave., Bethesda, MD 20817
Wheeler, Douglas L., 27 Mill Rd., Durham, NH 03824
Wheeler, James L., 2018 Yarmouth Court, Falls Church, VA 22043
Whelan, Lawrence, 208 Lantem Park La., N. Southbury, CT 06488
Whidden, Glenn, 13214 L'Enfant Dr., Ft.Washington, MD 20744
Whipple, David D., 9509 Watts Rd., Great Falls, VA 22066
Whipple, Col Howard W, USA5723 8th Avenue Dr., West Bradenton, FL 34209
Whipple, John L., P.O. Box 144, Cave Creek, AZ 85331
White, Adam C., 17278 Lakemont Dr., Culpeper, VA 22701
White, Dr. Cloyd T. Ph.D., DET 4 2STG Box 155, APO, AE 09815
White, Harry E., 333 East 55th St., Penthouse A, New York, NY 10022
White, Robert D., 6407 Stoneham Rd., Bethesda, MD 20817
White, Wells B., 9001 Southwick St., Fairfax, VA 22031
Whitehead, Harvey A. ,P.O. Box 572, Palmer, AK 99645
Whitlow, Capt Robert S., P.O. Box 1321, New Canaan, CT 06840
Whitney, Capt Frank D., USAR 1308 Biltmore Dr., Charlotte, NC 28207

Wiatrak, Kenneth, Metrolight Studios 5724 West 3rd St., Los Angeles, CA 90036
Wibalda, Maj Richard T., USAF2925 Darby Falls Dr., Las Vegas, NV 89134
Wideman, Lawrence G., 676 Neff Rd., Grosse Pointe, MI 48230
Wiggins, Lloyd G., 3239 London Dr., Yuma, AZ 85364
Wilbrant, Roger L., 7612 Mendota Place, Springfield, VA 22150
Wiley, Col G. R., USAR 777 Marina Boulevard, San Francisco, CA 94123
Wilkins, Capt Richard S., AUS 800 Parkview Dr., 4902, Hallandale, FL 33009
Will, Earl G., 312 Tallahassee Dr., N.E., St.Petersburg, FL 33702
Will, LtCol Thomas S., USAF4645 Aaron Court, Jefferson, MD 21755
Willard, Eugene J., 172 W. Queen Lane, Philadelphia, PA 19144
Willams, Bruce F., 1505 Ynez Place Rd., Coronado, CA 92118
Williams, BGen Charles, USAF 502 Sunhaven Dr., San Antonio, TX 78239
Williams, Eleazer A., 3804 Garfield St., NW, Washington, DC 20006
Williams, Garland W. Jr., 1001 Green Pine Blvd., No. B-2, West Palm Beach, FL 33409
Williams, LtGen James A., USA8928 Maurice Lane, Annandale, VA 22003
Williams, Col James H., USA712IG Rock Ridge Lane, Alexandria, VA 22315
Williams, Joseph V. III, 623 Ocoee St.,NW, Cleveland, TN 37311
Williams, Mrs. June Neff, 2072 Kedge Dr., Vienna, VA 22180
Williams, Kristin M., 8 South Wheaton Rd., Horseheads, NY 14845
Williams, Michael W., USN 664 Crescent Dr., Chula Vista, CA 91911
Williams, Philip R., 292 SE 30th Ave., Hillsboro, OR 97123
Williams, Dr. Robert J., 4508 Arberst Lane, Bethesda, MD 20814
Williams, Tracy L, 4540 Crest Rd., Fair Oaks, CA 95628
Williamson, Col Charles, USMC P.O. Box 1460, Mount Dora, FL 32757
Williamson, Eugene, 1008 Millbrook Dr., Greenville, NC 27858
Williamson, Richard E., P.O. Box 289, Florissant, CO 80816
Williamson, Cdr Robert C., USN3906 Butternut Ct., Brandon, FL 33511
Willner, Eddie H., 2703 Welcome Dr., Falls Church, VA 22046
Wills, Dennis G., 7461 Girard Ave., La Jolla, CA 92037
Willson, Charles E., 11001 Glen Rd., Potomac, MD 20854
Wilson, Col Daniel E., USAR P.O. Box 11567, Charlotte, NC 28220
Wilson, Ms Diann V., 16345 W. Dixie Hwy., No. 346, North Miami Beach, FL 33162
Wilson, Larry Donald, 7813 Perry Rd., Baltimore, MD 21236
Wilson, Robert E., P.O.Box 290, Annandale, VA 22003
Wilson, Sam, 10126 Spring Lake Terrace., Fairfax, VA 22030
Wiltamuth, Richard E., 1700 Kiva Rd., Silver Spring, MD 20904
Wing, CWO Virgil N., USN 3098 N. Acorn Court, Dale City, VA 22193
Winn, Col Arthur C., USA9505 Laurlin Court, Vienna, VA 22180
Wisniewski, Jerome J., RR. 1, Box 98B, Broad Run, VA 22014
Wold, Mark Christian, 715 Greenridge Ave., Earlville, IL 60518
Wolfe, Col H. G., USAP.O. Box 3514, Grand Central Station, Glendale, CA 91221
Wolfe, Leonard W, 410 Homer St., Newton Centre, MA 02159
Wolfe, Robert, 602 Crestwood Dr., Alexandria, VA 22302
Wolin, Ronald, 437 Bartell Dr., Chesapeake, VA 23320
Womack, Bruce L., 2834 Triway Lane, Houston, TX 77043
Wood, Lt Gen C. Norman, USAF 5440 Mt.Corcoran Place, Burke. VA 22015
Wood, Capt Sidney E. Jr., USN1614 Courtland Rd., Alexandria, VA 22306
Woodgate, LtCol Cecil L., USAP.O. Box F, Boulder, MT 59632
Woodruff, Ronald S., 101 McIntyre St., Wilmington, IL 60481
Woodson, LtCol Edward, USA 7101 38th Dr., SE, Lacey, WA 98503
Woodward, Ms Betty W., 3800 North Fairfax Dr., No 509, Arlington, VA 22203
Woodward, Dr. Lawrence, G. 4026 N. Tazewell St., Arlington, VA 22207
Wootten, Col Edward, USAF115 Haverhill Way, San Antonio, TX 78209
Work, Col Robert E., USAF19015 Sunnyside Drive, Saratoga, CA 95070
Wray, Dr.Samuel S. Jr., 2227 16th St., Newport Beach, CA 92663
Wren, Patrick L., USNR 15603 Gulf Fwy., No.1402, Webster, TX 77598
Wright, Maj Albert J., AUS3820 Ridge Rd., Annandale, VA 22003
Wright, Col Burchard, USAR6333 St. Andrews Circle, Ft Myers, FL 33919
Wright, BGen Corey J., USA 121 Lafayette Rd., No. 622, Syracuse, NY 13205
Wright, James L., 830 Monroe St., No. 208, Annapolis, MD 21403
Wright, Richard B., P.O.Box 4188, Sunriver, OR 97707
Wurzberger, W. Clark, 812 Paloma Ave., Burlingame, CA 94010
Wyatt, Mark, 3310 P St., NW, Washington, DC 20007
Wynecoop, LtCol Joseph, USAF 3832 Hillway Dr., Glendale, CA 91208

– Y –

Yarnall, Raymond T, P.O. Box 414, York Harbor, ME 03911
Yates, Ron E., 2174 University Dr., Naperville, IL 60565
Yatsevitch, Col Gratian M., P.O. Box 902, Camden, ME 04843
Yeates, Eugene F., 1311 Falismead Way, Rockville, MD 20854
York, John A., 5314 Black Oak Drive, Fairfax, VA 22032
Yosick, Thomas M., 2180 Garrett Rd., Hanover, PA 17331
Young, Maj. Keith D., USAF325 1/2 Eighth St., Coronado, CA 92118
Young, Ronald F., 1845 Las Galinas Avenue, San Rafael, CA 94903
Young, Warren H., 22 Laguna Seca St., Helena. CA 94574
Yu, David C.L., 2510 Morning Sun Dr., Hilltop Village Richmond, CA 94806

– Z –

Zacharias, Col George, USA 7736 Tauxemont Rd,, Alexandria, VA 22308
Zaid, Mark S., 1600 South Eads St., No I18-S, Arlington, VA 22202
Zammarella, Louis J., 11600 Connecticut Ave., Silver Spring, MD 20902
Zamory, David A., 8306 Lincoln Lane, No 104, McLean, VA 22102
Zaretz, Albert, 108-22 Queens Blvd., No 222, Forest Hill, NY 11375
Zarker, Alvin B., 11814 lndianhead Dr., Austin, TX 78753
Zaslow, Milton S., 9039 Sligo Creek Pkwy., No 308, Silver Spring, MD 20901
Zellmer, Ernest J., 668 Grant Court, Satellite Beach, FL 32937
Zemaitis, Bruno J., P.O. Box 145, Santa Maria, CA 93456
Zeman, Charles J., 137 Edgewater Dr., Edgewater, MD 21037
Zenowitz, Allen R., 2555 Pennsylvania Ave., NW, No 507, Washington, DC 20037
Ziegler, David, 4200 Wilson Blvd., No.850, Arlington, VA 22203
Zimmer, G.H. Jr., 9826 E. Watford Way, Sun Lakes, AZ 85248
Zimmerman, Col Thomas, USA800 Washington, Box 922, Oak Park, IL 60302
Zindroski, James E., 9512 Vista Drive, North Royalton, OH 44133
Zingsheim, Gerald A., 9440 Country Trail, Loveland, CO 45140
Zoche, Alfred, 159 Hazelwood River Rd., Edgewater, FL 32141
Zschock, Capt Charles W, USN 400 Madison St. , No 1206, Alexandria, VA 22314
Ztimbrum, William F., 3442 14th St., N. Naples, FL 33940

Documents

All documents reproduced in this book were compiled by the late Robert T. Crowley, once Deputy Director for Operations for the Central Intelligence Agency. All handwritten notes on them are Crowley's.

Although many paragraphs of the Driscoll Report have already been reproduced in the main body of the book, a complete, un-cropped copy of it is included as the first document in this section. The "Appendix" to this document, as mentioned in the cover letter, contains the sources for this report. Since most individuals listed in it might not have any specific knowledge about the assassina-tion of John F. Kennedy and certainly were not involved in it, it was decided not to include this list in the appendix of this book in order to protect the privacy of these individuals.

The second document reproduced here is a typewritten copy of a departmental memorandum by FBI Director J. Edgar Hoover of November 29, 1963, clearly indicating the strong concerns of the highest U.S. authorities to prevent a thorough and independent investigation into the background of Kennedy's assassination.

The third document is the carbon copy of an *aide-mémoire* writ-ten by Robert T. Crowley, like Hoover's memorandum addressing L. B. Johnson's concerns, but also referring to the tactics planned to distract the public from the ugly truth and briefly mentioning the problem of the fourth assassin Guidobaldo Fini who got away.

The fourth document is the so-called ZIPPER Document. Pages 7-11, consisting of obscene photos of J. F. Kennedy, have been omitted here for reasons of civility, but can be used to corroborate the authenticity of this document if it should prove necessary. Also, according to its table of contents, the original of this docu-ment contained "Copies of NSA communication intercepts on RFK" on pages 29-97. These pages were not found in the photocopies retrieved from R. T. Crowley's papers.

In order to be able to read and interpret this document properly, it is followed by a list of explained abbreviations used in it. Though without official letterhead and signature, this document is certainly the most intriguing of all, because it contains answers to almost all the Whos, Whens, Whys, and Hows one can possibly come up with regarding the Assassination of J. F. Kennedy. It was probably produced by the five persons mentioned in the distribution list in order to cover themselves, since this document clearly proves that the assassination of J. F. Kennedy was anything else but a private plot by a few CIA senior officers going rampant.

The last document is an official internal organizational chart of the CIA. Robert T. Crowley was second in command of the powerful "Directorate of Operations (Clandestine Services)." As such, he was also responsible for organizing the assassination of John F. Kennedy, in conjunction with his close associate, James Jesus Angleton, head of the CIA's Counterintelligence section. These top CIA leaders had discovered that Kennedy was passing the highest level CIA secrets to the Soviet Union.

DEFENSE INTELLIGENCE AGENCY
WASHINGTON, D. C. 20301

20 APRIL 1978

SUBJECT: Soviet Intelligence Report on Assassination of President KENNEDY

TO: Director

The following report has been prepared at your request in response to a Soviet report on the assassination of President John F. KENNEDY on 22 NOV 1963. The Soviet document (see Enclosure a) has been obtained from a fully reliable source and duly authenticated.

This report is an analysis of the Soviet document and is done on a paragraph-by-paragraph basis.

Material in this analysis has been taken from a number of sources indicated in the Appendix and is to be considered classified at the highest level. Nothing contained in this report may be disseminated to any individual or agency without prior written permission of the Director or his appointed deputy.

This agency does not assume, and cannot verify, the correctness of the material contained herein, although every reasonable effort has been made to do so. Any use of information contained in this report must be paraphrased and sources, either individual or agency, must not be credited.

VEDDER B. DRISCOLL
Colonel, USA
Chief, Soviet/Warsaw Pact
   Division
Directorate for Intelligence
   Research

1 Enclosure
Appendix

NOTE: The Russian language file is not attached to this report and exists in
      official translation only.

Driscoll Report, 19 pp. plus cover letter

ENCLOSURE A

THE SOVIET INTELLIGENCE STUDY (translation)

    1. On 22 November, 1963, American President John Kennedy was shot and killed during a political motor trip through the Texas city of Dallas. The President was riding at the head of the procession in his official state car, seated in the right rear with his wife on his left side. Seated in front of him was the Governor of Texas and his wife, also on his left side. The vehicle was an open car without side or top protection of any kind. There was a pilot car in front, about 30 meters, and the President's car was flanked by motorcycle outriders located two to a side roughly parallel with the rear wheels of the State car.

    2. The President and his party were driving at a speed of about 20 kilometers per hour through the built-up area of Dallas and greeted the many people lining the streets along his route. Security was supplied by the Secret Service supplemented by local police. There were two Secret Service agents in the front of the car. One was driving the car. Other agents were in cars following the Presidential vehicle and Dallas police on motorbikes were on both sides of the Presidential car but at the rear of it. There was a pilot car in front of the President's car but it was some distance away.

    3. The course of the journey was almost past all the occupied area. The cars then turned sharply to the right and then again to the left to go to the motorway leading to a meeting hall where the President was to speak at a dinner. It is considered very bad security for such an official drive to decrease its speed or to make unnecessary turnings or stops. (Historical note: It was just this problem that led directly to positioning the Austrian Heir in front of wating assassins at Sarajevo in 1914) The route was set by agents of the Secret Service and published in the Dallas newspapers before the arrival of the President and his party.

    4. After the last turning to the left, the cars passed a tall building on the right side of the street that was used as a warehouse for the storage of school books. This building was six stories tall and had a number of workers assigned to it. There were no official security people in this building, either on the roof or at the windows. Also, there were no security agents along the roadway on either side. All security agents were riding either in the Presidential car (two in the front) and in the following vehicles.

    5. As the President's state car passed this building, some shots were heard. The exact source and number of these shots was never entirely determined. Some observers thought that the shots came from above and behind while many more observers in the area stated that the shots came from the front and to the right of the car. There was a small area with a decorative building and some trees and bushes there and many saw unidentified people in this area. Many people standing in front of this area to watch the cars stated that shots came from behind them.

-1-

6. When the first shots were fired, the President was seen to lean forward and clutch at his throat with both hands. Immediately when this happened, the Secret Service driver of the President's state car slowed down the vehicle until it was almost stopped. This was a direct breach of their training which stated that in such events where firing occurred, the driver of the President's car would immediately drive away as quickly as possible.

7. At the same time as the first shot, there was a second one, this one from above and behind. This bullet struck the Governor, sitting in front of the President and slightly to his right, in the right upper shoulder. The bullet went downwards into the chest cavity, breaking ribs, struck his wrist and lodged in his left upper thigh. There were then two shots fired at the President's car. The first shot initiated the action and this one appears to have hit the President in the throat. If so, it must have been fired from in front of the car, not behind it.

8. Right at this moment, there was one other shot. The shell, obviously struck the President on the upper rear of the right side of his head, throwing him back and to the left. Also, at this time, blood, pieces of skull and brains could be seen flying to the left where the motorbike police guard was struck with this material on his right side and on the right side of his motorbike.

9. Immediately after this final shot, the driver then began to increase his speed and the cars all went at increasing speed down under the tunnel.

10. The fatally injured President and the seriously injured Governor were very quickly taken to a nearby hospital for treatment. The President was declared as dead and his body was removed, by force, to an aircraft and flown to Washington. The badly wounded Governor was treated at the hospital for his wounds and survived.

11. Within moments of the shots fired at the President, a Dallas motorcycle police officer ran into the book building and up to the second floor in the company of the manager of the establishment. Here, the policeman encountered a man later positively identified as one Lee Harvey Oswald, an employee of the book storage company. Oswald was drinking a Coca-Cola and appeared to be entirely calm and collected. (Later it was said that he had rushed down four flights of steps past other employees in a few moments after allegedly shooting the President. It is noted from the records that none of the other employees on the staircase ever saw Oswald passing them.) The elevator which moved freight and personnel between the floors was halted at the sixth floor and turned off so that it could not be recalled to persons below wishing to use it.

12. After meeting the police officer and apparently finishing his drink, Oswald went down to the main floor and left the building, unnoticed.

13. Oswald then went to his apartment by a public bus and on foot, dressed in new clothes and left the building. His apartment manager observed that a

-2-

police car stopped in front of the building and blew its horn several times. She was unaware of the reason for this.

14. Oswald was then stated to have been halted by a local police officer whom he was alleged to have shot dead. The only witness who positively identified Oswald as the shooter was considered to be unstable and unreliable.

15. Oswald then entered a motion picture house and was later arrested there by the police. He was beaten in the face by the police and taken into custody.

16. When the captured Oswald was photographed by the reporters, he claimed that he was not guilty of shooting anyone and this was a position he maintained throughout his interrogations.

17. All records of his interrogation, carried out by the Dallas police and the Secret Service, were subsequently destroyed without a trace.

18. During the course of the interrogations, Oswald was repeatedly led up and down very crowded corridors of the police headquarters with no thought of security. This is an obvious breach of elementary security that was noted at the time by reporters. It now appears that Oswald's killer was seen and photographed in the crowds in the building.

19. The American Marine defector, Lee Harvey Oswald, entered the Soviet Union in October of 1959. Initially, Oswald, who indicated he wanted to "defect" and reside in the Soviet Union, was the object of some suspicion by Soviet intelligence authorities. He was at first denied entrance, attempted a "suicide" attempt and only when he was more extensively interrogated by competent agents was it discovered that he was in possession of material that potentially had a great intelligence value.

20. Oswald, who as a U.S. Marine, was stationed at the Atsugi air field in Japan, had been connected with the Central Intelligence Agency's U2 intelligence-gathering aircraft program and was in possession of technical manuals and papers concerning these aircraft and their use in overflights of the Soviet Union.

21. The subject proved to be most cooperative and a technical analysis of his documentation indicated that he was certainly being truthful with Soviet authorities. In addition to the manuals, Oswald was able to supply Soviet authorities with a wealth of material, much of which was unknown and relatively current. As a direct result of analysis of the Oswald material, it became possible to intercept and shoot down a U2 aircraft flown by CIA employee Gary Powers.

22. On the basis of the quality of this material, Oswald was granted asylum in the Soviet Union and permitted to settle in Minsk under the supervision of the Ministry of the Interior. This was partially to reward him for his cooperation and also to remove him from the possible influence of American authorities at the Embassy in Moscow.

23. Oswald worked in a radio factory, was given a subsidized apartment in Minsk and kept under constant surveillance. He was very pro-Russian, learned

to speak and read the language, albeit not with native fluency, and behaved himself well in his new surroundings.

24. Although Oswald was a known homosexual, he nevertheless expressed an interest in women as well and his several casual romantic affairs with both men and women were duly noted.

25. Oswald became involved with Marina Nikolaevna Prusakova, the niece of a Minsk-based intelligence official. He wished to marry this woman who was attractive but cold and ambitious. She wished to leave the Soviet Union and emigrate to the United States for purely economic reasons. Since his marrying a Soviet citizen under his circumstances was often most difficult, Oswald began to speak more and more confidentially with his intelligence contacts in Minsk. He finally revealed that he was an agent for the United States Office of Naval Intelligence and had been recruited by them to act as a conduit between their office and Soviet intelligence.

26. The official material on the CIA operations was entirely authentic and had been supplied to Oswald by his controllers in the ONI. It was apparent, and Oswald repeatedly stated, that the CIA was completely unaware of the removal of sensitive documents from their offices. This removal, Oswald stated, was effected by the ONI personnel stationed at Atsugi air field. Oswald was unaware of the reasons for this operation but had been repeatedly assured that the mission was considered of great national importance and that if he proved to be successful, he would be afforded additional and profitable future employment. It appears that Oswald was considered to be a one-time operative and was expendable. His purpose was to establish a reputation as a pro-Russian individual who would then "defect" to the Soviet Union and pass over the U2 material. He did not seem to realize at the time he "defected" that once he had been permitted to live in the Soviet on an official governmental subsidy, returning to America would be very difficult, if not impossible.

27. Now, with his romantic, and very impractical, attachment to Prusakova, he was being pressured by her to marry and then take her with him back to the United States. Oswald was informed that this was not a possible option for him. He became very emotional and difficult to deal with but finally made the suggestion that if he were allowed to marry and return to the United States, he would agree to work in reality for the Soviet Union.

28. After referring this matter to higher authority, it was decided to accede to Oswald's requests, especially since he was of no further use to Soviet intelligence and might well be of some service while resident in America.

29. Marriage was permitted and his return was expedited both by the Soviet authorities and the Americans who were informed, via a letter from Oswald, that he was in possession of intelligence material of value to them. This valuable information was duly given to him, a reversal to be noted on his original mission!

30. Oswald was given prepared information of such a nature as to impress American intelligence and permitted to contact intelligence officials in the American Embassy in Moscow. He was then permitted by the Americans to return to the United States with his new wife.

31. In America, Oswald no longer worked with the ONI because he was not able to further assist them. Besides, he was viewed as dangerous because he had knowledge of the ONI theft and use of CIA documents.

32. While in America, Oswald then worked as a paid informant for the Federal Bureau of Investigation who had contacted him when he returned and requested his assistance with domestic surveillance against pro-Soviet groups. He was assigned, in New Orleans, the task of infiltrating the anti-Castro groups which were nominally under the control of the CIA.

33. It is noted that there exists a very strong rivalry between the FBI and the CIA. The former is nominally in charge of domestic counterintelligence and the latter in charge of foreign intelligence. They have been fighting for power ever since the CIA was first formed in 1947. Oswald has stated that the FBI was aware of this ONI-sponsored defection with stolen CIA U2 documents but this is not a proven matter.

34. Later, Oswald was transferred to Dallas, Texas, by the FBI and he then secured a position in a firm which dealt in very secret photographic matters. Here, he was able to supply both the FBI and Soviet intelligence with identical data.

35. FBI reports, kept secret, show clearly that Oswald was paid by the FBI as an informant.

36. In New Orleans, a center of Cuban insurgent activity, Oswald was in direct contact with FBI officials and worked for a Guy Bannister, former FBI agent. Oswald infiltrated the ranks of Cuban insurgents and reported his findings to the FBI.

37. At that time, the FBI was involved, at the request of the Attorney General, Robert Kennedy, in watching the clandestine activities of the CIA and its Alpha and Omega special commando groups, some of whom were in training in the New Orleans area.

38. The American President was greatly concerned that continued and fully unauthorized para-military action against Cuba might upset the balance he had achieved in seeking peace with the Soviet Union.

39. It is known from information inside the CIA and also from Cuban double agents that the CIA was, in conjunction with the highest American military leadership, to force an American invasion of Cuba.

40. These joint plans, which consisted of acts of extreme provocation by American units against American property and citizens, were unknown to Kennedy.

41. When the American President discovered that Cuban insurgents, under the control of the CIA and with the support of the highest military leadership, were embarked on a course of launching military action against American naval bases under the cover of being Cuban regular troops, he at once ordered a halt.

-5-

42. Kennedy also informed the Soviet Premier directly of these planned actions and assured him that he had prevented them from being executed. The Premier expressed his gratitude and hoped that Kennedy would be successful in enforcing his will and preventing any other such adventures.

43. The American President, unsure of the depth of his influence with the leadership of the American military and the CIA, ordered the FBI to investigate these matters and ordered the Director, Hoover, to report directly to him on his findings.

44. Oswald was a part of the FBI surveillance of the Cuban insurgents in the New Orleans area.

45. Oswald made a number of public appearances passing out pro-Castro leaflets in order to ingratiate himself with the insurgents.

46. At the FBI request, a local television station filmed Oswald passing out these leaflets and had this film shown on local stations in order to enhance Oswald's image. When his mission was finished, Oswald was then sent to Dallas to observe and penetrate the Russian colony there.

47. Two days after the shooting of the American President, the alleged assassin, Oswald was shot to death in the basement of the Dallas Police Department while he was being transferred to another jail. On the day of the assassination, November 22, FBI Chief Hoover notified the authorities in Dallas that Oswald should be given special security.

48. This killing was done in the presence of many armed police officers by a known criminal and associate of the American Mafia named Jack Rubenstein, or "Ruby" as he was also known. "Ruby" had a long past of criminal association with the Mafia in Chicago, Illinois, a major area of gangster control in America. "Ruby" had once worked for the famous Al Capone and then for Sam Giancana. This man was head of the Chicago mob at the time of the assassination.

49. "Ruby" was the owner of a drinking establishment in Dallas that specialized in dancing by naked women and was also a close friend of many police officers in Dallas. "Ruby" had been seen and photographed in the Dallas police department while Oswald was being interrogated. It should be noted here that suspect Oswald was very often taken by Dallas police out into the completely unguarded hallways of the building and in the presence of many persons unknown to the police. This is viewed as either an attempt to have Oswald killed or a very incompetent and stupid breach of basic security.

50. The timing by "Ruby" of his entrance into the guarded basement was far too convenient to be accidental. Also, the method of his shooting of Oswald showed a completely professional approach. "Ruby" stepped out from between two policemen, holding a revolver down along his leg to avoid detection. As he stepped towards the suspect, "Ruby" raised his right hand with the revolver and fired upwards into Oswald's body. The bullet severed major arteries and guaranteed Oswald's death.

51. Although "Ruby" subsequently pretended to be mentally disturbed, his actions showed professional calculation to a degree. This play-acting was continued into his trial and afterwards. "Ruby" was convicted of the murder of

and sentenced to death. H died in prison of cancer in January of 1967 after
an appeal from his sentence had been granted by the court judge. Information
indicates that he was given a fatal injection.

52. "Ruby's" statements should not be confused with his actions. He
was a <u>professional criminal</u>, had <u>excellent connections with the Dallas police</u>,
had been involved with activities in Cuba and <u>gun running into that country</u>
and some evidence has been produced to show that he and Oswald had knowledge
of each other.

53. Like Oswald, "Ruby" too had homosexual activities and one public
witness firmly placed Oswald in "Ruby's" club prior to the assassination.

54. In view of later developments and disclosures, the use of a
<u>Chicago killer</u> with local Mafia connections to kill Oswald is <u>not surprising</u>.
Stories of "Ruby's" eccentricity were highlighted by American authorities to
make it appear that he, like suspect Oswald, was an eccentric, single individual who acted out of emotion and not under orders.

55. As in the case of Oswald, there was never a proven motive for
"Ruby's" acts. <u>Oswald had no reason whatsoever to shoot the President</u>, had
never committed any proven acts of violence. Although he was purported to
have shot at a fascist General, it was badly presented and in all probability
was a "red herring" to "prove" Oswald's desire to shoot people. "Ruby", a
professional criminal with a long record of violence, claimed he shot Oswald
to "protect" the President's wife from testifying. This statement appears to
be an obvious part of "Ruby's" attempt to defend himself by claiming to be
mad.

56. It is obvious that <u>"Ruby" killed Oswald to silence him</u>. Since
<u>Oswald was not involved</u> in the killing of the President, continued interro-
gation of him leading to a court trial would have very strongly exposed the
weakness of the American government's attempt to blame him for the crime.

57. Silencing Oswald promptly was a matter of serious importance for the
actual killers.

58. That Oswald could not be convicted with the evidence at hand, his
removal was vital. He could then be tried and convicted in public <u>without any</u>
danger.

59. Rubenstein was not a man of intelligence but was a devoted member
of the American criminal network.

60. Just prior to the assassination, Rubenstein was in a meeting with
representatives of the criminal network and was told that he was to be held
in readiness to kill someone who might be in Dallas police custody.

61. It was felt that Rubenstein was a well-connected man with the
Dallas police department and that he might have access to the building
without a challenge. He was also informed that he could be considered a
"great hero" in the eyes of the American public. Rubenstein was a man of
little self-worth and this approach strongly influenced him in his future
actions.

62. A very large number of published books about the assassination have appeared since the year 1963. Most of these books are worthless from a historical point of view. They represent the views of obsessed people and twist information to suit the author's beliefs.

63. There are three main ideas written about:

    a. The American gangsters killed the President because his brother, the American Attorney General, was persecuting them;

    b. Cuban refugees felt that Mr. Kennedy had deserted their cause of ousting Cuban chief of state Castro;

    c. Various American power groups such as the capitalist business owners, fascist political groups, racists, internal and external intelligence organizations either singly or in combination are identified.

64. American officials have not only made no effort to silence these writers but in many cases have encouraged them. The government feels, as numerous confidential reports indicate, that the more lunatic books appear, the better. This way, the real truth is so concealed as to be impenetrable.

65. It was initially of great concern to our government that individuals inside the American government were utilizing Oswald's "Communist/Marxist" appearance to suggest that the assassination was of a Soviet origin.

66. In order to neutralize this very dangerous theme, immediately after the assassination, the Soviet Union fully cooperated with American investigating bodies and supplied material to them showing very clearly that Oswald was not carrying out any Soviet design.

67. Also, false defectors were used to convince the Americans that Oswald was considered a lunatic by the Soviet Union, and had not been connected with the Soviet intelligence apparatus in any way. He was, of course, connected but it was imperative to disassociate the Soviet Union with the theory that Oswald, an American intelligence operative, had been in collusion with them concerning the assassination.

68. The false defector, Nosenko, a provable member of Soviet intelligence, was given a scenario that matched so closely the personal attitudes of Mr. Hoover of the FBI that this scenario was then officially supported by Mr. Hoover and his bureau.

69. Angleton of the CIA at once suspected Nosenko's real mission and subjected him to intense interrogation but finally, Nosenko has been accepted as a legitimate defector with valuable information on Oswald.

70. Because of this business, Angleton was forced to resign his post as chief of counter intelligence. This has been considered a most fortunate byproduct of the controversy.

71. The FBI has accepted the legitimacy of Nosenko and his material precisely because it suited them to do so. It was also later the official position of the CIA because the issue dealt specifically with the

involvement, or non-involvement, between Oswald, a private party, and the organs of Soviet intelligence. Since there was no mention of Oswald's connection with American intelligence, this was of great importance to both agencies.

72. It is known now that the American gangsters had very close relations with the Central Intelligence Agency. This relationship began during the war when the American OSS made connections with the Sicilian members of the American gangs in order to assist them against the fascists. The man who performed this liaison was Angleton, later head of counter intelligence for the CIA. These gangster contacts were later utilized by the CIA for its own ends.

73. American foreign policy was, and still is, firmly in the hands of the CIA. It alone makes determinations as to which nation is to be favored and which is to be punished. No nation is permitted to be a neutral; all have to be either in the U.S. camp or are its enemies. Most often, the wishes of American business are paramount in the determination as to which nation will receive U.S. support and which will not only be denied this support but attacked. It is the American CIA and not the Soviet Union, that has divided the world into two warring camps.

74. American, and most especially the CIA, attempts to destabilize a Communist state i.e., Cuba, could not be permitted by the Soviet leadership. Castro was a most valuable client in that he provided an excellent base of intelligence and political operations in the American hemisphere. As the CIA had been setting up its own ring of hostile states surrounding the Soviet Union, Cuba was viewed officially as a completely legitimate area of political expansion. Threats of invasion and physical actions against Cuba were viewed by the Chairman as threats against the Soviet Union itself. It is an absolute fact that both the American President, Kennedy, and his brother, the American Attorney General, were especially active in a sexual sense. A number of sexually explicit pictures of the President engaging in sexual acts are in the official files as are several pictures of the Attorney General, taken while on a visit to Moscow in 1961.

75. The President was aware that a number of these pictures were in Soviet hands and acted accordingly. In addition to a regular parade of whores into the White House, it was also reliably reported from several sources that the President was a heavy user of various kinds of illegal narcotics. It is also known from medical reports that the President suffered from a chronic venereal disease for which he was receiving medical treatment.

76. In order to better cooperate with the Soviet Union, President Kennedy used to regularly keep in close, private communication with the Chairman. These contacts were kept private to prevent negative influences from the State Department and most certainly from the Central Intelligence Agency. The President said several times that he did not trust this agency who was bent on stirring up a war between the two nations. Through this personal contact, many matters that might have escalated due to the interference of others were peacefully settled.

77. The pseudo-defector, Oswald, became then important to the further-ance of the plan to kill the American President. He had strong connections with the Soviet Union; he had married a Soviet citizen; he had been noticed in public advocating support of Fidel Castro. His position in a tall building overlooking the parade route was a stroke of great good fortune to the plotters.

78. Oswald was then reported by the CIA to have gone to Mexico City on 26 September, 1963 and while there, drew considerable attention to his presence in both the Soviet and Cuban embassies. What Oswald might have done in the Cuban embassy is not known for certain but there is no record of his ever having visited the Soviet embassy in Mexico at that time. CIA physical descriptions as well as photographs show that Oswald was not the man depicted. This appears to be a poor attempt on the part of the CIA to embroil both the Soviet Union and Cuba in their affairs. It is understood that the actual assassins were subsequently removed in a wet action but that one apparently escaped and has been the object of intense searches in France and Italy by elements of the CIA.

79. From this brief study, it may be seen that the American President was certainly killed by orders of high officials in the CIA, working in close conjunction with very high American military leaders. It was the CIA belief that Kennedy was not only circumventing their own mapped-out destruct-ion of Fidel Castro by assassination and invasion but actively engaged in contacts with the Soviet Union to betray the CIA actions.

80. The American military leaders (known as the Joint Chiefs of Staff) were also determined upon the same goals, hence both of them worked together to ensure the removal of a President who acted against their best interests and to have him replaced with a weaker man whom they believed they could better control.

81. President Johnson, Kennedy's successor, was very much under the control of the military and CIA during his term in office and permitted enormous escalation in Southeast Asia. The destruction of the Communist movement in that area was of paramount importance to both groups.

ANALYSIS OF THE SOVIET INTELLIGENCE REPORT

1. The Soviet analysis of the assassination of President John F.
Kennedy contains material gleaned from American sources both <u>official</u> and
<u>unofficial</u> i.e., media coverage, etc. Some of this material obviously
stems from sources located inside various agencies. To date, <u>none of
these have been identified.</u>

2. It has long been a concern of the leadership and intelligence
organs of the Soviet Union that blame has been attached to them for this
assassination.

3. The Soviets felt in the days immediately following the assassination that a plot was being developed, or had been developed prior to the
act, that would serve to blame either the Cuban government or themselves
for this action.

4. It was felt that the <u>identification</u> of Lee Harvey Oswald as the
sole assassin was intended to <u>implicate the Soviet Union</u> in the act because
Oswald had been a very vocal supporter of the Marxist theory; had defected
to the Soviet Union and had married a <u>Soviet woman with intelligence connections.</u>

5. The strongly stated official policy of putting Oswald forward as
the sole assassin greatly alarmed the Soviet Union which had already
weathered the very serious Cuban Missile Crisis, a situation that came
perilously close to an atomic war between the two powers.

6. The Soviet leadership had established a strong, albeit secret,
connection between themselves and the American President but with his
death, this clandestine communications channel was closed.

7. The Soviets promptly dispatched a number of senior intelligence
personnel and files to Washington in order to reassure President Johnson
and his top aides that the Soviet Union had no hand in the assassination.

8. Johnson himself was a <u>badly frightened man who</u>, having witnessed
the murder of his predecessor, <u>lived in constant dread of a similar attack</u>
on himself. He also had no stomach for the kind of international brinkmanship as practiced by Kennedy and immediately assured the Soviets that he did
not believe they had anything to do with the killing.

9. The Soviets had learned of the plans formulated by the JCS to create
a reason for military intervention in Cuba in 1962-63. They believed then,
and still believe, that the killing of Kennedy was done partially to create
a causus belli insofar as the Soviet Union itself was concerned.

10. Their information indicated that while Kennedy had not permitted
these provocations to influence his policy, such could not be said for
Johnson. He was viewed as an <u>untried</u> individual and best reassured.

11. One of the strongest supporters of the Soviet point of view was
FBI director Hoover.

-11-

12. Because of the involvement of his agency with Oswald, it was in Hoover's best interest to absolve the Soviets of any complicity and maintain the accepted fiction of Oswald as a deranged person working without assistance of any kind and certainly without any connection to any U.S. agency.

13. It has been alleged that Oswald had also worked for the CIA. This has not been proven although it should be noted that Oswald was in direct contact with CIA agents, associated with the U.S. Embassy in Moscow, while in Russia and had been debriefed by that agency after his return from Russia.

14. Oswald was also intimately connected with De Mohrenschildt who was certainly known to be a CIA operative. Oswald's connections with this man were such as to guarantee that the CIA was aware of Oswald's movements throughout his residence in the Dallas area.

15. When Oswald secured employment at the Texas Book Depository, De Mohrenschildt, according to an FBI report, reported this to the CIA.

16. The existence and location of Oswald's mail order Mannlicher-Carcano rifle in the garage of his wife's friend, Ruth Paine, was also known to De Mohrenschildt at least one week prior to the assassination.

17. The background and development of the Presidential trip as hereinafter set forth is in parallel with the Soviet report.

18. The Dallas trip had been in train since late July of 1963. Texas was considered to be a key state in the upcoming 1964 Presidential elections. It was the disqualification of over 100,000 Texas votes, in conjunction with the known fraudulent voting in Chicago in 1960 that gave President Kennedy and his associates a slim margin of victory.

The actual route of Kennedy's drive through downtown Dallas was made known to the local press on Tuesday, November 19. The sharp right turn from Main St. onto Houston and then the equally sharp left turn onto Elm was the only way to get to the on ramp to the Stemmons Freeway. A traffic divider on Main St precluded the motorcade from taking the direct route, from Main St. across Houston and thence right to the Stemmons Freeway exit.

20. Just after the President's car passed the Texas Book Depository, a number of shots were fired. There were a total of three shots fired, at the President. The first shot came from the right front, hitting him in the neck. This projectile did not exit the body. The immediate reaction by the President was to clutch at his neck and say, "I have been hit!" He was unable to move himself into any kind of a defensive posture because he was wearing a restrictive body brace.

21. The second shot came from above and behind the Presidential car, the bullet striking Texas Governor Connally in the upper right shoulder, passing through his chest and exiting sharply downwards into his left thigh.

-12-

22. The third, and fatal, shot was also fired at the President from the right front and from a position slightly above the car. This bullet, which was fired from a underline{.223} weapon, struck the President above the right ear, passed through the right rear quadrant of his head and exited towards the left. Pieces of the President's skull and a large quantity of brain matter was blasted out and to the left of the car. Much of this matter struck a Dallas police motorcycle outrider positioned to the left rear of the Presidential car.

23. Photographic evidence indicates that the driver, SA Greer, slowed down the vehicle when shots were heard, in direct contravention of standing Secret Service regulations.

24. Reports that the initial hit on the President came from above and behind are false and misleading. Given the position of the vehicle at the time of impact and the altitude of the alleged shooter, a bullet striking the back of the President's neck would have exited sharply downward as did the projectile fired at Governor Connally purportedly from the same shooter located in the same area of the sixth floor of the Texas Book Depository.

25. The projectile that killed the President was filled with mercury. When such a projectile enters a body, the sudden decrease in velocity causes the mercury to literally explode the shell. This type of projectile is designed to practically guarantee the death of the target and is a method in extensive use by European assassination teams.

26. The disappearance of Kennedy's brain and related post mortem material from the U.S. National Archives was motivated by an official desire not to permit further testing which would certainly show the presence of mercury in the brain matter.

27. Official statements that the fatal shot was fired from above and behind are totally incorrect and intended to mislead. Such a shot would have blasted the brain and blood matter forward and not to the left rear. Also, photographic evidence indicates that after the fatal shot, the President was hurled to his left, against his wife who was seated to his immediate left.

28. The so-called "magic bullet" theory, i.e., a relatively pristine, fired Western Cartridge 6.5 Mannlicher-Carcano projectile produced in evidence, is obviously an official attempt to justify its own thesis. This theory, that a projectile from above and behind struck the President in the upper back, swung up, exited his throat, gained altitude and then angled downwards through the body of Governor Connally, striking bone and passing through muscle mass and emerging in almost undamaged condition is a complete impossibility. The bullet in question was obtained by firing the alleged assassination weapon into a container of water.

29. Three other such projectiles were recovered in similar undamaged condition. One of these was produced for official inspection and was claimed to have been found on Governor Connally's stretcher at Parkland Hospital. As a goodly portion of the projectile was still in the Governor's body, this piece of purported evidence should be considered as nothing more than an official "plant."

-13-

30. Soviet commentary on Oswald is basically verified from both KGB and CIA sources. Oswald, however, was not being run by the ONI but instead by the CIA. Their personnel files indicate that Oswald was initially recruited by ONI for possible penetration of the very pervasive Japanese Communist intelligence organization. Atsugi base was a very important target for these spies.

31. Because of a shift in their policy, the CIA found it expedient to exploit their U2 surveillance of the Soviet Union as a political rather than intelligence operation.

32. The Eisenhower administration's interest in the possibility of achieving a rapprochment with the Soviet Government created a situation that might have proven disasterous to the CIAs continued functions.

33. Internal CIA documents show very clearly that as their very existence was dependent on a continuation of the Cold War, any diminution of East-West hostility could easily lead to their down sizing and, more important, to their loss of influence over the office of the President and also of U.S. foreign policy.

34. It was proposed, according to top level CIA reports, to somehow use their U2 flights to create an increase in tension that could lead to a frustration of any detente that might result from a lessening of international tensions.

35. It was initially thought that certain compromising documents could be prepared, sent to the CIA base at Atsugi, Japan, and then somehow leaked to the aggressive Japanese Communists. However, it was subsequently decided that there was a strong possibility that the documents might not be forwarded to Soviet Russia and kept in Japan for use in the anti-west/anti-war domestic campaigns.

36. CIA personnel stationed at Atsugi conceived a plan to arrange for select documents to be given directly to the Soviets via an American defector. It was at this point that Oswald's name was brought up by an ONI man. A CIA evaluation of Oswald convinced them that he would be the perfect defector. Psychological profiles of Oswald convinced them that he was clever, pro-Marxist, a person of low self-esteem as manifested in his chronic anti-social attitudes coupled with homosexual behavior.

37. As Oswald had developed a strong friendship with his ONI control, it was decided to allow him to think that he was working for the U.S. Navy rather than the CIA.

38. Oswald was told that he was performing a "special, vitally important" mission for the ONI and would be given a very good paying official position when he "successfully returned" from the Soviet Union. CIA and ONI reports indicate that he was never expected to return to the U.S. after he had fulfilled his function of passing the desired documents to the Soviet intelligence community.

39. The subsequent interception and shooting down by the Soviets of a U2 piloted by CIA agent Gary Powers using the leaked CIA material was sufficient to wreck the projected Eisenhower/Khruschev meeting and harden the Soviet leader's attitude towards the West.

40. It should be noted that the Powers U2 was equipped with a delayed
action self-destruct device, designed to be activated by the pilot upon
bailing out. This device was intended to destroy any classified surveillance
material on the aircraft. In the Powers aircraft, the device was later
disclosed to have been altered to explode the moment the pilot activated it.
This would have resulted in the destruction of both the pilot and his
aircraft.

41. After his return to the United States, Oswald was a marked man. He
was a potential danger to the CIA, whose unredacted personnel reports
indicate that Oswald was considered to be unstable, hostile, intelligent and
very frustrated. He was, in short, a loose cannon.

42. While resident in Dallas, Oswald became acquainted with a George S.
De Mohrenschildt, a CIA operative. De Mohrenschildt, a Balt, had family
connections both in Poland and Russia, had worked for the German Ausland
Abwehr and later the SD during the Second World War. He "befriended" Oswald
and eventually an intimate physical relationship developed between the two
men. This infuriated Marina Oswald and their already strained relationship
grew even worse. She had come to America expecting great financial rewards
and instead found poverty, two children and a sexually cold husband.

43. It was De Mohrenschildt's responsibility to watch Oswald, to
establish a strong inter-personal relationship with him and to learn what
information, if any, Oswald might possess that could damage the CIA if it
became known.

44. The CIAs subsequent use of Oswald as a pawn in the assassination
was a direct result of this concern.

45. The connections of Angleton, Chief of Counter Intelligence for the
CIA with elements of the mob are well known in intelligence circles.
Angleton worked closely with the Sicilian and Naples mobs in 1944 onwards
as part of his duties for the OSS.

46. The connections of Robert Crowley, another senior CIA official,
with elements of the Chicago mob are also well known in intelligence circles.

47. The attempts of the CIA and the JCS to remove Castro by assassination
are also part of the official record. These assassination plots, called RIFLE
show the connections between the CIA and the Chicago branch of the Mafia.

48. This Mafia organization was paid nearly a quarter of a million
dollars to effect the killing of Castro but apparently kept the money and did
nothing.

49. Subsequent to the assassination, the CIA put out the cover story
that Castro had planned to act in retaliation for the attempts on his life.
This is not substantiated either from U.S. or Soviet sources.

50. While the American Mafia had numerous reasons for wishing the removal
of the President and, especially, his brother, the Attorney General, it does
not appear that they were participants in the assassination.

-15-

51. It is evident that contact was made between the Chicago Mafia and its counterpart in Sicily in an effort to locate putative assassins.

52. French intelligence sources have indicated that a recruitment was made among members of the Corsican Mafia in Marseilles in mid-1963.

53. French intelligence sources have also indicated that they informed U.S. authorities in the American Embassy on two occasions about the recruitment of French underworld operatives for a political assassination in the United States.

54. It is not known if these reports were accepted at the Embassy or passed on to Washington.

55. In the event, the Corsicans were sent to Canada where they blended in more easily with the French-speaking Quebec population.

56. Although the Chicago Mafia did not supply the actual assassins, they did provide the services of one of their lesser members, Jack "Ruby" Rubenstein, a small-time mob enforcer, in the event that Oswald was taken alive.

57. The use of Jack Ruby to kill Oswald has been explained by the official reports as an aberrant act on the part of an emotional man under the influence of drugs. The Warren Commission carefully overlooked Ruby's well-known ties to the Chicago mob as well as his connections with mob elements in Cuba.

58. Ruby's early Chicago connections with the mob are certainly well documented in <u>Chicago police files.</u> This material was not used nor referred to in the Warren Report.

59. Ruby's close connection with many members of the Dallas police infrastructure coupled with a very strong motivation to remove Oswald prior to any appointment of an attorney to represent him or any possible revelations Oswald might make about his possible knowledge of the actual assassins made Ruby an excellent agent of choice. If Oswald had gained the relative security of the County Jail and lawyers had been appointed for him, <u>it would have proven much more difficult to remove him.</u>

60. The Warren Commission was most particularly alarmed by attempts on the part of New York attorney Mark Lane, to present a defense for the dead Oswald before the Commission. Lane was refused this request. A written comment by Chief Justice Earl Warren to CIA Director Allen Dulles was that "people like Lane should never be permitted to air their radical views...at least not before this Commission..."

61. Ruby had been advised by his Chicago mob connections, as well as by others involved in the assassination, that his killing of Oswald would "make him a great hero" in the eyes of the American public and that he "could never be tried or convicted" in any American court of law.

62. Ruby, who had personal identity problems, accepted and strongly embraced this concept and was shocked to find that he was to be tried on a capital charge. Never very stable, Ruby began to disintegrate while in custody and mixed fact with fiction in a way as to convince <u>possible assassins</u> that he was not only incompetent but would not reveal his small knowledge of the motives behind the removal of Oswald.

63. In the presence of Chief Justice Warren, Ruby strongly intimated that he had additional information to disclose and wanted to go to the safety of Washington but Warren abruptly declared that he was not interested in hearing any part of it.

64. A polygraph given to Ruby concerning his denial of knowing Oswald and only attempting to kill him as a last minute impulse proved to be completely unsatisfactory and could not be used to support the Commission's thesis.

65. During his final illness, while in Parkland Hospital, Ruby was under heavy sedation and kept well supervised to prevent any death bed confessions or inopportune chance remarks to hospital attendants. An unconfirmed report from a usually reliable source states that Ruby was given an injection of air with a syringe which produced an embolism that killed him. The official cause of Ruby's death was a blood clot.

66. It was later alleged that Ruby had metastated cancer of the brain and lungs which somehow had escaped any detection during his incarceration in Dallas. It was further alleged that this terminal cancer situation had existed for over a year without manifesting any serious symptoms to the Dallas medical authorities. This is viewed by non-governmental oncologists as highly unbelievable and it appears that Ruby's fatal blood clot was the result of outside assistance.

67. Following the assassination, a number of persons connected with the case died under what can only be termed as mysterious circumstances. Also, the FBI seized a number of films and pictures taken by witnesses. These were considered to be too sensitive to leave in private hands.

68. Statements by Dallas law enforcement personnel, as well as similar statements by witnesses, that there had been "several" men in the area of the railroad yard adjacent to the roadway and that these men had "Secret Service" identification, created considerable confusion.

69. According to Secret Service records, the only Secret Service agents at the scene were in the motorcade itself and they had no agents in the railroad yard.

70. Witness and witness statements introduced before the Warren Commission were carefully vetted prior to introduction as evidence. The home movie of the assault was turned over to the FBI and a spliced version of it was released to the public. This doctored version showed Kennedy reacting in a way that was diametrically opposed to his actual reactions.

71. The concerns of Soviet intelligence and governmental agencies about any possible Soviet connection between defector Oswald and themselves is entirely understandable. It was never seriously believed by any competent agency in the United States that the Soviet Union had any part in the assassination of Kennedy.

72. Because of the emotional attitudes in official Washington and indeed, throughout the entire nation immediately following the assassination, there was created a potentially dangerous international situation for the

Soviets. Oswald was an identified defector with Marxist leanings. He was also
believed to be a pro-Castro activist. That both his Marxist attitudes and his
sympathies and actions on behalf of the Cuban dictator were enhanced simulations was not known to the Warren Commission at the time of their activities.

73. To bolster their eager efforts to convince the American authorities
that their government had nothing to do with the assassination, men like
Nosenko were utilized to further support this contention. It is not known
whether Nosenko was acting on orders or whether he was permitted access to
created documentation and given other deliberate disinformation by the KGB
and allowed to defect. A great deal of internal concern was expressed upon
Nosenko's purported defection by Soviet officials but this is viewed as
merely an attempt, and a successful one, to lend substance to his importance.

74. James Angleton's attitude towards Nosenko is a commentary on the
duality of his nature. On the one hand, Angleton was performing as Chief of
Counter Intelligence and openly showed his zeal in searching for infiltraters
and "moles" inside his agency while on the other hand, Angleton had very
specific personal knowledge that the Soviet Union had nothing to do with the
Kennedy assassination.

75. The senior Kennedy, it is known, was heavily involved with rum-
running during the Prohibition era and had extensive mob connections. He
had closely been associated with Al Capone, mob boss in Chicago, and had a
falling out with him over an allegedly hijacked liquor shipment. Capone,
Chicago police records indicate, had threatened Kennedy's life over this
and Kennedy had to pay off the mob to nullify a murder contract.

76. Anti-Castro Cuban militants view Kennedy's abandonment of their
cause with great anger and many members of these CIA-trained and led groups
made calls for revenge on the President for his abandonment of their cause.

77. Soviet attempts to gain a strategic foothold in close proximity to
the United States and certainly well within missile range, was intolerable
and had to be countered with equal force. At that time, the threat of a
major war was not only imminent but anticipated. In retrospect, all out
nuclear warfare between the United States and the Soviet Union was only
barely averted and only at the last minute.

78. The President's highly unorthodox form of personal diplomacy vis a
vis the Soviets created far more problems than it ever solved. When it
came to light, both the DOS and the CIA were extremely concerned that
sensitive intelligence matters might have been inadvertently passed to the
Soviets.

79. Reports from the CIA concerning Oswald's September/October visit
to Mexico City are totally unreliable and were rejected by the FBI as being
"in serious error." The reasons for Oswald's visit to Mexico are completely
obscure at this writing but the individual allegedly photographed by CIA
surveillance in Mexico is to a certainty not Lee Oswald. As the CIA had
pictures of the real Oswald, their reasons for producing such an obvious
falsity are not easy to ascertain at this remove.

80. The hit team was flown away in an aircraft piloted by a CIA contract

pilot named David Ferrie from New Orleans. They subsequently vanished
without a trace. Rumors of the survival of one of the team are persistent
but not proven.

81. A study of the Soviet report indicates very clearly that the
Russians have significant and very high level sources within both the
Central Intelligence Agency and the Federal Bureau of Investigation.
Their possession of material relating to certain highly classified
American military papers has been referred to the CIC for investigation
and action.

UNITED STATES DEPARTMENT OF JUSTICE
FEDERAL BUREAU OF INVESTIGATION

WASHINGTON, D.C.

1:39 p.m.   November 29, 1963

MEMORANDUM FOR MR. TOLSON
                MR. BELMONT
                MR. MOHR
                MR. CONRAD
                MR. DE LOACH
                MR. EVANS
                MR. ROSEN
                MR SULLIVAN

The President called and asked if I am familiar with the proposed
group they are trying to get to study my report - two from the House,
two from the Senate, two from the courts, and a couple of outsiders. I
replied that I had not heard of that but had seen reports from the
Senate Investigating Committee.

The President stated he wanted to get by just with my file and my
report. I told him I thought it would be very bad to have a rash of
investigations. He then indicated the only way to stop it is to
appoint a high-level committee to evaluate my report and tell the House
and Senate not to go ahead with the investigation. I stated that would
be a three-ring circus.

The President then asked what I think about Allen Dulles, and I
replied that he is a good man. He then asked me about John McCloy, and I
stated I am not as enthusiastic about McCloy, that he is a good man but
I am not so certain as to the matter of publicity he might want. The
President then mentioned General Norstad, and I said he is a good man.
He said in the House he might try Boggs and Ford and in the Senate
Russell and Cooper and he indicated Cooper of Kentucky whom he described
as a judicial man, stating he would not want Javits. I agreed on this
point. He then reiterated Ford of Michigan, and I indicated I know of
him but do not know him and had never seen him except on television
the other day and that he handled himself well on television.

The President then mentioned that Jenkins had told him that I
have designated Mr. DeLoach to work with them as he had on the Hill.
He indicated they appreciated that and just wanted to tell me they
consider MrDeLoach as high class as I do, and that they salute me for
knowing how to pick good men.

Hoover Memorandum, 5 pp.

I advised the President that we hope to have the investigation
wrapped up today but probably won't have it before the first of the week,
as an angle in Mexico is giving trouble - the matter of Oswald's getting
$6500 from the Cuban Embassy and coming back to this country with it;
that we are not able to prove that fact; that we have the information he
was there on September 18 and we are able to prove he was in New Orleans
on that date; that a story came in changing the date to September 28
and he was in Mexico on the 28th. I related that the police have again
arrested Duran, a member of the Cuban Embassy; that they will hold her
two or three days; will confront her with the original informant; and
will also try a lie detector test on her.

The President then inquired if I pay attention to the lie
detector test. I answered that I would not pay 100% attention to them;
that it was only a psychological asset in investigation; that I would
not want to be a part of sending a man to the chair on a lie detector
test. I explained that we have used them in bank investigations and a
person will confess before the lie detector test is finished, more or
less fearful it will show him guilty. I said the lie detector test has
this psychological advantage. I further stated that it is a misnomer to
call it a lie detector since the evaluation of the chart made by the
machine is made by a human being and any human being is apt to make the
wrong interpretation.

I stated, if Oswald had lived and had taken a lie detector test, this
with the evidence we have would have added that much strength to the
case; that there is no question he is the man.

I also told him that Rubenstein down there has offered to take a lie
detector test but his lawyer must be consulted first; that I doubt the
lawyer will allow him to do so; that he has a West Coast lawyer
somewhat like the Edward Bennett Williams type and almost as much of a
shyster.

The President asked if we have any relationship between the two
as yet. I replied that at the present time we have not; that there
was a story that the fellow had been in Rubenstein's
nightclub but it has not been confirmed. I told the President that
Rubenstein is a very seedy character, had a bad record - street brawls,
fights, etc.; that in Dallas, if a fellow came into his nightclub and
could not pay his bill completely, Rubenstein would beat him up and
throw him out; that he did not drink or smoke; that he was an
egomaniac; that he likes to be in the limelight; knew all of the
police officers in the white light district; let them come in and get
food and liquor, etc.; and that is how I think he got into police
headquarters. I said if they made any move, the pictures did not
show it even when they saw him approach and he got right up to Oswald

and pressed the pistol against Oswald's stomach; that neither officer
on either side made any effort to grab Rubenstein - not until after the
pistol was fired. I said, secondly, the chief of police admits he moved
Oswald in the morning as a convenience and at the request of motion
picture people who wanted daylight. I said insofar as tying Rubenstein
and Oswald together, we have not yet done so; that there are a number
of stories which tied Oswald to the Civil Liberties Union in New York in
which he applied for membership and to the Fair Play for Cuba Committee
which is pro-Castro, directed by communists, and financed to some extent
by the Castro Government.

The President asked how many shots were fired, and I told him three.
He then asked me if any were fired at him. I said no, that three shots
were fired at the President and we have them. I stated that out
ballistic experts were able to prove the shots were fired by this gun;
that the President was hit by the first and third bullets and the second
hit the Governor; that there were three shots; that one complete
bullet rolled out of the President's head; that it tore a large part of
the President's head off; that in trying to massage his heart on the
way into the hospital they loosened the bullet which fell on the
stretcher and we have that.

He then asked where they aimed at the President. I replied they were
aimed at the President, no question about that.

I further advised him that we have also tested the fact you could
fire those three shots in three seconds. I explained that there is a
story out that there must have been more than one man to fire several
shots but we have proven it could be done by one man.

The President then asked how it happened that Connally was hit. I
explained that Connally turned to the President when the first shot was
fired and that in that turning he got hit. The President then asked, if
Connally had not been in his seat, would the President have been hit by
the second shot. I said yes.

I related that on the fifth floor of the building where we found the
gun and the wrapping paper we found three empty shells that had been
fired and one that had not been fired; that he had four but didn't fire
the fourth; then threw the gun aside; went down the steps; was seen
by a police officer; the manager told the officer that Oswald was all
right, worked there; they let him go; he got on a bus; went to his
home and got a jacket; then came back downtown, walking; the police
officer who was killed stopped him, not knowing who he was; and he
fired and killed the police officer.

The President asked if we can prove that and I answered yes.

I further related that Oswald then walked another two blocks; went
to the theater; the woman selling tickets was so suspicious - said he
was carrying a gun when he went into the theater- that she notified the
police; the police and our man went in and located Oswald. I told him
they had quite a struggle with Oswald but that he was subdued and shown
out and taken to police headquarters.

I advised the President that apparently Oswald had come down the steps from the fifth floor; that apparently the elevator was not used.

The President then indicated our conclusions are: (1) he is the one who did it: (2) after the President was hit, Governor Connally was hit; (3) the President would have been hit three times except for the fact that Governor Connally turned after the first shot and was hit by the second; (4) whether he was connected with the Cuban operation with money we are trying to nail down. I told him that is what we are trying to nail down; that we have copies of the correspondence; that none of the letters dealt with any indication of violence or assassination; that they were dealing with a visa to go back to Russia.

I advised the President that his wife had been very hostile, would not cooperate and speaks only Russian; that yesterday she said, if we could give assurance sue would be allowed to remain in the country, she would cooperate; and that I told our agents to give that assurance and sent a Russian-speaking agent to Dallas last night to interview her. I said I do not know whether or not she has any information but we would learn what we could.

The President asked how Oswald had access to the fifth floor of the building. I replied that he had access to all floors. The President asked where was his office and I stated he did not have any particular place; that he was not situated in any particular place; that he was just a general packer of requisitions that came in for books from Dallas schools; that he would have had proper access to the fifth and sixth floors whereas usually the employees were down on lower floors. The President then inquired if anybody saw him on the fifth floor, and I stated he was seen by one of the workmen before the assassination.

The President then asked if we got a picture taken of him shooting the gun and I said no. He asked what was the picture sold for $25,000, and I advised him this was a picture of the parade showing Mrs. Kennedy crawling out of the back seat; that there was no Secret Service Agent on the back of the car; that in the past they have added steps on the back of the car and usually had an agent on either side standing on the bumper; that I did not know why this was not done - that the President may have requested it; that the bubble top was not up but I understand the bubble top was not worth anything because it was made entirely of plastic; that I had learned much to my surprise that the Secret Service does not have any armored cars.

The President asked if I have a bulletproof car and I told him I most certainly have. I told him we use it here for my own use and, whenever we have any raids, we make use of the bulletproof car on them. I explained that it is a limousine which has been armorplated and that it looks exactly like any other car. I stated I think the President ought to have a bulletproof car; that from all I understand the Secret Service has had two cars with metal plates underneath the car to take care of hand grenades or bombs thrown out on the street. I said this is European; that there have been several such attempts on DeGaulle's life; but they do not do that in this country; that all assassinations have been with guns; and for that reason I think very definitely the President ought to always ride in a bulletproof car; that it certainly would prevent anything like this ever happening again; but that I do not mean a sniper could not snipe him from a window if he were exposed.

The President asked if I meant on his ranch he should be in a bulletproof car. I said I would think so; that the little car we rode around in when I was at the ranch should be bulletproofed; that it ought to be done very quietly. I told him we have four bulletproof cars in the Bureau: one on the West Coast, one in New York and two here. I said this could be done quietly without publicity and without pictures taken of it if handled properly and I think he should have one on his ranch.

The President then asked if I think all the entrances should be guarded. I replied by all means, that he had almost to be in the capacity of a so-called prisoner because without that security anything could be done. I told him lots of phone calls had been received over the last four or five days about threats on his life; that I talked to the Attorney General about the funearl procession from the White House to the Cathedral; that I was opposed to it. The President remarked that the Secret Service told them not to but the family wanted to do it. I stated that was what the Attorney General told me but I was very much opposed to it. I further related that I saw the procession from the Capitol to the White House on Pennsylvania and, while they had police standing on the curbs, when the parade came, the police turned around and looked at the parade.

The President then stated he is going to take every precaution he can; that he wants to talk to me; and asked if I would put down my thoughts. He stated I was more than head of the FBI - I was his brother and personal friend; that he knew I did not want anything to happen to his family; that he has more confidence in me than anybody in town; that he would not embroil me in a jurisdictional dispute; but that he did want to have my thoughts on the matter to advocate as his own opinion.

I stated I would be glad to do this for him and that I would do anything I can. The President expressed his appreciation.

Very truly yours,

/s/ J.E.H.

John Edgar Hoover
Director

To: JJA

From: RTC

Date: Aug 10 1964

Subject: The President

Dear Jim:

The DCI has spoken with me recently concerning several contacts he has had with Jenkins, the President's man.

According to the DCI, the President has been privately expressing his growing concerns that "another Dallas" might be executed against him or his family.

The President is a man who is very easily, and badly, frightened. He is a highly emotional and very unstable individual who could become quite dangerous if his fears are not addressed.

I spoke with Hoover about this and as a good, personal friend of the President, has agreed to mollify him and put his irrational fears to rest.

Hoover has advised the President that certain "negative forces" are at work against those agencies who wish to protect and support the President.

The President has urged Hoover to find a way to "convince" these "troublemakers" to cease their negative remarks "in the best interests" of the nation.

This gives us the opportunity of silencing anyone who might express dangerous opinions about Dallas.

Hoover also suggested, and I agree, that instead of attempting to shut down controversial books, that we encourage the publication of "not" books. That way, the public will soon grow tired of questions and go on their merry way.

The forthcoming Commission report is a wonderful piece of creative writing and will be extensively promoted by our good friends at the NY Times.

-1-

Aide-Mémoire R. T. Crowley, 2 pp.

The question of the surviving member is still of concern but hopefully, the reward will flush him out.

I will get Allan to autograph a copy of the final Commission report for both of our personal libraries.

Crow

O P E R A T I O N   Z I P P E R   CONFERENCE RECORD

Table of Contents

Page 2......Statement of Policy

Page 3......Statement of Policy

Page 4......Statement of Policy

Page 5......Statement of Policy

Page 6......Statement of Policy

Page 7......Photographs, JFK

Page 8......Photographs, JFK

Page 9......Photographs, JFK

Page 10.....Photographs, JFK

Page 11.....Photographs, JFK

Page 12.....Synopsis of exeftive meetings and communications

Pages 12-28.Conference record

Pages 29-97.Copies of NSA communications intercepts on RFK

Summary of Conferences held March-November 1963

Reference: Operation ZIPPER

Date: 22 DEC 63

Participants:

DCI McCone, James Angleton, Robert Crowley, William Harvey,
DD/FBI Sullivan, LtCol Cass, USMC

Distribution as above

Statement of Policy

1. The removal of the President and the Attorney General
   from their positions because of high treason has been
   determined.

2. By their contacts with top-level intelligence officials
   of the Soviet Union and the subsequent release by the
   President and the Attorney General of the highest level
   security material to a government that stands in direct
   opposition to the United States, these individuals
   cannot be permitted to occupy their official positions.

3. By treating with the enemy on the Cuban issue and
   actively blocking legitimate military actions against
   a Soviet/Cuban armed enemy in close proximity to the
   United States, these individuals have endangered the
   people of the United States and permitted enemies of
   this country to actively place atomic weapons within
   the reach of many American cities.

4. Removal by impeachment or other legal means is considered unfeasable and too protracted.

5. Therefore, an alternative solution has been found to
   effect this removal.

6. This removal is the result of a consensus between the
   various concerned official agencies.

-2-

7. This opertation, codenamed ZIPPER, was under
   the direction of James Angleton of the Agency,
   assisted by Robert Crowley and William Harvey,
   also of the Agency.

8. The government departments directly concerned
   consisted of:

   a. The Central Intelligence Agency.

   b. The Federal Bureau of Investigation.

   c. The Joint Chiefs of Staff.

9. Other government agencies involved but not with
   specific knowledge were:

   a. The U.S. Department of the Treasury,
      Secret Service Division.

   b. The National Security Agency.

   c. The Naval Security Group.

   d. INTERARMCO.

   e. The U.S. Department of State, Passport
      Division.

10. Following the removal of the President, the
    new President, who had been fully briefed
    prior to the act, agreed "in the interest
    of national concerns" to appoint a special
    Commission chaired by the Chief Justice,
    for the purpose of "setting public concerns
    to rest." Mr. Angleton was in complete control
    of all evidence presented to this Committee
    and worked closely in conjunction with Mr.
    Sullivan of the FBI to ensure that nothing
    was brought before the Committee that it did
    not want to acknowledge.

11. As both the Vice President and the Director
    of the Federal Bureau of Investigation had
    been slated for replacement by the Kennedy
    faction, their support for this project was
    practically guaranteed from the outset.

12. The Vice President came to believe that an
    attempt would be made on his life at the
    same time and was greatly concerned for his
    own safety.

13. As the Vice President and the Director of the
    FBI were longtime neighbors and very friendly,
    the Director has repeatedly assured the President
    that he was not a target and that no shots

-3-

were fired at him in Dallas.

14. The President has been reassured but is still
    considered very leery of any possible such
    actions being taken against himself or mem-
    bers of his personal family.

15. One of the primary goals of ZIPPER, the re-
    moval of the Attorney General, has been dis-
    cussed repeatedly with the President by the
    DCI, and the President has agreed to gradually
    force him out of his position. He has stated,
    however, that the popularity of the AG is
    such that this removal must be performed with
    care.

16. Representative Ford, R, of Michigan, a member
    of the Commission, is working closely with
    Director Hoover and reports all incoming in-
    formation directly to him.

17. Full cooperation with friendly media sources
    has ensured that the public attention has been
    drawn to Oswald as the sole killer. The Presi-
    dent feels strongly that any attempt to por-
    tray Oswald as a tool of the Soviets is liable
    to create "too high a level of international
    tension" which the President feels, might
    lead to direct confrontation with the Soviet
    Union.

18. The President is not receptive to plans of the
    JCS, supported entirely by the Agency, to
    eradicate Castro and his Marxist government
    from Cuba. The President states that war almost
    occurred as a result of the last military
    attempt to dislodge the Cuban dictator and he
    does not wish to replay that aspect of the en-
    forcement of the Monroe Doctrine.

19. The President has indicated, however, that an
    escalation of U.S. military involvement in
    French Indo China is not unreasonable. Reports
    given to him by the Agency as well as the JCS
    on this subject have been well received.

20. The President's aide, Jenkins, has also sup-
    ported this idea and the Secretary of Defense
    has come down strongly in favor of it.

21. The President believes that his occupancy of
    the White House is due to the death of his
    predecessor and has a desperate desire to
    achieve a degree of legitimacy.

-4-

22. He has been advised that a war-time President
is always assured of reelection (i.e., Wilson,
Roosevelt) but only in the event that the war
is prosecuted with vigor and has attendant
military successes.

23. On a related topic, the French President,
DeGaulle, while in Washington for the late
President's funeral, held several conferences
with the new President as well as other
officials to include the Agency.

24. The General stated several times and with
some asperity that he had been the object of
a number of assassination attempts in the
past, some going back to the war, and that he
had grown tired of them. He stated that the
OAS attempts to shoot him or bomb him had
been known to members of the Agency who had,
in at least one case, assisted the OAS assassins.

25. The General also stated that he was aware through
French intelligence reports, that the assassins
of the President were French citizens.

26. Because it is viewed as vital that the French
become involved in NATO and to assuage the concerns of the General, guarantees were given
both by the President and the DCI that no
further actions would be undertaken that could
result in an assassination and further, that
the United States would actively support French
commercial interests in French Indo China in
return for French cooperation with NATO.

27. The French President agreed to this but made
several oblique threats to the President about
his reactions in the event of future Agency
"meddling" in French domestic and foreign
policy.

28. The General was reassured repeatedly on these
points and is now apparently in agreement with
United States aims in Southeast Asia. He made
several remarks about the trade in opium in
that area being extremely lucrative and stated
that he had his own problems with narcotics
traffic in the Mediterranean area.

29. It is not believed, and electronic surveillance
of the President's lines of communication
while in the United States does not support, the
possibility that he might have actual knowledge

-5-

of any American involvement, or projected involvement, in this sensitive area.

30. Both the Agency and the President feel that the
French President has "fired a shot across our
bows" but that these issues have now become
resolved. The President feels, however, that
the French will have to be watched carefully
in the future and that if American interests
become established in French Indo China, we
had best consider our own interests at that time.

31. In the matter of the Soviet Union, it is evident
that they were initially concerned that the
removal of Kennedy might be laid at their door-
step. As this was certainly one of the objectives
of the Agency as well as the JCS, it has been
necessary to repeatedly reassure their leadership that there would be no such intimations
in the future and, that in addition, there would
be no further attempts to execute any military
or overt clandestine operations against either
Cuba or its leader, Castro.

32. In the matter of the public perception of the
Dallas action, extensive use has been made of
Agency connections with major American media
organs, i.e., the New York Times and the Washington Post. The Times is strongly supporting
the Commission and its findings and we are
assured that they will continue to do so. The
same attitude has been clearly and strongly
expressed by the Post.

Synopsis of executive meetings and communications.

Note:

In most cases, the participants listed above were in attendance. In some cases, not noted, one or more of the participants were absent but subsequently fully informed of salient material discussed or were involved by telephonic participation in meetings.

In the following compendium, many meetings, conferences or telephonic communications are not fully covered.

Summary of Conferences held March-November 1963

✓ 1 MAR 63

8:30 AM- Noon

Conference with DCI, JJA, RTC. Implementation of ZIPPER. Presentation of RFK intercepts to DCI. Review of investigative data to date. DCI requests more data.

✓ 2 MAR 63

9:45 AM- 11:15 AM

Presentation by JJA and RTC to DCI of evidentiary material.

2:20 PM

Request by DCI for interview with Director/FBI.

4 MAR 63

8:15 AM-10:00 AM

Conference with DCI, JJA with Director/FBI and DD/FBI Sullivan.

7 MAR 63

8:30 PM- 12:06 AM

Conference with JJA and Sullivan.

Operation ZIPPER/Conference Record (cont.)

✓ 8 MAR 63

   2:02 PM-3:45 PM

      Conference with JJA, RTC in
      re RFK.

   4:15 PM- 4:48 PM

      Telephone conference JJA
      DCI concerning above meetings.

✓ 12 MAR 63

   8:30 AM- 9:23 AM

      Conference JJA and Sullivan.

   1:20 PM- 2:10 PM

      Lunch conference with JJA and
      RTC. Joined by DCI.

13 MAR 63

   9:10 AM- 9:30 AM

      Telephone conference by DCI
      with Walter Jenkins in re VP.
      Request for personal interview.

✓ 14 MAR 63

   9:45 AM- 10:23 AM
      and
   3:37 PM- 4:11 PM

      Conferences with JJA, Jenkins,
      RTC and telephone conference
      with WKH on ZIPPER. Views
      of VP are discussed. Extreme
      caution on part of VP subject
      of both conferences. Tentative
      acceptance of basic thrust of
      ZIPPER. VP to speak with DCI
      on 15 MAR.

✓ 15 MAR 63

   12:35 PM- 1:43 PM

      Luncheon conference with DCI,
      Jenkins and A. Fortas, Met Club.
      Present: JJA and RTC. Discussion by
      VP's aides of two conversations with
      DIR/FBI Hoover on ZIPPER. AF requests
      copies of telephone intercepts.

-13-

Operation ZIPPER/Conference Record (cont.)

√ 16 MAR 63

1:08 PM- 1:16 PM

    Telephone conference by RTC
    with SG in re U/C.

1:24 PM- 2:19 PM

    Telephone conference by RTC
    with JJA in re SG.

2:45 PM- 3:10 PM

    Telephone conversation by JJA
    with DCI in re SG.

3:32 PM-4:50 PM
    Telephone conference with WKH
    by JJA in re SG.

√ 18 MAR 63

8:44 AM-9:29 AM

    Telephone conference by JJA w SC/
    INTERARMCO in re weaponry
    and delivery.

3:04 PM-3:30 PM

    Telephone conferences with DCI
    and RTC in re SC analysis.

9:30 PM-11:27 PM

    Conference RTC with WJ and AF.
    Copies of RFK reports for VP.

√ 19 MAR 63

11:45 AM

    Telephone report by SG to RTC
    concerning need for US passports.

√ 20 MAR 63

3:27 PM-3:39 PM

    Telephone conference by RTC
    with SG in passports
    Affirmative response.

-14-

Operation ZIPPER/Conference Record (cont.)

✓ 21 MAR 63

11:55 AM-2:37 PM

    Lunch meeting with DCI, RTC, and JJA.
    Review of telephone surveillance on
    RFK. Report by JJA on Soviet Receipts.

✓ 25 MAR 63

9:45 AM-10:17 AM

    Telephone conference with Jenkins
    in re VP. RTC

28 MAR 63

3:15 PM- 4:25 PM

    Conference with DCI and JJA.
    Coordination of JCS objectives
    with ZIPPER.

✓ 4:45 PM-4:48 PM

    Telephone conference with Jenkins
    in re VP. RTC

✓ 4:55 PM-5:01 PM

    Telephone conference with DCI on
    VP. RTC

29 MAR 63

2:35 PM-3:15 PM

    Telephone conference with DCI with
    FBI/Sullivan.

6:60 PM-9:55 PM

    Conference with RTC and WKH ref-
    erence logistics of ZIPPER.

A P R I L

-15-

Operation ZIPPER/Conference Record (cont.)

3 APRIL 63

11:08 PM-1:21 AM

Telephone conference
between JJA and Amos
Manor, Israel, in re
possible cooperation
in ZIPPER.

4 APRIL 63

11:31 AM- 1:02 PM

Conference with JJA
and RTC in re Manor
assistance.

3:35 PM- 4:45 PM

Telephone conference
with RTC and SG.
Sicilian referral.

5:20 PM- 5:45 PM

Telephone conference
RTC, JJA in re SG
conference.

9 APRIL 63

8:31 AM- 8:45 AM

Telephone conference
JJA with LtCol Cass,
S'Domingo in re ZIPPER.
Agreement for conference.

9:08 AM- 9:14 AM

Conference with DCI and
JJA concerning Cass
meeting and SG progress.

-16-

Operation ZIPPER/Conference Record (cont.)

✓ 10:20 AM- 10:45 AM

      Conference with MC,
      JJA, RTC, WKH in re
      Cass and SG report.

1:20 PM- 4:35 PM

      Conference with MC,
      WKH in re continuation
      of RFK surveillance
      and possibility of
      additional NSA sur-
      veillance of subject.

5:25 PM- 5:50 PM

      Telephone conference
      with RTC and SG in
      re payments.

6:20 PM-8:15 PM

      Telephone conference
      with RTC and JJA in
      re SG payments.

8:30 PM- 9:05 PM

      Telephone donference
      with JJA and MC in re
      SG payments.

9:30 PM- 10;04 PM

      Telephone conference
      with JJA and RTC in
      re MC conference.

✓ 10 APRIL 63

8:24 AM- 9:30 AM

      Telephone conference
      JJA with DCI in re
      SG payments.

1:45 PM- 1:55 PM

      Conference DCI. Payment
      OK

Operation ZIPPER/Conference Record (cont.)

2:45 PM- 2:50 PM

    Conference, JJA, MC in re
    payments (SG)

3:20 PM-3:45 PM

    Telephone conference, JJA
    and RTC in re payments (SG)

4:40 PM- 4:55 PM

    Conference JJA, RTC, WKH
    in re ZIPPER.

5:10 PM-5:23 PM

    Telephone conference RTC
    with SG in re payments.

11 APRIL 63

1:45 PM- 1:56 PM

    Telephone conference with
    Jenkins in re VP.
    Clarification of DCI memo.

2:30 PM- 2:46 PM

    Telephone conference
    with Pentagon in re Cass
    meeting.

4:36 PM- 5:15 PM

    Meeting JJA and DCI
    on progress for ZIPPER.
    No direct contact between
    DCI and Cass.

13 APRIL 63

8:22 PM- 9:07 PM

    Telephone conference
    RTC and SC in re ZIPPER.

Operation ZIPPER/Conference Record (cont.)

14 APRIL 63

9:35 AM- 11:07 AM

    Conference with DCI, JJA, WKH.
    Reference update with WKH.
    Suggestion received from Lemhitzer
    ref LtCOL Cass. S'Domingo.

2:35 PM- 3:12 PM

    Telephone conference with LtCOL
    Cass in re ZIPPER.

√ 15 APRIL 63

12:35 PM-2:23 PM

    Conference with WKH and RTC con-
    cerning weaponry and logistics.
    INTERARMCO.

5:20 PM-5:45 PM

    Telephone conference with Jenkins
    in re VP. RTC

√ 18 APRIL 63

1:23 PM-1:25 PM

    Telephone conference with SC.
    INTERARMCO.

2:01 PM- 2:05 PM

    Telephone contact with SG in
    Chicago in re RTC meeting. RTC

2:25 PM- 2:31 PM

    Telephone conference with JJA
    concerning SG.

2:33 PM- 2:40 PM

    Meeting with DCI in re Chicago. RTC, JJA

19 APRIL 63

    Telephone conference with ARM in
    re LANCER SS protection. JJA

Operation ZIPPER/Conference Record (cont.)

√ 23 APRIL 63

    Conference with RTC and SG
    concerning logistics for ZIPPER.
    Chicago.

√ 24 APRIL 63

    Conference with RTC and SG
    concerning logistics for ZIPPER.
    Chicago.

3:09 PM- 3:33 PM

    Telephone conference with
    JJA and LtCOL Cass in re
    ZIPPER.

30 APRIL 63

9:31 AM- 1:45 PM

    Telephone conference
    with RTC and Jenkins in re
    VP. Further clarification on
    post-ZIPPER.

2:20 PM- 5:38 PM

    Conference DCI and Sullivan
    in re contact with Director/FBI.
    Supply RFK transcripts.

M A Y

√ 2 MAY 63

1:00 PM- 2:59 PM

    Conference with DCI, JJA, RTC,
    Sullivan in re intercepted
    phone conversations from Hickory
    Hill. Also, intercepted and
    decoded conversations from Soviet
    Embassy.

4:09 PM- 4:21 PM

    Telephone conversation RTC and
    SG on Marseilles contacts.

Operation ZIPPER/Conference Record (cont.)

4:30 PM- 5:37 PM

    Conference with RTC and
    JJA concerning SG referrals.
    Also Mass. sailboat plan.
    Rejected.

√ 5 MAY 63

2:02 PM- 4:45 PM

    Telephone conference between JJA,
    RTC. In re progress on ZIPPER.
    Subject of discussion.
    1. SS Presidential security.
    2. Projected Presidential visits,
       a. Inside US.
       b. Outside US.
    3. Disinformation in reports to
    White House aimed at disrupting
    channels of communication.
    4. Contact with NSA in re blocking
    of calls transmitting information
    to Soviet Union.
    5. Close coordination with JCS
    concerning military action against
    Cuba.
    6. Ascertaining attitudes of VP in
    re para 5.
    7. Communicating compromising material
    on President to Soviet Union...loss
    of confidence.
    8. Information on planned RFK prosecution
    of VP aides. To discredit VP and give
    motive for removing from the ticket in
    '64. Give to AF?

V 6 MAY 63.

9:34 AM- 10:21 AM

    Conference JJA with DCI in
    re 5 May conference. Approval noted.

11:10 AM- 3:17 PM

    Telephone conferences by JJA & RTC with:
    a. AJ in re VP
    b. JCS in re ZIPPER and plans
    c. SG in re team progress
    d. SC in re logistics

-21-

Operation ZIPPER/Conference Record (cont.)

√ 10 MAY 63

      Lunch conference
      DCI, Sullivan, JJA, RTC, WKH
      Discussion of progress of ZIPPER.
      Decision to launch disinformation
        program in re Soviets.
      Decision for dual payments to
        UC and to SG.

14 MAY 63

4:45 PM

      Report by SC in re weaponry.

√ 21 MAY 63

3:20 PM- 4:11 PM

      Conference DCI, RTC
      in re NSA communications
      surveillance.

24 MAY 63

2:25 PM

      Contact with source on AF1.

3:10 PM

      Conference DCI, JJA on subject
      payment for AF1.

√ 25. MAY 63

2:10 PM- 4:43 PM

      Conference, UClub, RTC, JJA
      WKH with rep Chair/JCS
      in re ZIPPER.
      Coordination of ZIPPER w. MARLINSTRIKE.

√ 27 MAY 63

9:45 AM- 12:00 PM
      &
2:30 PM- 5:52 PM

      Conference JJA, RTC in re ZIPPER

Operation ZIPPER/Conference Record (cont.)

28 MAY 63

8:32 AM- 9:01 AM

    Telephone conference JJA
    with LtCOL Cass in re ZIPPER.

11:34 AM- 12:30 PM

    Conference JJA, DCI in re
    NSA transcripts.

31 MAY 63

1:35 PM- 2:50 PM

    Conference JJA, AF in re VP
    Discussion of VP attitudes in re
    MARLINSTRIKE, ZIPPER.

3:00 PM- 3:21 PM

    Telephone conference JJA,
    JCS in re AF conference.

3:30 PM- 3:34 PM

    Telephone conference JJA,
    DCI in re AF & JCS.

J U N E

3 JUNE 63

2:20 PM- 3:05 PM

    Conference with DD Carter
    and GEN Blake, DIR/NSA
    concerning ZIPPER.
    1. NSA SIGINT surveillance
    of Cuba, Mexico and Dominican
    Republic.
    2. NSA domestic surveillance.
    3. Confirming reports on RFK
    conversations.
    4. TASS communications.
    5. Soviet internal communications.
    6. White House communications.

-23-

Operation ZIPPER/Conference Record (cont.)

✓ 4 JUNE 63

Lunch conference, DD/MC, JJA, RTC
in re Blake position.

✓ 6 JUNE 63

7:30 PM- 9:20 PM

Conference, JJA, RTC in re
NSA intercepts.

11 JUNE 63

9:55 AM- 10:02 AM

Telephone conference with AF
in re VP. Anxiety.

12 JUNE 63

12:30 PM- 12:45 PM

Telephone conference with LtCOL Cass, S'Domingo.

4:11 PM- 4:34 PM

Telephone conference with JJA &
A. Manor in re UC team.

5:30 PM- 6:45 PM

Telephone conference with JJA & AF in re VP.
More reassurances needed.

✓ 19 JUNE 63

11:35 AM- 12:40 PM

Telephone conference, DD/MC
with D/NSA Blake concerning
NSA intercepts.

1:45 PM- 1:50 PM

Telephone conference, DD/MC
with RTC concerning SG.

24 JUNE 63

Report from SG in re weapons.

5:39 PM- 5:51 PM

Telephone conference, DCI

Operation ∠IPPER/Conference Record (cont.)

and JJA, RTC and WKH.

25 JUNE 63

Receipt of NSA report.

3:09 PM- 3:30 PM

Telephone conference, WKH
with LtCOL Cass, S'Domingo.

26 JUNE 63

9:30 AM- 9:54 AM

Telephone conference. AF
to RTC in re VP. Agreement
in general.

10:07 AM- 10:09 AM

Telephone conference RTC
with DCI in re AF call.

11:30 AM- 11:45 AM

Telephone conference, RTC
with Lemnitzer aide in re
ZIPPER.

J U L Y

3 JULY 63

Arrival of B. Baumann from
Toronto.

4 JULY 63

Receipt of courier reports NSA

7:39 PM- 11:45 PM

Personal interview with JJA,
RTC, MC with Baumann.

5 July 63

Evaluation of AF 1 material by
JJA, WKH, RTC.

2:33 PM- 3:15 PM

Conference with DCI, JJA on
AF 1 findings. Negative.

-25-

Operation ZIPPER/Conference Record (cont.)

✓ 11 JULY 63

      Review by JJA on RFK and
      White House telephone transcripts.

11:00 AM- 12:15 PM

      Conference with JJA, MC and RTC
      in re intercepts.

16 JULY 63

10:45 AM- 11:14 AM

      Telephone conference with
      MC and Blake in re NSA intercepts.

1:45 PM- 5:15 PM

      Conference with BB, JJA, MC in re
      ZIPPER and UC team.

17 JULY 63

6:30 PM- 11:00 PM

      Conference with JJA & BB.

9:45 PM- 10:15 PM

      Telephone conference JJA & BB
      with SC in re weapons.

✓ 19 JULY 63

7:01 PM- 11:45 PM

      Conference with DCI, AWD, MC,
      JJA, RTC in re ZIPPER. Agreement
      in principle on all issues.

✓ 31 JULY 63

9:40 AM- 10:20 AM

      Telephone conference with CHAIR/JCS
      in re AWD, VP overviews.

11:30 AM- 1:29 PM

      Conference, MC, JJA, RTC in
      re ZIPPER. Transfer operation to
      WKH

-26-

Oper<u>a</u>tion <u>Z</u>IPP<u>E</u>R/<u>C</u>onference <u>R</u>ecord (cont.)

<u>A U G U S T</u>

<u>9 AUG 63</u>

1:30 PM- 2:10 PM

     Conference, WKH, JJA.
     Progress Report.

<u>16 AUG 63</u>

7:50 PM- 11:01 PM

     Conference, WKA, JJA.
     Progress Report.

✓<u>23 AUG 63</u>

8:15 PM- 10:19 PM

     Conference, WKH, JJA, <u>RTC</u>
     Progress Report.

<u>30 AUG 63</u>

7:50 PM- 8:45 PM

     Conference, WKH, JJA.
     Progress Report.

<u>S E P T E M B E R</u>

<u>6 SEPT 63</u>

3:19 PM- 5:12 PM

     Conference, WKH, MC, JJA.
     Progress Report.

<u>12 SEPT 63</u>

2:45 PM- 3:18 PM

     Conference, WKH, JJA.
     Progress Report.

✓ <u>20 SEPT 63</u>

10:20 PM- 1:45 AM

     Conference, WKH, RTC, MC.
     Progress Report.

Operation ZIPPER/Conference Record (cont.)

√ 27 SEPT 63

9:30 AM- 10:17 AM

    Conference, WKH, DCI, MC, JJA, RTC.
    Progress Report.

O C T O B E R

18 OCT 63

7:45 PM- 11:30 PM

    Conference, WKH, JJA.
    Progress Report.
    Dallas

24 OCT 63

11:20 AM- 11:22 AM

    Telephone conference, SG, JJA
    in re UC arrival Montreal.

N O V E M B E R

√ 1 NOV 63

8:40 PM- 12: PM

    Conference, WKH, RTC
    Progress Report.

14 NOV 63

1:45 PM- 1:50 PM

    Telephone conference, WKH, MC
    in re UC/Dallas.

-28-

Abbreviations used in the ZIPPER Document

AF	Abe Fortas, advisor of Lyndon B. Johnson
AF1	Air Force One
AG	Attorney General, Robert F. Kennedy
ARM	unidentified
AWD	Allen Welsh Dulles, former DCI
BB	Binjamin Baumann, Shin Beth (Israel)
D/NSA	Director NSA, Gordon Blake
DCI	Director of Central Intelligence, John McCone
DD/FBI	Deputy Director of Federal Bureau of Investigation, William Sullivan
JCS	Joint Chiefs of Staff of U.S. Armed Forces
JJA	James Jesus Angleton, CIA Counterintelligence
Lancer SS	Code name for Security Service of J. F. Kennedy
MC	Marshal Carter, senior officer of CIA, later NSA
MARLINSPIKE	Probably a plan designed to draw the United States into war with Cuba, a strong desire of the JCS and its Chief, General Lyman Lemnitzer.
Met.Club	Metropolitan Club, Washington, D.C.
NSA	National Security Agency
OAS	*Organisation de l'armée secrète*, Secret Army Organisation of former French officers who did not recognize the independence of Algeria
RFK	Robert F. Kennedy, Attorney General
RTC	Robert Trumbull Crowley, CIA Clandestine Operations
SC	Sam Cummings, INTERARMCO
SG	Sam Giancana, Chicago Mafia
SIGINT	Signal Intelligence
U/C	*Unione Corse*, Corsican Mafia
UClub	University Club, Washington, D.C.
USMC	United States Marine Corps
VP	Vice President, Lyndon B. Johnson
WJ	Walter Jenkins, advisor of Lyndon B. Johnson
WKH	William King Harvey, senior officer CIA

Organization of the CIA

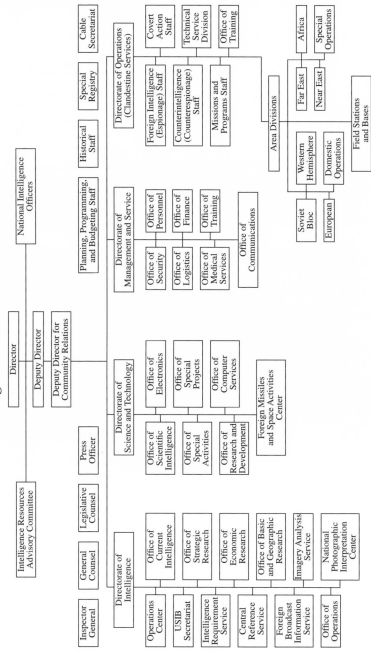

Index of Names

Names mentioned in documents and authors referred to in footnotes are not listed. Entries in footnotes only are set in italics.

Coming Soon!

Gregory Douglas, *The Last Nazi Refuge.*
In 1948, Heinrich Müller, Chief of Hitler's
Secret State Police (Gestapo), was hired by
the Central Intelligence Agency as the
world's foremost expert on Communist es-
pionage. It was Müller who supplied Joseph
McCarthy with Gestapo information on
communist spies in America. This was the
genesis of McCarthy's witch hunt against
communists. This book presents a complete
translation of Müller's confidential journals
kept during his years in Washington but

**Adolf Hitler's most loyal
Henchman in U.S. Service
After World War II**

also reveals other information about Müller's post-war activities. It
is a fascinating inside look at the early days of the CIA, the Truman administration's attempts to rid themselves of those communists Roosevelt permitted to function in the American government,
and gives an insight into one of the most fascinating, powerful and
unknown figures in both Hitler's Third Reich and Truman's Washington.

Gregory Douglas, *Federal Blood Guilt*
Secret CIA documents reveal one of the
biggest hypocrisies of modern times: The
U.S. Federal Government, which for decades has been at the forefront of a merciless
international war on drugs, is, in fact, one of
the biggest traffickers of illegal narcotics in
the world. The head of this monster, which
has poisoned uncounted thousands of young
people all over the world, is the CIA itself.
No American politician, however coura-
geous, can oppose this "patriotic" cartel without risking his life!

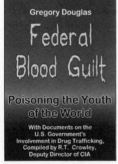

Gregory Douglas

**Federal
Blood Guilt**

Poisoning the Youth
of the World

With Documents on the
U.S. Government's
Involvement in Drug Trafficking,
Compiled by R.T. Crowley,
Deputy Director of CIA

**Check our website at
www.MonteSanoMedia.com**